How To Escape Your Comfort Zones

How To Escape Your Comfort Zones

The Secrets of Unbundling Your Life

Lee Johnson

with

Albert Koopman

PENGUIN BOOKS

PENGUIN BOOKS

Published by the Penguin Group
27 Wrights Lane, London W8 5TZ, England
Viking Penguin, a division of Penguin Books USA Inc, 375 Hudson Street,
New York, New York 10014, USA
Penguin Books Australia Ltd, Ringwood, Victoria, Australia
Penguin Books Canada Ltd, 10 Alcorn Avenue, Toronto, Ontario, Canada
M4V 3B2
Penguin Books (NZ) Ltd, 182-190 Wairau Road, Auckland 10, New Zealand
Penguin Books, Amethyst Street, Theta Ext 1, Johannesburg, South Africa

Penguin Books Ltd, Registered Offices: Harmondsworth, Middlesex, England

First Published by Penguin Books 1995

ISBN 0 140 250220

Typeset by Iskova Image Setting
Printed and bound by Creda Press
Cover photograph: The Image Bank

Contents

Acknowledgments — vii

Preface — ix

1. What are Comfort Zones? And Why Should We Escape? — 1

2. Mapping Out Your Journey — 9

3. Stage 1: What Exactly is a Comfort Zone? — 14

4. Stage 2: Preparing Yourself for the Escape — 76

5. Stage 3: Taking Time Out to Get to Know Yourself — 142

6. Stage 4: Stimulating The Motivation and Readiness for Change — 206

7. Stage 5: Getting in Touch With Yourself by Living in the 'Now' Moment — 216

8. Stage 6: The Vital Importance of a Mentor/ Soulmate/Guide — 246

9. Stage 7: The Final Nudge — Action and Integration — 267

References — 282

Acknowledgements

To John, Alison, Pam, Alistair, Michael, Samantha and all those at Penguin Books South Africa who believed in our work when it really counted.

To Albert, my catalyst, partner and friend — what more need I say?

To Mavis, whose wisdom helped me to accept that loneliness is a small price to pay for being special; and who guided me through the agony of turning unfolding wings into an art.

To Mom and Dad, Sandra, Darryl, Desirée and Wayne: my wish is that this book will help us all to understand each other and ourselves better and enable us to love all those around us more.

To Lorraine, whose infinite capacity for love, forgiveness and courage kept her running beside the train until she discovered her own shiny tracks.

To Rowan, whose wonderful sensitivity and maturity has rendered so deceptively simple the transition from son to intellectual and spiritual friend.

To Kyle, whose empathy and reverence for all living things and spontaneous ability to share his love with all those around him are continuing inspirations.

To Carole, famous astrologer and writer who has been a valued adviser, an inspiration to be published, and a true friend.

To Peter, professor, critic and friend who spent so much valuable time reading, analysing and encouraging my work and giving such fresh and intelligent insights.

Finally, to all those other friends, colleagues and willing ears who endured and encouraged my thoughts and theories and explorat'ons, and who read my manuscript through various stages of its evolution, and whose conversations added great wisdoms and insights: Carol B, Chris, Corinne, Gail, Janet, John C, Marino, Merlin, Paddy H, Roelene, Wanda. Also to Felix, Jon and Luke for the InfraManagement designs and implementation;

Veronique, Mariza and Lauren for their work on the cover design; and last (but by no means least) Peggy, without whom the Course wouldn't have happened.

Preface

Let's get one thing straight up front. The objective of this book is not to make you wealthy. Nor is it designed to increase your status in a material sense, or your power over others. Nor is it a trendy self-empowerment fad book, or an attempt to force some esoteric religious or New Age movement down your throat. In fact, this book is diametrically opposed to most of these things.

Simply, it is a book for anyone who wants to discover the pearls hidden deep inside the crusty shell of their everyday lives — those inner qualities that are the most noble, most valuable, most eternal qualities you possess; the qualities that will give perspective and meaning to your life. The qualities that will bring true inner peace and fulfilment.

It's a book about how to set free the 'real you' locked deep inside the complexities of your life. It's a common-sense, back-to-basics guide to help you break down the imprisoning castle walls that are holding you back from real happiness and self-fulfilment. It's about undergoing a permanent inner transformation that will change your whole life for the better. It's for people who want to live instead of merely existing. Anyone who feels trapped or manipulated, or vaguely lost and in need of guidance. Anyone who's feeling 'There must be more to life than this...' Anyone who feels stagnant, who wants to move ahead, who's tired of trying to live up to standards and expectations they don't really believe in. Anyone who wants to understand what life is *really* all about.

The motivation for writing this book has been largely the result of my own attempts to find meaning and permanent truths within the impermanence of life, and to try to share with others the lessons that I have learned along the way. It is thus largely a personal journey, because although I have had formal training and a university degree in psychology, and indeed practised professionally for a short time, my most valuable classroom has been life itself. I have found that it is simply too easy to be a grandstand philosopher and offer advice from the outside; real wisdom comes from getting down into the arena of personal experience. But having said that, one of the most gratifying and exciting things about doing research for this book during the past few years was to find academic and scientific corroboration and justification for many of the 'principles' that I established as a result of my personal experiences.

If reading this book sometimes makes you feel uncomfortable or angry or indignant, that's a good sign. Feeling discomfort is one of the most important steps in acknowledging that you are in a Comfort Zone. When I gave the original manuscript to some of my colleagues and friends to read for their input and opinion, I was amazed when some of them expressed concern because they felt the book was directed specifically at them and was therefore a kind of 'personal message'. Which, of course, is like saying that the horoscope in your daily newspaper is a 'personal message' just for you! Even my case studies (although based on actual people and events) have been disguised and combined and creatively embellished in a way which I felt would best illustrate the point I am making. As such, they are universal.

So when I thought about the reactions of these people, it was proof that I had somehow touched a nerve or held up a mirror, and that they had recognised something about themselves and felt uncomfortable. This was wonderful! If this book can create discomfort — the starting point and an essential catalyst in acknowledging and escaping a Comfort Zone — then I will have succeeded at least partially in my objective. So if the shoe fits, don't be afraid to wear it.

I don't expect this book to answer all your questions, and I don't see it as a panacea for the world's problems. I am still — and will forever be — on my own perpetual search for answers. In the words of Omar Khayyam, 'I have learnt nothing from life, except my own amazement at it.' So, I am only planting seeds. Some will fall on fertile soil and begin to grow immediately.

Others may lie dormant for months or years until the rains of insight come.

I sincerely hope you will find things of value in it — enlightenment or enrichment, or some small piece in the great jigsaw that we call Life. If you do, I can take little credit: as Isaac Newton said, 'If I have seen farther than other men, it is because I have stood on the shoulders of giants.'

In this regard, I would like to express my appreciation for the invaluable guidance and insights of some very special mentors and enlightened friends, especially Johannesburg psychologist Mavis Derman, as well as all the others who proof-read and contributed to the book through suggestions and constructive criticisms.

Most of all, I would like to acknowledge the wisdoms and insights of my good friend Albert Koopman whose programme Goal Source and our many long conversations late into the night were both inspirational and catalytic in the writing of this book. It, in turn, has been the catalyst for Albert's writing a new book called *The Inner Shift*, as well as motivating our working together to apply these principles in a corporate context and form the basis of our new, Vancouver-based company InfraManagement which aims at establishing a new paradigm of management for corporations and businesses.

I have also primarily Albert to thank for translating my Comfort Zones principles and my often idealistic theories into a practical course with the same name as this book, and his wife Peggy for all her assistance in assembling the material for the course. It has been extremely gratifying and sobering to see how this course actually *works*. Almost everyone who read the initial manuscript, and several people who attended our very first pilot course, reported that it had given them a completely new perspective on their lives, and some subsequently made major and dramatic changes for the better. I sincerely hope this book can also do the same for you.

Lee Johnson
Johannesburg
January 1995

1

What Are Comfort Zones? And Why Should We Escape?

We all have our own Comfort Zones — havens of security, familiarity and comfort. But why, you may be asking, *should* we escape? Surely a Comfort Zone is our reward for hard work, the place we've struggled for so long to get to? The place everyone wants to be? And wants to stay?

These are good questions. But don't be fooled — because there's a lot more to Comfort Zones than meets the eye.

The first problem is that Comfort Zones *are* comfortable — at least superficially. And because they're comfortable, they lull us into a false sense of security and well-being. Yet the very fact that you have started reading this book proves that, despite your 'comfort', you have a vaguely uncomfortable feeling that this may not be altogether a good thing.

That's good! Feeling uncomfortable is a really positive sign; it's when we are blissfully oblivious that we've got a real problem. It's when we're *not* uncomfortable that we aren't motivated to confront our true feelings and simply run away from them — and are doomed to remain trapped in those Comfort Zones.

Slipping into a Comfort Zone is a simple process. When we are comfortable, our activities and behaviour tend to take on familiar patterns. Patterns become habits; habits become routines; and before we know it those routines become a rut. And the only difference between a rut and a grave is the depth of the excavation!

1

Of course, the most obvious of all is the *material* Comfort Zone. It's one of the easiest to get trapped in, and one of the most difficult to escape from. After all, it's the embodiment of the Great American Dream; the pursuit of success and wealth and all their external symbols. Perpetuated by movies and soap operas and reinforced by advertising, the material Comfort Zone seems, for most people, to have become the very purpose of life.

But there are also many other less obvious Comfort Zones. I'm talking about the invisible prisons of social and parental conditioning, of societal and cultural norms, of systems and rules and conventions, and a thousand other factors that are all just bricks in the walls of the prisons that surround us and prevent us from growing.

If we look at them objectively, Comfort Zones are almost inevitably states of limbo, secure castles in which we have imprisoned ourselves or allowed ourselves to be imprisoned by others. We perpetuate − and grow − those high walls by not being aware of them, or by refusing to recognise that they're there. And so we compromise and rationalise and convince ourselves that it's simply our 'fate' to be in our current situation... and, after all, we could be worse off, couldn't we?

Mostly, we don't even *realise* we're in Comfort Zones. And so we simply shut off any ideas of the alternatives, of the options that lie outside our own narrow existences. Because it feels so safe and comfortable within, even to think of venturing outside our castle (and I'm not necessarily talking about a *physical* escape) seems foolish and risky and scary.

And the fact is, it *is* risky and scary. But definitely not foolish.

Recognising that we are trapped in a Comfort Zone − and that there's a whole lot more to life beyond the walls of our self-imposed limitations − is the first step towards escaping it and gaining mature wisdom and insight into our lives. Like the alcoholic, whose healing process can only begin once he has stood up in front of his peers or looked into a mirror and *admitted* that he is an alcoholic, so we can only begin to escape our Comfort

Zones when we admit that we are trapped in them. Until that moment of honest self-confrontation, *nothing* can happen.

A second important step is accepting the fact that risk and pain are essential and inescapable components of this escape, as they are of any change or transition. In its most trite form it's a question of 'no pain, no gain'. Until we confront this fact, and until we muster the courage to leave behind the temporary and unfulfilling 'myths' of security and familiarity and material possessions (and they *are* myths, no matter how real or vital they may seem to you now), we can never begin the process of discovering our true selves and learning what is truly meaningful and fulfilling and worth while in life.

The honesty to confront yourself in the mirror of truth

It's all about *honesty*. Honesty with those around us, but most of all honesty with ourselves. In order to become our true selves, we must have the courage to *be* ourselves and follow our *own* dreams. If we can't do that, then the life we're living isn't our own. Isn't that a terrible admission — that the life you're living isn't your own? How can we ever be self-fulfilled or at peace when we are lying to ourselves?

Real honesty also means bridging the gap between 'Who I am' and 'What I do'; and between 'Ought to be' and 'Is'. It is *being* what you believe in; letting every action and behaviour be an expression of who you are inside. And you simply can't do that until you recognise and realise to what extent your life is being restricted, and how many of your actions are motivated by external forces rather than inner desires.

Only you can admit that you *are* trapped in Comfort Zones. But, like the alcoholic who can't begin to be cured until he has the honesty to confront that fact and commit himself to doing something about it, you have to go through the same process in escaping your Comfort Zones. And, unfortunately, nobody can do it *for* you — even though, as you'll see later, there are people who can lead you to the water (as this book does), but then it's up to you to decide whether you want to drink.

How do we recognise these Comfort Zones?

There are many different types of Comfort Zones and, as I said earlier, most of the time we aren't even aware that we're in them. And you can't solve a problem until you know exactly what that problem is. So, how do you recognise your own particular Comfort Zones?

You already know about material Comfort Zones, and they're fairly easy to identify. But let's look at another simple example.

You may be trapped in a dead-end job, hating every moment, resenting your boss, your circumstances, your pay package. And yet you just carry on from one dreary or stressful day to the next. You dream of winning the sweepstakes or hitting that huge jackpot, and walking into the boss's office, telling him his fortune, and walking out into a new life — perhaps retiring to a desert island. (Don't we all have these dreams some time or another?)

Problem is, your chances of winning the sweepstakes or hitting that big jackpot are about as remote as your Fairy Godmother appearing, or a Knight in Shining Armour arriving on a white steed to rescue you, or any of the other unrealistic fantasies we invent to make our realities tolerable.

The reality is that you have to get real.

You have to realise that *you* are the Knight in Shining Armour, that you are the Fairy Godmother who can miraculously change your life for the better. *And you can only do that when you can see things in true perspective.* You can see the lush green fields and mountains of the world that lie beyond your Comfort Zones only when you have broken down the high castle walls that imprison you. Yet most people find it more comfortable simply to remain where they are, to make excuses and compromises.

But why do you put up with a life of compromise? Why do you continue to suffer, escaping only in day-dreams? The truth is that although you may be unhappy and unfulfilled, this discomfort is relatively more comfortable than the alternative — like waking up one morning and walking into the boss's office and handing in your resignation.

4

You are afraid of the void beyond — the unknown world. What else will you do? Will you find another job? What will it pay? What will your friends/family think? That's why, even if actually offered another job, most people still find it very disconcerting and disturbing to actually 'take the leap', to find the courage to leave behind their Comfort Zone and accept the risks and unknowns of a new job. And even when they've decided, they often have difficulty taking the step of actually *doing* the things necessary to implement the change: writing the letter of resignation, telling the boss, making a firm and final date for leaving.

Being stuck in a lousy job is only one example of being trapped in a Comfort Zone. There are many other examples: an unhappy or stagnant relationship, an unfulfilled marriage, restrictive social or religious norms, a smothering small town with no future, an inhibiting, aggressive, over-competitive city.

The fact is, unless things become completely intolerable, or until you are fired or retrenched or dumped and are forced to do something about it, *it's more comfortable to stay where you are than to confront and risk change.* And so you stay put. And become more and more trapped.

Perhaps your own particular Comfort Zone is mainly a psychological or emotional one; perhaps you are inhibited from progressing in your life by some past, often long-forgotten incident or traumatic experience or parental reproach or religious rule or societal norm.

For example, you may have been brought up in a time when pre-marital sex was considered taboo by society. Entrenched by what you heard in church. Made more real by someone you know becoming pregnant and being ostracised by family and friends. And twenty or thirty years later, even though the attitudes of society have changed dramatically, even though your parents and teachers and church ministers may all be dead, your attitude and behaviour is still governed by an amalgam of all your past lessons and entrenched beliefs. And this may be inhibiting your entire life, affecting your relationships with members of the opposite sex, preventing you from making a full

5

and satisfying attachment... leaving you trapped in your Comfort Zone of loneliness.

Invariably, each Comfort Zone is unique to each individual and very complex in its uniqueness, being an amalgam of many factors interacting powerfully with one another. And even once you *recognise* your own particular Comfort Zones, and realise that you're trapped, why don't you simply escape? Unfortunately, it's a lot harder and a lot more complex than it seems — and for these reasons you don't simply walk out on your lousy job.

Although you may be lonely and unhappy and unfulfilled, the truth is that the discomfort you feel is relatively more comfortable than the alternative — that is, asserting yourself against everything on which you have based your past behaviour, changing your entrenched beliefs to fit the new *changed you* within a changed society. In short, simply being honest with yourself in what you really want and desire in life, and having the courage to go out and get it.

But why this obsession with change and growth? Why can't we just stay where we are, secure in our Comfort Zones?

Many people asked me this question when I first started working on this book and exposed them to my ideas. They asked me how I could be so arrogant as to expect everyone to think as I did — namely, that *growth* is the most important and worthwhile task we all have in life, and that stagnation is therefore the most worthless.

My answer is that these are not just my subjective thoughts and opinions — they are in fact *universal truths*. This is my reasoning:

Everything in the entire universe is in a constant process of movement, of progress and growth. Decay and death are not only valid parts of this eternal and ubiquitous process — they are essential aspects of it... for only through decay and death can new birth begin.

And yet man, with his rational mind capable of contemplating his own destiny, seems to have the dubious talent and desire consciously to suspend or delay or manipulate this process in himself.

For example, medical science prolongs an often fatally diseased physical life; social mores and the institution of marriage often prolong fatally diseased relationships; psychological hang-ups and defence mechanisms such as rationalisation perpetuate and prolong fatally diseased emotional, material and spiritual wastelands — those most insidious of traps that I call Comfort Zones.

Unless we recognise the fortresses we have built around us, unless we confront our own honesty, unless we recognise that risk and pain and death of the familiar and the comfortable are essential companions to the inescapable process of growth and rebirth, and should therefore be welcomed and embraced, we cannot even begin to break down the restraining walls and lower the drawbridge to a new and fuller existence.

I think Morris West expressed it perfectly in his book *The Shoes of the Fisherman*:

> It costs so much to be a full human being that there are very few who have the enlightenment or the courage to pay the price... one has to abandon altogether the search for security and reach out to the risk of living with both arms.
> One has to embrace the world like a lover.
> One has to accept pain as a condition of existence.
> One has to court doubt and darkness as the cost of knowing.
> One needs a will stubborn in conflict but apt always to total acceptance of every consequence of living and dying.

That's what escaping Comfort Zones is all about — *to abandon altogether the search for security and reach out to the risk of living with both arms.*

If you're not prepared to do that, if you'd prefer to keep your security bubble of rationalisations and illusions and self-deceptions intact rather than confront truth and your own honesty, if you're not prepared to take the risks and face the consequences, then burn this book now. Because once you've begun the journey, once you have taken the blinkers off your eyes and your mind and your soul, you will never be able to fool yourself again. You will either have to continue the journey, or live for ever with the knowledge that you are living a compromise.

And *that* is the most uncomfortable Comfort Zone of all.

Key points to remember from Chapter 1

1. We all become trapped in Comfort Zones — be they material, emotional, psychological or spiritual.

2. You can't think straight, or make real and valid decisions about your life, or progress towards true inner peace and fulfilment, until you acknowledge that you *are* trapped in Comfort Zones and consciously decide that you *want* to escape from them. (*Now please read that again!*)

3. Escaping your Comfort Zones is a long, slow, gradual process. It is a rejuvenation and a strengthening of the psychological and emotional and spiritual 'inner you' that, once completed, will make your present practical problems seem insignificant, or at least far easier to handle.

4. That process — that journey — begins with the first step. And that means confronting the fact that you *are* trapped in certain Comfort Zones, and making the decision that you *want to* and *will* escape from them.

5. The process can be painful and scary. But *no* change happens without turbulence and discomfort. As you progress, you will learn to accept and even welcome these things as inescapable parts of the process — a simple price to pay. It'll be as natural (and as inevitable!) as paying a toll as part of your journey on the Interstate or Autobahn.

6. The process is inevitable. But the longer you leave it, the harder it will be to escape. So make the decision to start *now*. Because all you have to lose are your own self-deceptions and illusions. And all you have to gain is inner peace and self-fulfilment.

2

Mapping Out Your Journey

We can't control or predict what Fate does to us.
But we CAN control how we REACT to these things.

Escaping your Comfort Zones is like going on an inner journey. And when you make a journey, you need a map. Otherwise, the chances are you'll go around in circles and never reach your destination. It's also important that you pass through each of the key places *in the correct sequence* if you are to take the shortest route. Finally, you need to stop along the way every now and then to rest and regain your energies.

So, since you are about to take one of the most important journeys of your life, I'd like to give you a 'map' showing you how to get to your destination of escaping from your Comfort Zones. And along the way I'll give you 'resting places'. These may be simple illuminating stories, or summaries of key points, or exercises for you to do. *Don't skip these resting places. They are very important to you.*

To begin with, here are the key stages you must pass through, in sequence:

Stage 1: What exactly is a Comfort Zone? (Chapter 3)

Here you will learn more about what Comfort Zones are, and some of the things that cause them, and some of the reasons why you become trapped in them.

You'll learn that you aren't alone in being trapped in Comfort Zones, and you'll see how some of the most famous people in history have described the pain and fear of escaping, and finally their ecstasy of freedom and inner peace.

You will also learn that a *crisis* can be the best opportunity to confront and escape the limitations to your freedom... or become just another excuse simply to go deeper inside your castle.

Stage 2: Preparing yourself for the escape (Chapter 4)

One of the most critical steps is deciding that you want to and will escape. Here you will learn that escaping from a Comfort Zone and going through the transition from dependency to non-dependency is an absolutely natural and common process in life, that it is something you have already done successfully many times before, and that it is absolutely essential — a step that you *have* to take before you can continue growth of any kind.

You will also learn how to overcome the fear of losing what you are now clinging to so stubbornly, by gaining insight into the importance of wholeness/individuation/self-actualisation through perpetual growth and conscious forward movement, and the need to integrate these values into every aspect of your life.

We also explore the effect that your growth and transformation process will have on others around you — and look at what to do when your escape is being resisted or blocked by these people.

We look at one of the most important components of happiness and self-fulfilment — Love.

Finally, we explore levels of spirituality and awareness, and their relevance to confronting and escaping your Comfort Zones.

Stage 3: Taking time out for yourself (Chapter 5)

Here you need to really get to know yourself. Who are you, deep down — the *real* you? What do you *really* want in life? And what exactly is stopping you from getting there? Isolating yourself for a while — literally 'taking time out' — is an important step.

How you use this time by yourself is even more important — so you'll find a whole lot of exercises to help you discover these things for yourself, and the mechanisms for helping you achieve your goals.

You'll learn about the vital importance of self-esteem as part of the process of escaping, and explore the importance of interacting effectively with other people.

Finally, there are still more questions to help you discover who you really are inside, and what you really want in your life.

Stage 4: Stimulating your motivation and readiness for change (Chapter 6)

The journey is long and the going often tough. So unless you are convinced that the destination is worth it, you might be tempted to stop or turn back.

This short chapter is designed to motivate you by observing the process in somebody else, and also to caution you not to expect miracles or overnight cures. It's a long, arduous journey, but once you have started each step — no matter how small — is taking you closer to your goal. And further from the prison of your Comfort Zones.

You will learn that you have the right to be who you are and do what you truly feel and want to do, rather than what you *should* or *have to* do. You will discover the enormous relief of just being *you*... and being proud of it. And you will learn how increasingly important this transition will be as you grow older, how this journey you are taking could be one of the most valuable investments you could make in your entire life.

Stage 5: Getting in touch with yourself by living in the 'now' moment (Chapter 7)

Life is not yesterday or tomorrow. It's *now* — that fleeting, elusive moment when the future ticks by into the past.

Here you will learn how to recognise, and have more of, and make more of, those moments of genuine *living*, as opposed to merely existing, and how by doing this you will learn who the 'real you' is deep inside, and set yourself free to experience the full joy of living. You'll learn about 'islands' and how, in the turbulent seas of life, these are vital to regenerate your energies and strengthen you emotionally, physically and psychologically.

You will also learn the importance of balance in Mind, Spirit and Body, and how genuine happiness and inner peace depends on complete harmony of all the elements of your life. Concentrating too much on one — especially if that one is material success or security — inevitably leads to disharmony and unhappiness.

Stage 6: The vital importance of a mentor/soulmate/guide (Chapter 8)

Here you will learn how to recognise — and find — mentors to guide and help you on your journey. Like the Wise Old Man or Spirit in all the world's legends and myths who magically appears and gives the hero the key to unlock the door or the magic sword to slay the dragon, your mentors will help you on your journey.

You will also learn what to do when you yourself are called upon to be a mentor.

Then we look at how you can overcome one of the most daunting obstacles to escaping your Comfort Zones, namely how to get rid of old, damaging emotional baggage.

Finally, we examine an even more daunting task: how to overcome your ego and attain the inner peace of humility.

Stage 7: The final nudge — action and integration (Chapter 9)

This stage is a short synopsis to help you review your own journey so far, to understand that each person grows at a different pace. But no matter how much or how little you may think you have personally grown so far, the acorns have been planted and are simply lying dormant until you allow them to germinate and grow into mighty oaks.

Yet what's the use of travelling a great distance and then turning back just before the final bend in the road or the final crest of the hill? (Unless you decide that's where you *want* to stay and temporarily put down roots.) And so we give you hints on how to take those final and most vital steps of all, and how to turn those acorns into mighty oaks through *action* and *integration*.

You will also learn that once you've escaped one Comfort Zone, you can't rest. You may get trapped in another Comfort Zone — or you may question what you've done, and be tempted to go back to where you started from.

You'll also learn how to recognise some rather unexpected Comfort Zones in your everyday life and how your journey can have some remarkable effects on your life in unexpected ways. Finally, we briefly discuss Comfort Zones in the workplace and how managements and employees alike can benefit by recognising the importance of merging You-in-the-Organisation with The-Organisation-in-You.

START YOUR ENGINES...

So now you know where you're going. And you have a map of how to get there.

Please don't be annoyed if you encounter some repetition or philosophical side-tracking. These are intended and have their own purpose.

And if you are still having doubts about whether to take the first step or not, remember the most important lesson from Chapter 1: **You can't think straight, or make good decisions about your life, or progress towards inner peace and fulfilment, until you escape from your Comfort Zones**.

So, start your engines, or lace up your walking boots. Your journey has just begun.

3

Stage 1

What Exactly Is A Comfort Zone?

*The obscure we see eventually. The completely
apparent takes a little longer.*

E R Morrow

I define a Comfort Zone as a state of passive acceptance of
external controls.

It's where you resign yourself, consciously or unconsciously,
to a set of circumstances or a series of factors without making
any real effort actively to make any change or improvement, or
even question the boundaries that limit and constrain you.

In this definition, a Comfort Zone is therefore much more
than just a material environment that is 'comfortable' —
although, as we have seen, these 'material Comfort Zones' are
some of the most obvious and also some of the most difficult to
escape from. Here are just a few examples of other types of
Comfort Zones:

- A Comfort Zone can be a religion, with all its rules and
  conditions and parameters. You simply accept everything at
  face value, often because you have grown up with it and have
  never stopped to question anything. And you have been told
  that questioning anything is wrong — even heretical,
  blasphemous or sinful.

- A Comfort Zone may be a formal, structured hierarchy which positions you as a lesser being within an organisation. You are a lowly clerk or secretary, or middle management, and the upper echelons are completely out of reach unless you sleep with the boss or play golf with the directors or someone dies and you might be in line to fill his shoes.

- A Comfort Zone may be a relationship or a marriage which has stagnated and is no longer a dynamic interaction which enriches both parties, or perhaps it's become a boring backwater where you have accepted your 'role'. For example, it's your 'duty' as a husband to bring home the money, to fix the kettle, to change the light bulb. Or it's your 'duty' as the housewife to wash the dishes, change dirty diapers, make the children's lunch, play taxi driver for all their activities. And for both, it's your 'duty' not to get separated or divorced.

- A further example could be a discriminatory Comfort Zone based on your religion, your sexual inclination, your long hair, your physical impediment, your gender or your skin colour. (I believe discrimination is based on the fact that people, or groups of people, are trapped in a Comfort Zone which says that they are right in having certain religious beliefs, certain sexual inclinations, having short hair or being of a certain gender or skin colour or culture — and anyone who does *not* fit their own familiar and safe patterns is seen as a threat to their entrenched beliefs.) Yet many people are prepared passively to accept such discrimination — and I have a personal example to relate.

Growing up in South Africa, I was amazed that so many so-called 'non-whites' simply accepted their lot under the apartheid system over a period of many, many years. As a foreign exchange student in Detroit, Michigan in the late sixties, I saw even worse racial discrimination than I had known in South Africa. But the difference was that in the United States far more people were not prepared to remain in their 'Comfort Zones' of passive acceptance, and spoke out vehemently or expressed their anger in violent confrontation. It took the Nelson Mandelas of this world to eventually change things in South Africa, and to restore to so many 'non-whites' the pride and self-confidence to assert their rights.

Dependency and control

You may say, 'Ah, but in apartheid South Africa it wasn't just a passive acceptance. In the police state environment they *couldn't* assert themselves for fear of being arrested, tortured or worse.'

True. And yet *coercion* is one of the most important (and ironically often one of the least recognised) elements of the Comfort Zone which we'll call Dependency/Control. In almost all Comfort Zones, in fact, there is a *dependency* element: dependency on a breadwinner or a boss or a company for money; dependency on a partner for emotional security, companionship, sex; dependency on a religion for spiritual security; dependency on a system for a myriad aspects of daily life.

And where there is dependency, there is inevitably *control*. Someone who has power over you in some way or other, and who can exert that power either blatantly or subtly and manipulate your life. It works this way: because you are dependent on someone you allow them to describe the boundaries of your freedom and coerce you into compliance with what they want you to do or not to do.

Such coercion/dependency relationships, and their resultant Comfort Zones, can be on a personal level, or on a group or community level, or even on a national scale. Looking back at growing up in South Africa, I am appalled at how easily I simply accepted what was happening around me and did nothing to change it. I was anything but a racist; in our rock band we used to back 'black' and 'Coloured' (mulatto) singers in the days when we could have been thrown into jail for it. I never encouraged or agreed with or participated in entrenching apartheid. And yet, indisputably, I allowed apartheid to happen around me.

16

Rationalisation and denial

With what I know now, I realise that I was in a wonderfully secure Comfort Zone on a national scale: I was one of the privileged 'whites'. I simply accepted that that was the way things were in my life.

And I suppose my reasoning went something like this:

'Our government must know that they're doing, so I suppose they're right in saying apartheid is the solution to a problem that nobody else in the world has been able to solve. Even in the Bible they talk of "hewers of wood and drawers of water". Let's face it: our blacks are pretty well off, even if they haven't got the vote. Don't thousands of them stream in from neighbouring countries to work on our mines? So, it can't be that bad.

'True, there are some things that annoy me. I'd love to have TV (it only arrived in South Africa in 1975 after many years of the government's telling us that it was an evil medium that could be abused by dark powers and undermine the country); I'd like less restrictive censorship; I'd like lots of things the rest of the world have — but, hey, these things are a small price to pay for peace and stability and prosperity. And, anyway, if I step out of line, I could lose my privileges and be thrown into jail or deported...'

Control and dependency. Carrot and stick. Rationalisation and denial and avoidance of the truth. What insidious jail wardens they are!

THE UBIQUITOUS COMFORT ZONE

So many Comfort Zones. Racial and sexual discrimination, manipulation, religious distinctions, control and dependency, lesser beings, unequal rights, material prisons.

'Ridiculous!' you may say. 'I'd never allow myself to be shackled and limited like that!'

And yet, consciously or unconsciously, we all do. Because a Comfort Zone *is* exactly that — *comfortable*. It's a stage of your life or career or marriage where things seem to be going fine; where you seem to feel relatively contented and stable. But have you really thought about it? Are you all that you can be in life? Have you achieved all your dreams? Are you *really* completely happy and contented and fulfilled? Are you being completely fair and spiritual in your attitudes and actions towards others?

If you answered Yes to any of these questions, you're either a very, very rare individual, or you're fooling yourself. Because, as we have seen in Chapter 1, the walls of our Comfort Zones are often too high or too secure to allow us to see beyond them.

Fortunately, the dividing line between *comfort* and *stagnation* is very fine, and no matter how hard we try to avoid growth, over time every Comfort Zone inevitably becomes a *Dis*comfort Zone (see Figure 1 on page 19). And the more discomfort we feel, the more motivated we are to escape.

The tragedy is that by the time this happens, by the time things become completely intolerable, many people are too old to escape, or their lives have become too complex and the strings tying them down too numerous (like Gulliver in Lilliput) and thus collectively too strong to break, or they have lost the physical or emotional energy to make any change at all. I'm sure you know some of these people in your own world: people eking out the dregs of their lives in unfulfilling jobs and dead-end relationships. Sad and lonely couples sitting across the table from each other with lifeless eyes and immobile faces. People dining out on the dreams and memories of the past... seemingly oblivious that life happens *now*.

There's another devious thing about Comfort Zones: they're masters of disguise and camouflage. And so they're often very difficult to acknowledge and recognise, simply because many of the castle walls have their foundations deep in our subconscious, or way back in our forgotten past. Also, there is probably no such thing as a single, simple Comfort Zone but rather a complex interrelationship of several Comfort Zones simultaneously.

But the point is that there are critical times in the development of any Comfort Zone when we *should* and *can* escape. If we pass beyond those critical periods without taking action, it becomes almost impossible to escape:

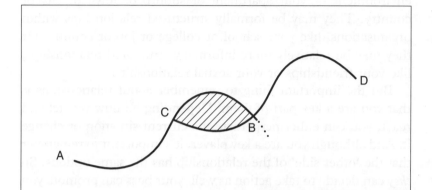

In Figure 1, the line A-B represents a normal growth curve from birth through maturity to decline.

If we take this to represent our period of stay in a Comfort Zone, we see that there is a critical phase (the shaded area) during which we can at any time make a 'quantum leap' from inevitable decline to a new growth curve (C-D) which will take us to much higher levels.

The last chance we have is when the old growth curve is on the decline and has reached 'critical' levels of discomfort. This crisis juncture is possibly our last (and often our best) chance to make the change. But if we miss this chance, or if we delay the 'leap' for too long (ie past the point where the old growth curve intersects with the new one), it becomes virtually impossible to make the change.

And then we're stuck, trapped in our old Comfort Zone for ever.

A Comfort Zone is a relationship

All Comfort Zones have to do with our subjective interpretation of the world around us, and are therefore always about 'relationships' — our relationship to systems and social structures, to opportunities and restrictions, to the environment, and especially to the people who make up our total world.

They may be relationships concerning physical things, like your appearance or your disabilities; they may be your living environment — your apartment or suburb or town or city or country. They may be formally structured relationships within organisations, like your school or college or job or country. Or they may be relatively more informally structured relationships, like your friendships or your sexual relationships.

But the important thing to remember about relationships is that you are a key part of them. Depending on how *you* act and react, you can either perpetuate the current situation or change it. And although you are a key player, it's important to remember that the 'other side' of the relationship has the same options. So *they* can decide to take action as well: your boss can promote you or fire you; your romantic or marriage partner can decide to drop you and see someone else — and so on. But it's important to remind yourself that *you* are always an equally important part of the relationship, and that you also have rights and powers. It's up to you to *assert* those most basic of human rights.

And remember: it *is* in your hands to do it.

The escape comes from within

Each Comfort Zone is completely unique — simply because each person is unique. And each Comfort Zone is always a complex interrelationship of many unique factors. All of these factors, and their interrelationships, are important bricks in the unique walls of your own individual castle. But the basic building materials of Comfort Zones, and the principles for *escaping* them, are the same for everyone.

While most people look for 'external' ways to escape (winning the jackpot, changing jobs or towns or countries), the *real* escape is inextricably linked to a personal inner transformation from the 'old' you to a 'new' you. It is a journey of enlightenment and increasing insight through self-honesty. It reaches right down into the depths of your inner self, way beyond the superficialities and carefully constructed illusions we cling to.

Yes, you *can* escape physically by leaving your marriage, changing jobs, moving house or even emigrating, winning a jackpot — and, of course, these can be very important catalysts in precipitating the *real* escape. But remember that it's still the same old you within your new circumstances — whatever they might be. You can't escape from yourself! So, unless there's been an inner transformation, you simply take your Comfort Zone mentality along with you — no matter how hard or far you try to run away.

Martin Flanagan, whom Caroline Jones calls 'One of the most interesting and original journalists in Australia' in her book *The Search for Meaning* comments that 'Though we are intellectually, emotionally and sexually frank these days, few people dare to speak of the soul's journey. It's been said that twentieth century man is a soul in search of meaning, and one of the principal ways we achieve meaning is through connections — both with ourselves and with other people.'

Don't be scared off by this talk of 'souls' and 'journeys'. No matter what your beliefs or religious inclinations, what we are talking about here is the *inner you* — the part of you that thinks and contemplates your life. Think of your body as a kind of car you drive around in on earth. It's just flesh and blood and bones, a purely mechanical (though incredibly complex and marvellous) vehicle. Now think of the 'inner you' as the *driver* of that vehicle. You can decide where you want to go and how you will get there, and whether you are going to let yourself be controlled by the obstacles that 'Life' or 'Fate' place in your path, or whether you are going to negotiate your way successfully past them.

Who *is* the 'inner you'?

[Author's note: The next seven pages may seem a bit arduous and difficult to follow, like a particularly steep little hill on your journey. Don't despair! The road beyond is easier.]

This is probably one of the oldest and most enigmatic questions to have been asked from the very dawn of time, and it has been explored exhaustively by philosophers, scientists, writers and poets — as well as ordinary people.

In ancient Greek times, Plato separated mind and body into two separate 'substances' — immortal soul and mortal body. Aristotle disagreed, and believed that the mind and body are one integrated unit; that one without the other makes no sense.

During the Renaissance from the 14th to the 16th centuries, Western man increasingly divorced himself from the religious and social restrictions of the Middle Ages. René Descartes (1596-1650) drew a clear distinction between the *immortal religious soul* (which he saw as the *ephemeral mind* which inhabits the body as a 'homunculus', a miniature person with magical powers supposed to be in the pineal gland of the brain), and the *body* which, in common with the body of animals, he saw simply as a biological mechanism.

And so these different views continued: the Christian religion talks of the 'soul'; some Eastern religions talk of the 'Overself' — a kind of extra-dimensional sum of who you are over all your incarnations and lives, and who directs each life in such a way that important lessons are added to the sum of who you are on an eternal plane; others believed that our existence was purely biological and coincidental, and that there was no perpetuation after death. And so it has been going on through the ages.

However, for our immediate purposes we jump to the twentieth century where these questions were finally examined in a structured and 'scientific' manner. Sigmund Freud, for example, formulated his famous psychoanalytical theory which says we all have an *instinctual* energy called **libido** which is pleasure-seeking and survival-oriented. Jordaan and Jordaan in their book *Man in Context* go on to explain:

> This libido or instinctual energy is regulated in accordance with two principles: **the pleasure principle** (immediate gratification of needs, wants and desires) and the **reality principle** (which suspends immediate gratification in order to experience greater pleasure later) (ie because immediate gratification is not always possible or realistic).

I don't think anyone can argue with that. We all do have a kind of inner energy which drives us, and it's obvious that some of our desires are controlled by other factors which inhibit us. But then Freud went on to say that this libido is regulated within three psychic systems which he called the **Id**, the **Ego** and the **Superego**.

Jordaan and Jordaan explain:

The term **id** refers to all subconscious impulses regarded as uncontrolled, primitive and animal. The source of these demands is in the body, and they demand immediate satisfaction. For example, the uncontrolled urge to eat, to physically attack another person, or for sexual satisfaction, can be ascribed to id impulses. Because id impulses are the product of a blind, unconscious and powerful instinctual energy, discipline, self-control, morality and fear for the consequences of certain forms of behaviour are not part of the id.

[Author: Think of the id as a naughty child who just wants and demands something without any consideration whatsoever for anybody else, or any regard for the consequences. For example, he wants to play with matches and throws a tantrum if his desire is blocked by his father telling him not to.]

The second psychic system, the **ego**, is based mainly on the reality principle. In order to produce behaviour which is appropriate for the satisfaction of instinctual drives, people must have contact with reality, and they must be able to foresee the consequences of their behaviour. But the ego must also have a certain tension tolerance for it to be able to better cope with the tensions remaining after satisfaction has been postponed, or when satisfaction can be achieved only in a roundabout way.

[Author: Think of the ego as the same child who has tried playing with matches and has got burnt. His desire is now

tempered by the memory of his pain, and his 'satisfaction' may now be achieved by watching his father light a fire.]

The third system is the **superego** (conscience). This system arose because society imposes certain ethical and religious standards on the behaviour of its members, which may or may not be disregarded. If these standards, or the standards people set for themselves, are transgressed, people experience feelings of guilt and anxiety. In order to avoid feelings of guilt and anxiety, and also the punishment for any transgression, people obey (via their ego) the demands of their superego.

[Author: Think of the superego as the same child who knows that his father will disapprove if he plays with matches, and now will not play with matches even if he's left on his own with a whole boxful because by doing so he will feel anxiety and guilt and risk a possible spanking.]

What's most interesting about Freud's theory is thus the interaction among these three systems. Jordaan and Jordaan continue:

> The ego can thus be seen as a sort of intermediary between the demands of the id and the superego. There is, therefore, a power struggle or conflict between the id (which demands immediate satisfaction of its instinctual drives), the ego (which chooses appropriate behaviour for achieving the satisfaction) and the superego (which forbids certain behaviour). In such a situation it is the ego's task to arrange a compromise.
>
> These compromises, however, are the root of many evils and self-deceptions. Because the id impulses are so powerful and primal, they cannot simply be shoved out of the way — the ego must do something with them. So in order to regulate and control the id impulses, the ego can utilise various *defence mechanisms*.

24

[Author: Such as denial, rationalisation and other self-deceptions — and we'll have a lot more to say about these in the next chapter!]

In the context of this book, we could then assume that Comfort Zones originate in the *superego* and that your 'escape' depends on your training your *ego* to allow more of the *id* out and be less subservient to the rules of the superego.

But there's more to it than this. I believe Freud's theory is incomplete. I believe there is a vital 'missing link' that needs to be added to the id, ego and superego equation to make it valid in the context of escaping Comfort Zones, and which should be integrated into your practical, everyday life through a 'Life Skills Delivery System'.

I have called this vital missing link the **Infra-ego**.

The Infra-ego

The infra-ego is what I believe is the real 'inner you'. This is in many ways similar to Freud's superego — namely, an internalised set of values that may have their roots in external systems (societal norms, parental guidance and advice, religious dos and don'ts), but which have been critically considered and selectively included into a *personal values system*. But that's where the similarity ends.

Whereas Freud's superego is externalised in the way the ego interprets and processes these values in a *conscious sense*, so this infra-ego is externalised in how you act and react, *even in instinctual ways*. It does this because such actions represent your true inner self — *independent* of outside factors such as social or parental disapproval or punishment, independent of personal guilt or anxiety; independent, in fact, of all defence mechanisms such as rationalisations, denials, projections. Such actions are simply your inner honesty and integrity in the most basic sense.

In this way there is true interaction between 'Who I am' and 'What I do' — the true interaction of all aspects of your life into 'wholeness'. This is entirely consistent with the Humanistic and existentialist school of psychology that began in the sixties and which attempted to expand on Freud's psychoanalytical theory by maintaining that humans must be studied *holistically*.

Jordaan and Jordaan explain:

> One of the most important principles of existentialism is that human beings have a free will — we choose our own destiny and the realisation of our inherent human potential. It is only through the realisation of our potential that we can live an authentic and meaningful life. People who do not realise their potential are not victims of their unconscious. They are victims of their own refusal to grow and become fully mature people by choice.

It is therefore the *integration* of this 'free will' into the 'automatic' processes that take place in the interaction among the id, the ego and the superego that provides a better definition and a more complete explanation of man and his behaviour. And it is only when this element of free will is consciously and frequently implemented that you can be a complete, individuated, inner-driven person. *But only when your free will is liberated and regulated by your infra-ego, can you ensure that your actions and behaviour will be altruistic and spiritually mature.*

This, I believe, is the true goal of individuation and achieving your 'inner self' — the true pinnacle to aim at. And the true path to follow in escaping your Comfort Zones.

What is the infra-ego, and how does it work?

When I gave my original *Comfort Zones* manuscript to various experts to read prior to publication, there was no single thing that attracted more comment than this infra-ego concept. I had included it almost as a throwaway, and nobody was more surprised than I by all the attention and interest it aroused.

I was then forced to go back and think about it a great deal myself, so that at least I could understand it better. So here are my thoughts up to now:

It seems to me that the infra-ego is a fourth dimension to Freud's psychoanalytical theory in that it not only forms a *foundation* for the others (and underpins them), but it also *governs* them all (ie the id-ego-superego interaction dynamics). This is the closest definition I can give at this stage:

The infra-ego is a personal value system independent of external influences such as societal norms and authority. It exists on a spiritual level, transcendent of present time and circumstances. It is the sum total of your deepest innermost convictions, and it is the determinator of how you will act instinctively, even when there is nobody around to see you — when you don't have to have your behaviour judged by those around you, or by norms that you have learned through contact with the world around you. It is a system of internalised norms that have been gained on a spiritual and eternal dimension, and are ultimately your innermost conscience and the essence of who you really are, stripped of all cognitive processes.

In its simplest explanation, I believe that the infra-ego is thus your *spiritual genetic self*. Just as we are biologically the product of the genetic material of all our ancestors, so I believe that there is also a kind of spiritual genetic material that has also been passed down to us; the sum total of all the lessons learned in the spiritual growth process of all our ancestors. And this could be true even if you don't believe in reincarnation.

The infra-ego is, in my opinion, entirely consistent with the humanistic movement in psychology — that is, seeing man as a holistic being; that he is affected daily and in a lifetime growth context by a multitude of factors around him. It also gets to the core of the whole age-old question in psychology of NATURE vs NURTURE — the role played by the genetic pool, and that played by the environment, and their relative importance in shaping the individual by adding a new dimension to the equation: the dimension of *spirituality*.

27

In terms of this new theory, it is not only Nature (ie biological/genetic factors) and the environment/experiences with the world around you, that determine who you are, but it is also an element that *precedes and supersedes* both Nature as well as Nurture. It could, in fact, be an important 'proof' of reincarnation.

In a practical sense, the infra-ego operates on *two levels*:

(1) In the sense of 'spiritual levels' (ie where you are born into this world on an eternal scale of reincarnated lifetimes in your quest and journey towards self-perfection and based on all past lessons and experiences — the sum total of who you are in the sense of spiritual maturity) it is a *personal value system*, and that part of you that adds the concept of 'responsibilities' to the concept of 'rights'.

(2) In the sense of a practical interaction between, and implementation of, the 'Who I am' and 'What I do' concept, it is the expression of your spiritual level even in an instinctual way, when nobody's watching or will ever find out what you've done. It also explains phenomena such as the puzzling 'honour among thieves' concept, as well as giving new insight into human qualities such as perseverance, determination, internalisation of 'no pain, no gain' principles, courage to confront change as set out in Comfort Zones, and many other areas.

Even from these few initial thoughts and observations, it is obvious what a vast subject the infra-ego is. I believe it should become the subject of a major research programme and would probably require the formulation of new scientific methods even to conduct such research.

One of the ways in which my partner Albert Koopman and I plan to pursue the subject is through our practical workshops and courses on How to Escape Your Comfort Zones, and by asking course franchisees and participants to assist us by filling in a questionnaire and corresponding with us. The key to such research would be to try to isolate and prove the existence of the infra-ego by separating it from Nature (biological factors) as well as Nurture (environmental factors) and show that it precedes and supersedes them both.

It will hopefully show, in essence, that some people start life on different rungs of the spiritual ladder − the ladder of real, eternal growth towards the perfection of the organism we call the *soul*, or what Eastern religions call the 'Overself'. On reflection, the infra-ego is, in fact, the *'personality'* of the Overself; it is the *externalisation of the Overself*; and, as such, it corresponds quite closely with what we call 'values'.

What are values?

Try this quick exercise. You are walking along a street and find a wallet. It is crammed full of money − more than you would earn in six months. There is also a card with the owner's name and address. Would you:

- Keep the money and throw away the wallet?
- Keep half the money and send the wallet to the rightful owner anonymously?
- Contact the owner and negotiate a reward before you return the wallet?
- Contact the owner and give the wallet and contents back intact, without any conditions or expectations of a reward?
- Refuse any reward even if you were offered one?

Once you have decided *what* you would have done, think about *why* you would have done it. This indicates the motive behind the action − your *values*.

Values are what govern how you act when nobody else can possibly know or find out what you did. Values are deep-rooted internal 'rules' that you live your life by, even when those rules are in conflict with what society expects or demands of you; even when the majority of people would act in another way, or not disapprove of your acting in that way; or when you can easily justify your negative actions with realistic reasons and excuses.

In your new life journey, in the quest to discover the real you, it is the recognition and refinement of these inner values that — more than anything else — lead to true inner peace and self-fulfilment.

In a world driven by materialism and personal success and gratification of needs and desires, values are what give meaning to your life. Your progress up Maslow's Hierarchy of Needs — no matter how rapid or impressive — is futile unless it is underpinned by a fundamental *value system*. Indeed, it is impossible to reach the highest level of Self-Actualisation until you have a well-developed value system in place.

More than that: we believe that this value system could be the 'missing link' in Freudian psychoanalytical theory, that the ego-id-superego equation is incomplete without the infra-ego. This infra-ego, this value system, is the foundation on which all psychology might be found to rest; it could even be the key to a unifying theory of all psychological theories.

But let's leave all that to the academics to puzzle over. All we are concerned with at this stage is how values affect us in our escape from our Comfort Zones.

Where do these values come from? Why do some people have them, and others not? Why are some better developed than others?

Most of these values are found in sacred texts and taught by all religions as the rules or conditions for entry into Heaven or Nirvana or to attain perfection. And since all religions ultimately have to do with living the 'good life' and improving oneself spiritually in the quest for perfection, these rules or commandments or values are *eternal truths*.

These rules or values are then perpetuated and retaught (to a greater or lesser extent) by parents and teachers. Unfortunately, as in the game of 'Broken Telephone', they become diluted and warped in time, according to the circumstances and insights (or lack thereof) of each individual, and according to the society where he or she grows up. They are also amended and changed through varying interpretations, often to suit the needs of the individual or to justify their contravention.

30

If everyone lived according to the same undiluted set of values, there would be no crime or injustice. Life on earth would, in fact, be exactly like Heaven. No need for laws, or police forces or armies or weapons or prisons.

Which brings us to a very important question:

What if, in your quest for self-honesty and self-expression, you have *not* got a fundamental value system? What if your actions are not underpinned and governed by a well-developed set of values?

The answer is simple: you would inevitably violate the rights of others. Your actions (or at least some of them) would be egocentric (ie relating to the self, to personal gain, to satisfying selfish needs and desires).

In your new journey in life, in your quest to attain true inner peace and self-fulfilment, values are an absolutely vital component of true growth. Without them, all the rest is just a meaningless charade.

Values and spiritual levels

Before we leave the issue of values, there are more puzzling questions.

Why is it that two children, brought up in the same home by the same parents and within the same country's laws and the same religion, often have completely different sets of values? Why are some people's values so strong that they will be true to them even if this results in personal loss or discomfort or discredit — or worse, as many famous martyrs have demonstrated?

Are values inherent at birth? Are they like genes? In other words, are they part of the 'equipment' we are born with — like talents, physical strength, beauty or IQ level? Are we in fact born on a certain 'spiritual level'? If so — and there certainly seems to be sufficient evidence to believe this — is this proof of reincarnation? Of an accumulation of values and spiritual knowledge in some part of us that is not physical and is therefore eternal? That has experienced and learned many things even before we were born?

xploring the infra-ego, with all its implications and extrapolations, will hopefully provide many of these answers. As the authors of this book, we would greatly welcome any suggestions or thoughts or contributions. If you have any insights or personal experiences which you believe may be useful in any way, we would greatly appreciate your sharing your thoughts with us. It goes without saying that your contribution would be acknowledged in any publication which might result from our research. You will find address details at the end of this book.

Hello! We've gone way off the track!

When you're on a journey, you'll sometimes spot something interesting beside the road and stop to take a closer look. I must confess I'm more guilty than most. In fact it has become something of a family joke that when we're on holiday I stop frequently, or take a side-road to examine some waterfall or to view an ancient ruin or a monument. Yet I have never failed to be enriched or enlightened by these excursions.

So I make no apology for my digression, because I believe that things like the infra-ego and spiritual levels and values are very important aspects of our quest to escape our Comfort Zones.

But — to summarise where we were, and where we're supposed to be going:

We were trying to understand exactly what Comfort Zones are, and what kinds of Comfort Zones there are. We were trying to understand how we get trapped in them, and what factors and what qualities within us cause us either to remain trapped or have the courage to escape.

So, let's continue!

The incredible power of your mind

One of the most important things to know about Comfort Zones is that you can't escape your castle until you know you're in one. And because the castle walls are subjective and primarily the constructions of our own minds, we have to recognise the incredible power (both positive and negative) of the mind in creating and using what psychologists call *defence mechanisms* to delude us into accepting what are often gross compromises in our lives.

These defence mechanisms are exactly what they say they are: they are ways of defending and protecting our ego from unpleasant realities in our lives. For example, *denial* is a psychological refusal to grant the truth of a statement or even hard facts. This is illustrated by the amusing story of the proud mother watching her son at a military passing-out parade and smugly telling her neighbour, 'Look, Johnny's the only one in step!' Just try to explain to this mother that her Johnny is the only one *out* of step and watch how angry she will get with you, and how doggedly she will continue to try to prove you wrong.

There are many kinds of defence mechanism. We use the mechanism of avoidance as a kind of ostrich-with-head-in-the-sand way of not confronting unpleasant truths; or the mechanism of *rationalisation* to produce a self-satisfying (but inadequate and often quite untrue) reason for our behaviour or that of others. For example, a woman finds out her husband uses bribery and back-handers in his business, but rationalises his behaviour by reasoning that 'It's tough doing business these days − every man for himself − and sometimes these things are necessary. Doesn't everyone do it anyway? I mean, look at our government! Also, I know he's only doing it to provide better for me and the kids... so it's OK.' If we remember the example of Johnny's mother above, try to imagine how difficult it is to convince someone that they are using defence mechanisms when the issues are far more complex, far more emotional, far more personal. I am increasingly amazed and appalled at the unbelievable powers of self-deception!

Of course, we all use these mechanisms to a greater or lesser extent in our everyday lives. That's completely human. But there's a danger that the balance can tip and we may start living more in our 'invented' world than in the real one.

I remember very vividly when I first encountered an example of this. In my final year of psychology I had to visit a mental hospital in my home town of Bloemfontein in South Africa and encountered a patient who, in real life, had been a lowly junior clerk on the South African Railways. The problem was, this man now believed that he was Napoleon Bonaparte. He strutted arrogantly around the ward, barking orders to his fellow patients and boasting (not with too much historical accuracy!) about his great victories, and frequently referring to the matron as 'Josephine'.

On the surface he seemed very happy. I recall asking my professor about the morality and ethics of our would-be profession: was it not cruel to shatter the illusions of this Emperor and bring him down to earth with a bump, back to a world where he was just an insignificant nobody, a little grey man living in a dull grey world, with no hope and no future? The answer was self-evident. His world (no matter how appealing) *was only an illusion*, and if he hoped to function and realise his potential as a real human being he had to be brought back to the world of reality. In effect, as therapists we had to be cruel to be kind.

I have related this example because the same holds true for anyone wanting to escape their Comfort Zones. We sometimes have to be cruel to ourselves in order to be kind to ourselves. We have to accept the pain of confronting our inner honesty. It is an absolutely vital step in escaping our Comfort Zones to examine critically − even brutally − all their aspects in order to separate illusion from reality. To recognise who the 'real you' is, separated from the 'you' that others expect you to be, or that has been conditioned by society and parental influences, without fooling yourself through denial or rationalisation or other self-deceptive and self-protective mechanisms.

Don't ever underestimate the immense power of your mind in being able to create perceptions that are as real as reality itself ... but also never underestimate its ability to shatter those illusions and lead you out of your Comfort Zones. It's all in your mind and, unless you are psychotic and need professional therapy, you can use this mind power in a positive way to improve your life.

No doubt there are as many types of Comfort Zones, and as many reasons for those Comfort Zones, as there are human beings on earth. And yet I believe that if we can learn the basic principles, we can successfully apply them to all individual instances — just as we can drive almost any vehicle once we have learned the basics of driving. So: here's another example of a Comfort Zone.

Comfort Zones can be pure fantasy

The dividing line between everyday 'fantasy Comfort Zones' and believing you're Napoleon Bonaparte is perilously thin. Almost everyone day-dreams and has fantasies about themselves, about being rich and famous, about living on a desert island.

And these are all very natural and pleasant thoughts, because having dreams is often the most important motivation and starting point for you to turn them into reality. But when you are more in love with your dream than with the reality of your life, you've got a problem. Let's look at such a case.

Case study: Ned

Ned is trapped in a lonely world populated by himself and three tanks of tropical fish. He has few acquaintances and even fewer friends, and makes a meagre living as a free-lance interior decorator, although his real talent lies in the fine arts. And yet his paintings are restrained and over-structured: a mirror of his soul. The one spontaneous work he produced was snapped up by a gallery, but he lacks the confidence or the inner peace to reproduce this spontaneity.

Several years ago he was married and emigrated to Brazil, where for a while he pursued a happy and successful career. Then his world fell apart: he was divorced and moved back to Zimbabwe where he worked for a large design company. Yet he couldn't shake off his past, and was forever making plans to move back to Rio and somehow resurrect the good times. He would set the date, put in his letter of resignation, and then retract it when the time drew near. He would make excuses about

---

its not being 'the right time', or not being able to leave his ailing father who was entirely dependent on him. And then a few months later the cycle would start all over again.

Finally, his employer grew tired of Ned's ambivalence and decided to make him confront reality. When Ned wanted to retract his umpteenth resignation, his boss gently refused and enthused about the new life and the new opportunities Ned would have in Brazil. When Ned said that he had to postpone his departure because he couldn't get a tenant for his apartment, his boss found a friend who was willing to take it. When Ned couldn't find a home for his fish, his boss offered to take them himself. Finally, there were no corners left to hide in and, unable to confront the self-deception of his fantasy Comfort Zone, Ned 'escaped' into a private world and the security of a mental institution. Years later, he still continues his lonely existence, living on the dreams of one day going to Brazil.

WHY DO WE ALLOW OURSELVES TO BECOME TRAPPED?

Why do we allow ourselves to become trapped in pools of stagnation when everything mitigates against this? Because, as I have said earlier, everything in the universe is in a constant state of growth and progress, and only man with his rational mind has the ability consciously or unconsciously to suspend and suppress this growth and cocoon himself in 'safe harbours', or to allow circumstances or other people to do this to him. Yet this is not natural; it goes against all the laws of Nature to allow ourselves to become trapped in Comfort Zones.

I found these thoughts echoed in Arthur Koestler's book *Janus*, in which he talks about the natural process of perpetual growth as '... the active striving of all living matter towards the optimal realisation of the planet's evolutionary potential'. Of course, I would like to expand his 'living matter' to include all things organic and inorganic, but I like his stress on the words *active striving*. If you want to grow, if you want to escape your Comfort Zone, you have to actively *do something about it*.

36

It's also interesting to note that biologist and Nobel Prize winner Albert Szent-Györgyi coined the term 'syntropy' which he defines as 'the innate drive in living matter to perfect itself'.

Marilyn Ferguson, who is in my opinion one of the brightest and most enlightened of all modern writers, is far more optimistic when she talks of this process of inner growth as being a worldwide phenomenon which she calls 'the Aquarian Conspiracy', that it is a *transformation* and an *evolution* of the entire species of man that has only just begun, spearheaded by an enlightened few who are often seen by their friends and family as being touched in the head. Many leading magazines and books have in recent years echoed her belief and are talking about a major trend towards spiritual enlightenment and progress towards a new spiritual age on earth.

But, if we all have this 'innate drive' within us, why do we fight against it by allowing ourselves to become trapped in Comfort Zones? And if there is indeed a major trend towards increased spiritual awareness, and if growth and forward progress are such natural and inevitable processes, why do we inhibit this by getting trapped in Comfort Zones? To explain, I'll try to illustrate some of the most common reasons *why* we become trapped.

ONE: WE'RE IN A COMFORT ZONE BECAUSE WE CHOOSE TO BE THERE

The first reason could be that, particularly in our materialistic world, everyone quite naturally strives for pleasure and comfort and tends to avoid risk and pain. In this regard, a Comfort Zone is nothing more than an egocentric hedonism, a conscious or subconscious relegation of your greater self to a stagnant backwater of life, and a stubborn and immature refusal to confront the question of what is the true potential of your life. By clinging to material and emotional security, you are not allowing yourself the chance to expand your existence to experience the full richness of life. Like Jonathan Livingston Seagull, you must overcome the fear of leaving the security of your warm and comfortable nest if you really want to fly.

So, yes, it is very pleasant to be in a Comfort Zone. But the longer you stay, the more you become enmeshed in the web of material possessions and status and security — all of which are only temporary and all of which can suddenly be taken from you, despite all your efforts. Your home could be swallowed up by an earthquake or washed away by a flood or destroyed by fire. You could have a heart attack or a stroke, or the breadwinner could be run over by a bus. (And haven't the world's insurance companies made a mint out of exploiting all these fears of loss!) You could lose everything through a stock market crash or an unscrupulous employee or partner. Your spouse could run off with another man or woman. The list is endless.

And so you become more and more possessive; more jealous of what you've got; more neurotic and paranoid about losing them. And more and more trapped in your Comfort Zones.

Compare this to developing an attitude that these things are all only temporal and therefore relatively unimportant in the greater scheme of things, that they are on the lower levels of any true measure of man's development and success in life. (We'll discuss this in depth later under Spiritual Levels and Maslow's Hierarchy of Needs.) I'm not saying that they are unimportant — just that in this age we have attached far too much importance to them.

But let's face it: the modern world's values have become screwed up. And we have to recognise that as being one of the main reasons why people feel lost and unfulfilled and aimless — because the entire basis of their life is no longer centred on permanence and inner values and truths, but on ephemeral values imposed by others around us. Escaping your Comfort Zones is an inner evolution and transformation — a return to the 'real you'.

And that's where we believe this book is different from so many other 'self-help' books that concentrate on making you more successful, wealthy, powerful, important. *How to Escape your Comfort Zones* is about finding a richer, more fulfilled inner self based on a return to genuine values and eternal truths. As we said in the introduction, this is not a 'religious' book, although you will find that almost every religion on earth points out the importance of these deep values and principles. So there must be something in it — and we believe that 'something' is the key to finding true inner peace and self-fulfilment.

By this, I am not in any way negating religion or any God you may choose to worship; nor am I saying that *you* are God. You were created with a wonderful capacity to think and reason, and even to contemplate your own origins and destiny. You have freedom of choice; the freedom to decide which God you believe in (if any) and which of His (or Her!) teachings to obey or reject. And yet it is this very freedom of choice that makes your faith so powerful and which to me is the essence of real love, be it towards your God or your fellow man. It goes without saying that an all-powerful God could simply force you or manipulate you to love and obey Him, if He wanted to. And yet He gives you the right to decide for yourself.

I am also not advocating that by living your life according to deep inner values and eternal truths you need necessarily live a life of austerity and poverty. All it means is having the right *perspective* of material wealth and possessions; that you earn them honestly; and that they never become your purpose or mission in life, or excuses for corruption and dishonesty. We must take care that material possessions never become a Comfort Zone prison which prevents us from seeing greater truths and pursuing more meaningful things in life.

The all-important question must be asked: If money and success and status are so vitally important, then how come many rich and successful and important people are often desperately unhappy and unfulfilled? Why do success and money often go hand in hand with corruption, manipulation, selfishness, hypocrisy? And in a world which has religiously pursued materialism and personal success for so long, why are there still so many shells of human beings — the kind of people T S Eliot described as 'hollow men'?

The world and society and the media also often lead us on the wrong path. Life is difficult in the face of the confusing signals that encourage materialistic and ephemeral goals, rather than eternal and spiritual ones, that stress the importance of social acceptance and the mechanisms for achieving this (status symbols, the nice house in a good suburb, and so on) which are entrenched by advertising and the media (television in particular!) more than anything else.

Wear Calvin Klein jeans or Nike sneakers. Drive a Mercedes Benz or a BMW. (There's nothing wrong with any of these products — the very fact that they are the best of their kind is the reason why they are so desirable!) The messages continue: Be slim, have straight teeth, get rid of the wrinkles, have bigger (or smaller) boobs. Watch 'Lifestyles of the Rich and Famous'. Succeed, succeed, succeed. And wear the badges to prove to the world how great you are.

In short: we get trapped in material Comfort Zones because we *want* to. Because everyone keeps telling us that we're not succeeding in life unless we have all these things. If we can't keep up with the Joneses, we feel we're failures — and the people around us are often only too quick and eager to reinforce this belief.

To me, there is something desperately wrong and desperately sad about a world that has become so spiritually destitute that it has totally lost perspective on what is important and what is not. Of course, materialism and false values are not unique to our times, but they seem to be more entrenched than ever before.

The wisdom of Thoreau

You have only to read great American philosopher Henry David Thoreau's *Walden* to see the folly of such things and to realise how such external symbols — far from being badges to show the world how great you are — often demonstrate spiritual immaturity and warped values. The truth is that material

40

success and its symbols can deceive and seduce you away from the things that are really important in life, the things that will bring you true peace and happiness and inner fulfilment.

Two hundred years ago, Thoreau became sickened by the values of society around him in Concord, Massachusetts and decided to 'take time out' by going to live beside Walden Pond in a forest belonging to his friend Ralph Waldo Emerson. In his own words, he wanted '... to live deliberately, to front only the essential facts of life, and to see if I could not learn what it had to teach, and not, when I came to die, discover that I had not lived... I wanted to live deep and suck out all the marrow of life... to drive life into a corner, and reduce it to its lowest terms.' And his objective is even clearer when he says, 'Rather than love, than money, than fame, give me Truth.' Living beside Walden Pond, he searched for and wrote about that Truth.

Using simple logic, Thoreau decided that the most precious commodity we have is *time*. No matter whether we die young or old, each of us has X number of days to live, so everything we do must be measured according to how much time it takes. For example, he looked at his neighbours, the farmers of Concord, and found that '... for the most part they have been toiling twenty, thirty or forty years, that they may become the real owners of their farms.' This, Thoreau concluded, was far too high a price to pay. And so he built a log cabin, using an axe to chop down trees. He created a comfortable home which served essentially the same function as the mansion on the hill, and he only had to 'spend' six months of his life to get it. In addition, he had the benefit of fresh air, sunshine and healthy exercise. To Thoreau's thinking, *that* was a bargain.

Thoreau also stripped bare the warped values of society, from fashions to commerce. His simple logic is as valid today as it was then; his simple truths difficult to argue with in terms of inner peace and self-fulfilment: 'I was rich, if not in money, in sunny hours and summer days, and spent them lavishly.' Or, 'I would rather sit on a pumpkin and have it all to myself, than be crowded on a velvet cushion.' At one stage he refused the gift of a doormat because he thought the time spent shaking it would be wasted — that 'Life is frittered away by detail.'

(Just look at all the unnecessary, time-wasting detail of our own lives. This is often a reason why we can't even recognise that we are in Comfort Zones: we become so bogged down by everyday practical problems and chores that we forget our greater purpose or who we are. That's one of the reasons why I recommend 'Taking Time Out' (see Chapter 5) and creating regular 'islands' in your life as one of the most important steps in escaping your Comfort Zone. You need to get to know your real self by temporarily removing yourself from those confusing 'smoke screen' complications in your life.)

As Thoreau became closer to Nature, he started recognising the interconnectivity and integral similarities with mankind. Every aspect of Thoreau's scenery represented to him the human soul, that invisible presence men have called spirit, self or personality. Walden Pond itself he saw as representing life eternal, 'a perennial spring' forever brimming with fresh water from its hidden bottom. Like the soul, Walden 'had no visible inlet or outlet except by the clouds and evaporation'. Like man's character, '... perhaps we need only to know how his shores trend and his adjacent country or circumstances, to infer his depth and concealed bottom.' How true this is of people: we need only to examine the things they do to determine what their true character is and what their values are. Their behaviour, their actions and reactions, are a mirror of their inner being, of their spiritual level.

As I was reading *Walden*, the question that puzzled me most was why on earth Thoreau ever returned to the falseness and superficiality of the people and society of his day — why he chose once again to become part of everything he had criticised so vehemently. Finally, I found the answer:

Thoreau finally left the pond 'because he had more lives to live, and could not spare any more time for that one'. He returned to Concord, carrying a message to his fellow country-men: '... be a Columbus to whole new continents and worlds within you... explore the private sea, the Atlantic and Pacific Ocean of one's being alone.'

It was only in doing research for this book and especially in reading Thoreau and Joseph Campbell's analogies in myths and legends that I realised that this 'return to the unenlightened' is an inevitable part of every spiritual journey. You will find you return to what appears to be some place you've been before, and are tempted to say, 'Been there, done that!' with some annoyance, until you discover that you have 'Been there, done that' as another person entirely; that you have returned with a completely new perspective. And so the lessons you learn (and the lessons you can teach to others) are completely different too.

I have used Thoreau to illustrate that he knew the value of the 'inner journey' and a return to genuine values in attaining inner peace and fulfilment. By leaving the 'Comfort Zone' of Concord society and exposing its follies, he risked ridicule and criticism. He accepted the risk of loneliness and won the treasures of Nature and insight and self-actualisation. He won the value of living in the 'now' moment and 'sucking the marrow out of life'.

And with a full acceptance of living, came a full acceptance of dying and an understanding of it as merely a natural passage in one's eternal growth. For example, in describing how leaves decay and bring forth new life, Thoreau writes, '... they teach us how to die. One wonders if the time will ever come when men, with their boasted faith in immortality, will lie down as gracefully and as ripe.'

Is that inner peace, or is that inner peace?

Ah, you say, but *I'm* not a great philosopher. *I'm* not a Thoreau.

Maybe you aren't. But you can go on your own journey and you can discover the same truths – and the same inner peace – that he did. As another great philosopher, Nietzsche, said: 'This is my way; what is *your* way? *The* way doesn't exist.' Each Comfort Zone is unique. Each escape is unique. Because you are unique.

So, to sum up about being trapped in a material Comfort Zone because we *want* to be trapped: Nobody can deny that we need money to live and pay our mortgage and rent and put food on the table and pay for our children's education and, of course, enjoy some of the great pleasures of life that money can help us get. But the vital thing is to maintain perspective and balance, and to recognise that material possessions are often some of the highest and most impenetrable castle walls trapping you in a Comfort Zone.

And, as Koestler reminds us:

> As long as he succeeds in his efforts he enjoys a certain amount of security and superficial happiness and content-ment, but his betrayal of his higher self, of inner values, leaves an inner emptiness and insecurity which will become manifest when anything goes wrong in his pursuit for success. And even if nothing should go wrong he often pays for his human failure with ulcers, heart attacks, or a general disturbing sense of misdirection and superficiality... he will live life only as a veneer; an empty shell.

Yes, the price of success is tragically high. Because no matter how much you have, there is always someone who has more. And intense competitiveness results in innumerable human tragedies ranging from bickering and household quarrels to theft and embezzlement, to ulcers and heart attacks and nervous breakdowns, perhaps even to the desperate solution described by Arthur Miller in his great play *Death of a Salesman* where Willy Loman could not confront the reality that he was a failure, when he could no longer fool himself or anyone else that he was a great salesman, he simply could not face life any longer. The whole materialistic ethic of the modern world is summed up in the Requiem of the play when Happy says: 'Willy Loman did not die in vain. He had a good dream. It's the only dream you can have — to come out number-one man.'

Death of an advertising man

Being number-one man was a dream I myself got caught up in for a long time. And I succeeded: at school I was always top of the class academically, and one of my sportsmasters once told my father that I was capable of representing my country in any one of three sports. At university I graduated cum laude and won the academic medal — which was even more significant in that I couldn't afford to attend classes full time and did both my degrees through evening classes. When I became a rock musician, our group made records and won the local equivalent of a Grammy Award. I wrote the lyrics for over a hundred recorded songs, and co-wrote a rock opera which featured international stars Oliver Reed and Michael York. And when I became an advertising copywriter, I was soon winning local and international awards for creativity, and was creative director of several leading agencies before starting my own. From a zero base, we enjoyed meteoric growth and within three years we employed some fifty-five people with billings of over twenty-five million a year.

Indubitably, I was a Success. And yet I felt terribly empty inside. More than anything, I hated some of the things I came across with alarming frequency: superficiality, expediency, corruption, greed, bribery and back-handers, immoral egocentrism and back-stabbing for the sake of a buck. Even within my own company, I increasingly failed to see eye to eye with some of my partners. I found myself wondering if it was all worth it — and I couldn't dodge the answer.

When I contemplated giving it all up, I often wondered whether growing up in the 'hippie era' with its anti-establishment stance and 'opting out' philosophies was my motivation for escaping the rat race. Yet I was no longer a teenager with a grandstand philosopher's view of life: I had worked my butt off and had beaten the 'establishment' at its own game. And that by playing the game with complete honesty and integrity.

At that point, Fate intervened. Our biggest client had long expressed disapproval with certain aspects and members of our agency and suggested that we create a new division so that I could personally handle his business while they continued with the rest. Unfortunately this didn't go down too well with my partners, and eventually ended in a bitter legal battle. My client stood by me and, as a token of my gratitude for their loyalty, I bartered my own share price to protect them when my partners threatened to drag them into the legal morass. (I never told my client about this. If any of them should read this, it will be the first they know about it.) I then negotiated with a friend from a competitive agency to take over the entire account, worth many millions of dollars, in return only for a guarantee that all my loyal staff who had walked out with me would be employed. I personally got nothing — but at least my integrity was intact.

When it was all over, I was utterly disillusioned with human beings, and with advertising in general.

I went through a long period of anger and emotional limbo, during which time of confusion I capitulated to the Comfort Zone of 'security' and accepted the job of creative director of one of the country's biggest advertising agencies to try to get some stability into my life. From day one, it was a disaster. I was shackled creatively and muzzled by an autocratic management hierarchy, and after three years of sheer torture I finally got out.

By then, my personal confrontation and transformation was finally starting to take root, and I decided to concentrate on doing things I loved, with people I liked and respected, in my own time. It's a decision I've never regretted.

I still love many aspects of advertising, and until very recently I still consulted for major agencies and found it a valuable contribution to my cash-flow while I was developing my career as a writer and Comfort Zone escapee. Especially, I enjoyed working with advertising people and found them a very valuable stimulus for my writing.

But the difference was that I was now playing according to my own rules: I was in control of my life, concentrating on doing things I loved, with people I liked and respected, in my own time. And, most importantly, I was escaping my materialistic

Comfort Zone — the one I'd spent so many years desperately wanting to be in.

TWO: WE'RE IN A COMFORT ZONE BECAUSE WE ARE TOLD TO BE THERE

As we have seen, the first example of materialistic Comfort Zones is also an example of being 'forced' by others to be there — encouraged by society, the media, advertising, material social norms, the opinions of our 'friends' and colleagues. Because we attach so much importance to these material things and these social approvals, *we become dependent on those who provide these things*. Our bosses. Our companies. Our husbands. Our parents if we're young, or our children if we're old. Or the government — the 'System' — for social security or pensions.

And so the important players and figures of authority in these *dependency relationships* become very powerful jailers keeping us trapped in our castles. They have only to dangle the keys to perks or profit shares or titles, or threaten us with the dungeons or the torture chamber, and we have almost no option but to oblige. But material needs are only one small part of the dependency equation.

In so many other important ways we have become *conditioned* to be dependent on, and to obey, people who have power over us. From the moment we were born we were completely dependent on our mothers for survival — for food, drink, warmth, security, love. When our fathers appeared in our lives, they became the second figure of authority, and so on.

As we grew up we learned that if we were good and obeyed our parents and teachers, we would be rewarded: a pat on the head, a smile, a cookie. But if we disobeyed and acted contrary to their wishes, we were punished: a frown, a beating, standing in the corner, extra homework, disapproval, denial of privileges. We became *conditioned* to obey people who had control over us — mainly because we were totally dependent on them.

47

And even when we become old enough to think for ourselves and question these figures of authority, many of us still allow this dependency/control relationship to continue. In the army, at college, in our first jobs. And in our personal relationships. And their influence is frighteningly powerful.

The incredible power of 'authority' over people

A series of remarkable experiments was conducted by Dr Stanley Milgram in the Psychology Department at Yale University in the early seventies to assess how obedient the average person was to authority − in this case represented by a white-coated professor.

Volunteers were told that the experiment was to find out whether punishment had a positive effect on a student who was seated in a kind of electric chair with an electrode attached to his wrist. The volunteers had to ask the student questions, and if he answered wrongly they were to administer an electric shock. (Unbeknown to the volunteers, the 'student' was a hired actor briefed to react to these non-existent shocks.)

The volunteers were seated in front of an impressive-looking 'shock generator' with switches that allowed the voltage to be increased from 15 to 450 volts. If the 'student' answered incorrectly, the volunteer had to 'punish' him by giving him a shock, starting at 15 volts and increasing each time by a further 15 volts.

Of course the 'student' played along and reacted with increasing alarm and discomfort to each non-existent shock, starting with mild grunts at about 75 volts and progressing to screams of pain at about 150 volts. At 315 volts, after a terrible scream, the 'student' cried out that he no longer wanted to continue with the experiment and then refused to answer any more questions. The professor, however, told the volunteer that a non-answer should be treated as 'incorrect' and dealt with accordingly. After three 'shocks' at the maximum of 450 volts, the experiment was stopped. Remember, the volunteer really believed the shocks were real!

When a panel of thirty-nine psychiatrists was asked before the experiment to predict what would happen, they predicted that virtually all the 'volunteers' would flatly refuse to obey the professor; that a sadistic few (four per cent of volunteers) would possibly go up to 150 volts, and that only a pathological one in a thousand might go all the way to 450 volts.

But, incredibly, the results proved them to be absolutely wrong. Amazingly, *well over sixty per cent of the volunteers*, acting under no greater coercion than the authority of a 'professor' they had never met before, pushed the shock level up to the maximum 450 volts as a pure obedience response to an authoritarian request.

This experiment was repeated by various researchers in Germany, South Africa, Italy and Australia. Not only were the results confirmed, but the percentage of 'obedient' volunteers was even higher — as high as eighty-five per cent in Munich.

If we consider that the 'professor's' power over his volunteers was far less than, say, that of a boss over his workers, or a husband over his wife, or parents over their children, we can begin to understand just how frighteningly powerful an influence figures of authority can have on our lives.

What is even more frightening is Dr Milgram's conclusion that 'ordinary people, simply doing their jobs [*Author: Or simply going about their daily lives!*], and without any particular hostility on their part, can become agents in a terribly destructive process. *Moreover, even when the destructive effects of their work becomes patently clear, and they are asked to carry out actions incompatible with fundamental standards of morality, relatively few people have the internal resources needed to resist authority.*'

If this innate obedience to authority — whether it be to an individual, a system, a government or a religion — is so incredibly powerful a part of us, can you imagine how it affects every aspect of our everyday lives? Without even thinking about it, we have become conditioned like Pavlov's dogs to respond in a predetermined way.

And that way is in direct conflict with *you*. Because the fact is that obedience to authority *is* 'blind' in so many instances. It is so much a part of us that we aren't even aware of its influence. And yet it affects almost everything we do — and are — in life.

How this obedience to authority can influence everyday life

When I was in Munich recently I visited Dachau — the notorious Nazi death camp. I had expected it to be in some remote part of the countryside, hidden from the world. Yet, incredibly, it seemed to be right in the middle of a middle-class suburb. Obviously the city has grown since the War, but nevertheless it was very close to civilised society. The citizens in the surrounding area must have been aware of what was going on. So why didn't they stop it?

In retrospect, and having confronted my own lack of action in apartheid South Africa, I can only conclude that the ordinary, decent folk simply closed their minds to the atrocities and accepted that the Powers That Be were acting in the best interests of the people who had voted them into power; the Powers that were in control of the country were doing what was best for Germany.

But apart from such obvious and universally known examples of people's blind obedience to authority, I have seen the principles of Dr Milgram's experiment enacted many times in my own experience of life. A gentle, God-fearing accountant who resorted to the most heinous manipulation of figures on the instructions of a devious managing director. A financial director who tapped into the company's pension fund to balance the figures to make the chairman look good to his overseas principals. I could go on and on, but I have chosen just these two examples to show how two average, honest men became criminals not because they wanted to line their own pockets but through simple, unquestioning obedience to figures of authority.

It's the same principle used by every army in the world. Break down the individual, teach him not to think for himself but merely to react without thinking to a command. And its legacy is tragically evident in millions of unmarked graves all around the world.

Blind obedience to authority? Bullshit. If there was one thing I as a parent was determined to teach my two sons, it was to become independent thinkers and be intelligently critical of figures of authority and their rules and regulations. Not anarchistic or anti-establishment. Just intelligently critical. And true to themselves.

The same principles of obedience to authority are evident in most relationships — and even more so in societies when one sex dominates. 'Male chauvinism' has become the most commonly known enemy of the past twenty years in the Western world, and I see it around me in virtually every relationship. True, the 'woman's role' has been institutionalised over many years by 'social norms' emanating from a long legacy of male-dominated societies, and the over-reaction in the sadly often hysterical and irrational 'women's lib' movements has, in many instances, only harmed the cause rather than helped it.

I have been fortunate to have been involved for most of my working life in careers and environments where gender played almost no role — where women earned their right to be regarded as equals or superiors simply by performing as well as, or better than, their male counterparts. And although I can remember myself being pretty chauvinistic at times when I was younger, I have since learned not to be so petty and small-minded and egoistic. I get angry when I am confronted by someone trying to claim authority or respect simply on the basis of his or her own chauvinism. Yet it is a sad reality that many people allow themselves to be limited and manipulated and dominated by such immature attempts to control or feel important.

To quote Koestler again:

Only the free man who has emancipated himself from authority — authority that threatens and rewards, that controls and protects — can he make use of his power of reason and grasp the world and his role in it objectively, without illusion but also with the ability to develop and to

51

make use of the capacities inherent in him. Only if we grow up and cease to be children dependent on and afraid of authority and figures who control and manipulate our lives can we dare think for ourselves; but the reverse is also true.

Koestler sees man as being essentially Janus-like (hence the title of his book), that is, having two faces in eternal conflict since each is possessed of two opposing tendencies: an *integrative* tendency to function as part of the larger whole (ie the society, family, company), and a *self-assertive* tendency to preserve his individual autonomy. He believed that when these two opposing tendencies are in balance with each other, all is well; when one dominates then it leads to emotional disturbance.

It may therefore be said that in the modern world with its over-emphasis on dependency relationships (to spouses and parents and teachers and bosses and societies and governments and religions and fashions and status symbols), man is dominated by *integrative* tendencies and thus needs to stimulate his *self-assertive* tendencies in order to re-establish balance. (That is, escape his Comfort Zones!)

Yet, as I have mentioned earlier, integration is vitally important. No man is an island. Nobody can function completely independently of the world around him. And so what we need is to establish and maintain a healthy *interrelationship* between the two; preserving our autonomy without ignoring the need to integrate this with the systems and organisations and relationships that we are part of. If we allow either one to dominate, or if we are on a different spiritual level to those around us, we're in trouble — as the following case study will show.

Control/dependency case study: Claire

This woman has vastly superior talent, intelligence and spiritual insight to her weak, egoistic and manipulative husband — yet she allows him to pamper his ego and exercise his inferiority complex by telling her what she can and can't wear, who can and can't be her friends, what time she has to be home, and so on. And no matter how hard her friends have tried to make her aware that she has the right to assert her independence, she simply continues to be fifty per cent of who she could and should be, and every day allows herself to become more and more entangled in a web of control and dependency – partially because her husband believes it is her 'role' as a woman to be subservient to her husband, partially because he is paranoid about the attentions other men pay her (she is extremely attractive) and therefore watches her movements like a hawk, but mainly because he controls the purse strings and uses them to tie her down. Having recently made a great deal of money in his import-export business – mainly through parasitical relationships entered into primarily for acquiring business – he has not only predictably acquired all the toys of the *nouveau riche*, but also used his new-found power to ensnare Claire even more securely. And bring her down to his own spiritual level.

Of course, a control/dependency relationship cannot exist without the participation of both parties. And as much as her husband exerts the control, so Claire *allows* him to do it because of the deep-rooted nature of her dependency needs. Apart from the portcullises of materialistic comforts and needs, Claire also has a very complex series of emotional and psychological walls to her castle. These range from self-imposed responsibility for the welfare of her parents and brother who live in the guest cottage of Claire's home, to guilt and emotional baggage from several failed relationships, to a paranoia about losing her 'security' which has its origins in her childhood when her family lost everything in being forced to flee their country of birth when a new regime took over. And all of these vulnerabilities and skeletons in the cupboard are exploited by her husband in an ongoing attempt to maintain total control over her life.

Manipulation and capitulation. Control and dependency. And because she is terrified of bursting her bubble of security, she continues to defend and justify his actions and the low opinions others have of him, and to rationalise other aspects of her life in her Comfort Zone. And I have mentioned only some of the parapets of Claire's castle – we won't even go to the depths of the dungeons and look at her husband's perverse sexual whims and the pornographic videos he takes of her, or his beating her when drunk or high on dope or cocaine, or boasting that he used occult mantras to 'will' the conception of a late (and from her point of view, completely unwanted) child which was simply the final padlock on her prison door in guaranteeing her dependency for several years to come.

Can Claire ever escape from so complex and convoluted a Comfort Zone? When she is alone she often shows that she is aware that she is trapped and manipulated, and admits she doesn't love her husband (although she enjoys the material benefits of his business success), and confesses that she isn't happy or fulfilled in her life. She constantly talks of doing something that will make her financially independent and allow her to have her own free will once more.

But she refuses to see that apart from her dreams and schemes being unlikely to come to fruition (especially since because of the demands of the child she doesn't have the time, the capital or the self-confidence, and because her husband is unlikely to support anything that will lessen his control over her), such 'external solutions' are simply not the answer.

She must undergo an *internal* transformation, a rejuvenation and a strengthening of her emotional and spiritual inner self before she can even begin to think of escaping. And yet she has resisted using her obvious intelligence and insight to confront the truths of her existence and take the first step towards taking full responsibility for her own life, taking control of it, and escaping her Comfort Zones. External 'escapes' can be an important catalyst for change, but they must be accompanied by an inner transformation if they are to have any lasting benefit of personal growth.

Avoiding the truth isn't the answer

And until she undergoes an inner transformation, Claire will simply continue to allow her castle walls to grow higher and higher around her by continuing her denials and avoidance of the truth and rationalisations to make her life seem rosy. But, as Marilyn Ferguson writes in quoting Thomas Kühn:

> Avoidance is a short-term answer, like aspirin. Avoidance settles for dull chronic pain rather than brief acute confrontation. Kühn also points out that 'Denial, however human and natural a response, exacts a terrible

price. It is as if we settled for living in the anterooms of our life . . . Denial is a way of life. More accurately, it is a way of *diminishing* life; a kind of self-deceiving camouflage to make life seem more manageable. Our ability to deny — to block our experience — is an evolutionary dead end. Rather than confronting the honesty of our experience and *transforming* pain, conflict and fear into actions that will put them behind us, we often divert or dampen them with a kind of unwitting hypnosis.

'Over a lifetime, more and more stress accumulates. If there is no release, our very consciousness — our feeling of being alive in the moment — narrows. The floodlight of life shrinks into the slender beam of a flashlight. We lose our vividness of colours, sensitivity to sounds, peripheral vision, sensitivity to others, emotional intensity. The spectrum of *awareness* becomes even narrower. The real alienation is not from the world but from *ourselves*.'

Can you think of anything worse than being sentenced to life imprisonment in a control/dependency Comfort Zone? Living on self-deceptions, rationalising unpleasant truths, avoiding reality? And yet you hold the keys to escaping in your hands.

But only if you undergo a profound inner transformation — that is, make the decision intellectually and emotionally to escape your Comfort Zone by becoming *truly yourself*, by asserting your own needs and desires and resisting those who try to control and manipulate you — can you be free to think, to love, to attain a new perspective and orientation on life . . . and be freed from the slavish devotion to the shackles of the previous 'rules' and 'shoulds' and 'musts' and 'cans and can'ts' that dominated and suppressed and limited your life.

But, be warned:

It takes considerable strength and courage to escape your Comfort Zones. As Sigmund Freud is quoted in *The Ethic of Honesty*: 'Some lives are so pent-up that a neurosis may be the least of the evils possible in the circumstances.' But — like the alcoholic — the longer you avoid confronting your problem, the worse it will become. The longer you put off taking the first serious step to escape, the more likely it is that your castle walls will eventually grow to the extent that 'a neurosis may be the least of the evils possible in the circumstances'.

If you think this is the case with you, perhaps you need to consult a professional therapist to help you get off the rack and out of the dungeons so that at least you can *see* your castle walls. You may need anti-depressants, or a very strong and caring mentor. Yet, no matter how high the walls of your castle, I am convinced that you *can* escape. All the natural laws of the universe are on your side. All it takes is for you to make the decision that you will open your mind to confronting the realities and truths of your life; that you be receptive to advice and what may often be painful revelations. What can you possibly lose — apart from lies and self-deceptions and illusions?

So, ask yourself this question: 'Am I going to continue being a diamond lost in a coalyard, a pearl trapped inside a wrinkled and crusted shell, or am I going to take the advice of a character from Brunner's *Shockwave Rider*: "You shall know the truth, and the truth shall make you you." '

As always, it's your decision. And yours alone.

THREE: WE'RE IN A COMFORT ZONE BECAUSE IT'S BECOME A HABIT

We go through daily life in various levels of consciousness. When we are confronted with something new or challenging, we shift into a higher level of consciousness in order to be receptive to the new stimuli and react accordingly. But for most of the day, for most of our familiar activities, we operate largely in 'automatic mode'.

To illustrate this, Koestler talks about the process of driving a car. When we are learning to drive, we have to concentrate carefully on every detail of this complex operation — from the simple mechanical details of manipulating an accelerator, clutch, brake, steering wheel, rearview mirror, and so on, to the more difficult process of co-ordinating all these operations into driving smoothly and safely under vastly differing conditions. And yet we can soon master all these things to the degree where driving becomes automatic — ie without conscious awareness of our actions. We can listen attentively to the radio, hold a conversation, take in the scenery, while the actual process of driving has been shifted to a lower level of consciousness.

If, however, a dog were suddenly to run across the road, we would instantly shift to a higher level of consciousness and awareness to handle the crisis.

Daily living is much the same. Most of the things we do have become *habits*. It is a process which starts in infancy and never stops. And when we are trapped in Comfort Zones, most of our living is in 'automatic mode' — we are not really living, but simply existing. Koestler describes it even better: 'The condensation of learning into habit is accompanied by a dimming of the lights of awareness.'

In order, then, to stimulate an 'escape' from your Comfort Zone, it is obvious that you need to shift your life out of automatic mode into higher levels of mental, physical, emotional and spiritual activity.

This is one of the most important steps in the process, and the exercises which I will later recommend to help you get in touch with the 'real you' through isolation, through stimulation of all your physical senses, through honest self-examination and through the entire process of reading this book and applying the steps, are all vital components in helping you to live life at a higher level of awareness and thus achieve greater fulfilment and enjoyment. Can you now understand why I constantly refer to the need to 'embrace life with both arms'?

These are only three of the possible reasons why we become trapped in Comfort Zones. Most people will find all three valid, in varying degrees, to their own situation. Everyone likes to be comfortable; there are elements of control and dependency in almost every relationship, and almost anything eventually becomes a habit.

Of course there are many more reasons why we find ourselves in Comfort Zones. After reading the first draft of my manuscript, one of my more enlightened and perceptive friends who herself has done extensive research in a similar field, immediately identified three more. She felt that although I had discussed these factors in a general sense, they were important enough to be highlighted as Comfort Zones in their own right.

FOUR: WE'RE IN A COMFORT ZONE BECAUSE WE DON'T EVEN REALISE WE'RE THERE

For whatever reason — be it lack of education or insight, or ignorance, or the fact that our castle walls are such successful and effective screens in blocking out options, or the fact that our rationalisations are so entrenched that we simply refuse to see the truth or even consider the possibility of the truth, or that our egos simply can't accept that we have wasted our lives on something worthless — we sometimes are genuinely not aware that we are trapped in a Comfort Zone, or we simply refuse the possibility of becoming aware.

And so, sadly, even when you try to talk to such people and enlighten them, they often immediately put up such barriers in their minds that the words fall on deaf ears. In fact, the very process of trying to enlighten them makes them fearful and uncomfortable, and immediately causes them to scurry back behind the security of their castle walls where they simply dismiss your advice as misguided nonsense.

This completely natural defence mechanism is used to protect the ego and justify the person's life and circumstances, and the decisions they took to be there. We are so afraid of the truth because acknowledging it will be like pulling off a security blanket and leaving ourselves exposed and naked to the world — and this would *force* us to take action which would disrupt and shatter everything we have clung to for so long.

FIVE: WE'RE IN A COMFORT ZONE BECAUSE WE'RE AFRAID *NOT* TO BE THERE

Here we are motivated almost entirely by gross insecurity. No matter how unpleasant the environment or circumstances, we put up with them because we are petrified of losing even the little security it offers. The very thought of being alone and taking responsibility for our own lives is too threatening and frightening to accept.

I guess this fear of *not* being in a Comfort Zone — and its logical companion, fear of escaping a Comfort Zone — is the most essential component of all Comfort Zones and the main reason why people overstay their welcome in them. (More about this later.)

The problem is that everything in our Comfort Zone is so *familiar*. And it's completely natural to feel comfortable with familiar things around us and to be reluctant to forsake them for new, unknown, untried alternatives. But — like leaving the familiar and safe haven of our homes to go to the scary classrooms and strange teacher on our first day of school — it's an absolutely essential step to growth.

SIX: WE'RE IN A COMFORT ZONE BECAUSE WE'VE JUST GIVEN UP, OR WE'VE BECOME TOO DAMAGED TO FACE THE THOUGHT OF MOVING ON

This kind of Comfort Zone is like a safe harbour to which we have retreated in order to repair the damage after we have been battered by life's turbulent seas. Once in dry dock, we simply cannot face venturing outside the harbour again and confronting the dangers of the world beyond.

Perhaps our lives and emotions really have been too damaged (escaping in this condition would be as risky as putting to sea in a leaking boat!) and we need professional therapy to repair them. And so we give up; we resign ourselves to a compromised life.

Even if we are aware of that, we simply don't have the courage to face the alternative.

I have mentioned only six possible reasons why you might become trapped in a Comfort Zone. Of course, there are many more reasons, and many more types of Comfort Zones. I am sure you could think of many that are unique to your own personal life and experience. I'll give you an example of one in which I found myself — a kind of *Justice* Comfort Zone.

A personal dilemma

I was going through a particularly turbulent stage of my life when, having been badly betrayed in both a personal and a business relationship, I was learning all about the pain of escaping Comfort Zones. My head was filled with innumerable questions about ethics and morals and principles and 'spiritual levels' — those invisible mechanisms that determine how people behave in a crisis situation or when their own survival is threatened. During this time of confusion I dabbled in several different businesses to try to find some direction, and came across an anomaly where it seemed some people in a certain industry were receiving money that wasn't due to them ... and of course, this was depriving others of income that was rightfully theirs.

On the surface it seemed simple: 'Justice' had to be done. And not only would I be righting a wrong, but it also seemed a good business opportunity where I could act as an agent for the wronged parties and collect the money on their behalf. (In most cases they weren't able to do it themselves — which was half the problem.) I did extensive research and gathered piles of documentation to prove my case. I took legal counsel from the top experts in the country to make absolutely sure of my facts. Then I met with representatives of the industry in question and laid my case before them.

I might just as well have thrown a lighted match into a barrel of gunpowder. With a few notable exceptions, their reactions ranged from indignation to near apoplexy. In retrospect, I can understand their alarm at the thought of losing a large slice of their annual incomes and the possibility of retroactive claims which I suggested with naïve insensitivity when the meeting became heated, and which would have ruined many of them completely.

But while I could understand and forgive their fear and their anger, and no matter whether my interpretations or observations were correct or justifiable or not, what *really* dismayed me was certain individuals' hypocrisy in protesting about their 'rights' when they were clearly violating the rights of others. Even more disturbing was the fact that some of my 'friends' in the industry whom I had loyally supported and given business to for many years, turned against me and condemned me, threatening to block me with the force of the entire industry. I was later told that at one of the meetings, a certain individual whom I can only imagine was too cowardly to confront me face to face, apparently had one of the loudest mouths of all in putting me down. The sad irony is that I had personally helped this same individual escape the drudgery of a dead-end, low-class job and given him the vital breaks to help get his business started in a lucrative new career which would catapult him and his family into a life path they could never even have dreamed of before. Apart from giving him invaluable advice and even hands-on input, I used my influence to get him blue-chip, high-profile work to build his portfolio, his credibility and his bank balance, and even to arrange early payment to help his cash-flow. I have a note from this same individual saying that he owed his entire business to me, and that he would be eternally grateful for what I had done. How shallow and ephemeral 'eternal gratitude' can sometimes be!

Angry and hurt by such hypocrisy and appalling ingratitude, I think I would have been quite justified in pursuing the course of justice and even retaliating personally — especially since I was in a position where, for example, I could have utterly destroyed the loudmouth with a stroke of my pen. And yet I was torn inside: if I did any of these things, it would be in conflict with everything I believed in spiritually. Also, many other innocent people would get hurt as well, some of whom were good friends of mine, genuine and loyal and decent people whom I didn't want to see hurt in any way. In fact, hurting or destroying people was the very furthest thing from my mind — I had simply wanted to right a wrong, to correct what I saw as an injustice, and in doing so exploit a good business opportunity for myself. Legally, morally, and ethically I believed I was absolutely in the right; that I had my country's laws and the best legal advice available to support my opinions. Also, I knew that if I opened the issue to the industry media, or to those who were losing out, I would have instantly gained the support of hundreds of people and representative bodies far more powerful than the ones threatening to block me. Yes, Justice *should* be done ... and that concept of Justice was in my opinion clearly defined by all the rules and laws and the concepts of right and wrong that I had grown up with. It was a lovely, safe Comfort Zone I could easily hide behind to justify my actions if I took them. And yet it wasn't quite as simple as that.

I found myself confronted with *subjective* complications — my personal relationships, my guilt that I was somehow not 'doing my duty' (although by informing industry leaders I could argue that it was also up to them to take it further!), my pride and my ego, material gain. Above all, half of me was tempted by the primal urge of retaliation and 'revenge', while my other half told me to be forgiving and compassionate and spiritually mature. It was a dilemma of enormously complex proportions ... and I had to confront the 'rules' of my own 'Justice Comfort Zone' which allowed me to act with the 'approval' of our country's laws and my old ingrained belief system of right and wrong, or decide personally what was *really* 'right' or 'wrong' in terms of my own evolved inner-driven beliefs and judgement. In the end, compassion and spiritual maturity and my own values won the day. I did nothing, and let the matter die a natural death.

Since then, many of these people personally apologised and expressed gratitude for my discretion and compassion. Others, no doubt, were either too embarrassed or too afraid to risk opening Pandora's Box again, or were simply lacking in elementary courtesies, and said nothing. Some possibly didn't even have the intelligence or insight to comprehend the morality of the issue, or the far-reaching implications it could have had in their careers and personal lives, and gloated over how they had 'beaten me' and 'scared me off'.

In retrospect, I often wondered if I had done the right thing. I had broken down the walls of my 'Justice Comfort Zone' by relying on my *own* evolving judgement and deciding that what was 'right or wrong' in this case was determined by external man-made laws; the laws *I* was trying to be true to were *eternal*: altruism, love, compassion, tolerance, mercy. Did I do the right thing in walking away? You be the judge.

All in all, it was a period of extreme pain, confusion and contemplation for me — a time when I had to exercise the utmost personal restraint and spiritual discipline. But, like all difficult life stage transitions, and like all escapes from Comfort Zones, it was also a catalyst for valuable personal growth. Amongst other things, it led me to start seriously examining the whole concept of values and spiritual levels... the deep-down reasons why people behave and react as they do. Why, for example, had some of the people stabbed me in the back, while others (who had just as much to lose, and in addition risked the disapproval of their fellows for supporting me), stayed loyal to me? Why are some people genuine, and others shallow and hypocritical? Why have some people got 'class' while others have none at all? What exactly *is* 'class'? What exactly *are* values? Are they connected? Are people born with values, or can they be learned? Do some people come into the world on different spiritual levels to others? Would this explain an anomaly like 'honour among thieves'? What exactly is 'integrity'? And how do you recognise it, given the fact that many people wear masks and hide their true nature behind carefully constructed façades?

In retrospect, there is no doubt that this incident was the key catalyst for my formulating and developing my theory about the 'Infra-ego', and it also provided much food for thought about Comfort Zones in general. I began to speak to experts and read as much as I could to search for answers, and especially to find out if anyone else had experienced what I was going through. I was amazed at what I found.

YOU'RE NOT ALONE IN YOUR COMFORT ZONE!

As I said before, everybody is trapped in some Comfort Zone or other; often several at the same time. It's nothing to be ashamed of. I've shared some of my own with you in this chapter. But each is unique, and each escape is therefore unique. But the basic principles, the keys to escaping, are the same.

Perhaps it will help if you can see how some of the greatest men and women who ever lived were trapped in Comfort Zones. And how it felt to be in them. And how it felt to escape.

Let's start with an analogy from the famous Greek philosopher Plato who wrote of people living inside a cave, chained in such a way that their backs are to the mouth of the cave. All they can see are the shadows on the wall in front of them, of people and animals passing by the cave mouth. Because they know nothing else, these shadows and reflections of the cave wall are their reality. And if one of these people should be released from the chains and actually go to the cave mouth itself, the *real* reality would probably be too blinding to comprehend. Certainly, it would be painful to confront. And even more painful to come to terms with the fact that they had wasted a large part of their lives believing in an illusion.

Sound familiar? For many people trapped in Comfort Zones, Truth and Reality are often too blinding to comprehend or accept. And so they go back to their chains, preferring to keep believing in the 'truth' that is familiar to them.

Now let's look at a poet. The great Dante Alighieri had to confront his disillusionment with the world around him when, after being elected as one of the chief magistrates of Florence, he attempted to rule justly amidst violent political struggles and corruption. Yet in 1302 he was convicted in absentia of refusing to recognise the Pope's authority in civil matters. It was an offence of which he was proud and would not repent. He rejected 'their' rules in favour of his own values and authority. As a consequence, he was dispossessed and banned from his native city. His words in the opening stanzas of *The Divine Comedy* express powerfully the psychological impact of this trauma:

> In the middle of the journey of our life, I came to myself within a dark wood where the straight way was lost. Ah, how hard it is to tell of that wood, savage and harsh and dense, the thought of which renews my fear. So bitter is it that death is hardly more.

The pattern is the same, isn't it? Here Dante was in a wonderful set of Comfort Zones: a respected figure of authority, comfortably well-off, enjoying status and power. Yet he risked the pain of asserting his own inner values — what *he* believed was right — and suffered the painful 'escape' from it all. The rest is history. Instead of being forgotten as some obscure little civil servant, he will always be remembered for his brilliant philosophical writing much of which, by the way, is in itself symbolic of a spiritual journey.

How about someone a bit more recent? Let's look at a woman — Eleanor Roosevelt. Gail Sheehy tells the story in her excellent book *Passages*:

> Eleanor Roosevelt, a woman who was afraid of being alone, wrote in her diary at age 35: 'I do not think I have ever felt so strangely as in the past year... all my self-confidence is gone and I am on the edge, though I was never better physically than I feel now.' Her husband had taken on a younger, prettier, gayer companion. She saw herself suddenly as older, discarded, a failed woman. The disassembling process had begun.

[Author: In other words, she had started confronting the truth and escaping her Comfort Zones.]

Later, at the age of fifty-seven, she could look back to write:

Somewhere along the line of development we discover who we really are, and then we make our real decision for which we are responsible. Make that decision primarily for yourself because you can never really live anyone else's life, not even your own child's. The influence you exert is through your own life and what you become yourself.

THE IMPORTANCE OF CRISIS AS A LEARNING EXPERIENCE AND CATALYST FOR GROWTH

In the case of both Dante and Eleanor Roosevelt you will have noticed a very important similarity: both were confronted with a crisis, and both *used* this crisis (whether consciously or unconsciously) as a stimulus for self-confrontation and for escaping their Comfort Zones. And for growing into better, greater, more fulfilled, self-actualised people.

A crisis can be a very powerful catalyst and a stimulus to growth, and you should never allow yourself to fall too long into deep depression or go into 'panic mode' because of a crisis, but should rather see it as an opportunity for catapulting yourself out of your Comfort Zones.

Other examples of famous people include writers Eugene O'Neill and Joseph Conrad, artists Paul Gauguin (at thirty-five he left his boring career in banking, walked out on his wife and his old life, and had become the leading Post-Impressionist painter by the age of forty-one) and Goya, architect Frank Lloyd Wright, visionaries Mahatma Gandhi and Sigmund Freud, and Nostradamus (his wife and all his children died of the plague while he was away as a doctor healing people in other villages in France. During his years of wandering in a depressive stupor, he became more introspective and began writing his great predictions, culminating in his famous prophetic Quatrains).

There are countless other examples. You yourself probably know a few people who have similarly confronted a crisis and used it as a vehicle for growth.

Like Ingrid, in our next case study:

Case study: Ingrid

After a disastrous first marriage where her husband habitually assaulted her, Ingrid found herself repeating the nightmare. Tom, a former heavyweight boxing champion, was insanely jealous and when even an innocent smile passed between Ingrid and another man at a party he would threaten the unfortunate individual and then beat his wife black and blue when they got home. The birth of their daughter did little to change his ways, nor did his increasingly heavy drinking. And yet Ingrid, still traumatised by her first marriage, couldn't admit to herself that she had made the same mistake again. So she hid behind such defence mechanisms as denial and avoidance of the truth, and complex rationalisations, and simply refused to confront her reality.

After several black eyes, innumerable bruises, and a broken nose and arm, Ingrid was reduced to a hollow, subdued shell. She lost contact with her old friends; even her visits to her step-parents became less frequent as she withdrew into herself. When questioned, she refused to incriminate her husband in any way; on the contrary, she would express her belief in him as a good and kind man at heart, wonderful with his daughter, and merely going through a temporary difficult phase of life. Ingrid was dragged down further and further, losing all respect for herself to the point where she didn't care if she bathed or washed her hair for weeks on end. She herself drank more and more, until the meagre family funds ran out and they had to start pawning their furniture for liquor.

Then Tom began to turn his attentions to the daughter, and this finally tipped the scales in Ingrid's head. While her husband was at work she gathered together her few clothes in a battered suitcase, wrapped her daughter in a shawl on her back, and hitched a ride with a long-distance truck driver friend, not even telling her family that she was leaving or where she was going. She took refuge with an old school friend on the other side of the country and began the long process of rebuilding the shattered fragments of her life, regaining her self-esteem and confidence, and making a new world for herself and her daughter.

I'll say it again: *a crisis can be a very powerful catalyst and stimulus for growth*. And though none of us welcomes crises and tragedy and pain, when they do happen to us we should try to see them as *positive learning opportunities* that can allow us to begin a completely new phase of our lives. It's as if the walls of your castle have come tumbling down in an earthquake, and you've run outside to escape the falling blocks of stone. Now you're standing on the drawbridge of your castle... freedom beckons ahead, scary though it might be, while the relative comfort and security of the castle lures you back. The crisis has created your chance for freedom.

So, ironic though it may sound, a crisis can be your best shot at escaping your Comfort Zones.

WHY IS A CRISIS A CATALYTIC OPPORTUNITY FOR GROWTH?

Although we try to avoid crises like the Plague, it is important to recognise that any 'crisis' in your life is a perfect opportunity to shift yourself into a higher mode of awareness. Like the dog running across the road in front of your car, *you do not choose the crisis, but you are forced to handle it.* Are you going to go into a panic (which is the natural reaction if you are lacking in self-confidence or don't have sufficient 'life skills') and simply withdraw and become defensive, or are you — like Ingrid — going to take action and negotiate your way past the obstacle and continue the journey?

Let's look at the dog-in-the-road analogy. If you have become a skilful and confident driver, you will simply apply a little pressure to the brakes and swerve past the dog or, if there is oncoming traffic (and perhaps a car close behind you), you may even choose to run over the dog rather than endanger your passengers' lives. But after the incident you will continue with your journey, a little shaken perhaps, but nevertheless in total control.

If, however, you are unskilled or lacking in confidence, or if your spouse constantly nags and criticises you and tells you how you should be driving, or keeps on grabbing the steering wheel, you may be so lacking in confidence and 'free will' that you cause an accident, or land in a ditch, or are so shaken that you ask someone else to drive.

Or let's say your free choice to act is hampered not only by nagging and criticism, but by your childhood memory of a horrific accident that killed your parents or best friend. And what if the car isn't yours — it's been borrowed from a friend or a father or a boss. Or you've got a baby on the seat beside you. These things will also affect the way you react to the crisis.

Life's like that in many ways. And that is why you need to become as skilful and confident as possible in driving your own life forward, without allowing the 'back seat drivers' to influence you negatively. You need to accept full responsibility for your own life and not let yourself be influenced by negative or complicating factors around you. *You need to take control and stay in control.*

I'll repeat that, because it's vitally important: *You need to take control and stay in control.* If Ingrid could do it, given her frightening circumstances which were a lot worse than most of ours, then you can too.

'Huh!' I can hear some of you thinking. 'That's easier said than done. If you only knew how impossible/difficult my circumstances are, you'd know that's out of the question.' And you're right. I don't know your circumstances, and perhaps they are too complex and difficult for me even to imagine. But I never said it was easy. All I'm saying is that you need to search for ways of getting more control over your own life. This may be something as simple as changing your daily routine to accommodate some small thing you want to do. Or it may be actually telling those around you what your true feelings are about something that annoys you. No matter how small or insignificant it may seem, anything you do to shift your life out of automatic mode into higher levels of mental, emotional and spiritual activity is a step in the right direction.

By the same token, any 'crisis' in your life is a perfect opportunity to shift yourself into a higher mode of awareness. Like the dog running across the road, you do not choose the crisis, but you are forced to handle it. Are you going to go into a panic and retreat even deeper inside your Comfort Zones castle, or are you going to negotiate your way past the obstacle and continue your journey?

Remember, it's your choice. You simply have to confront the crisis and not run away from it; you have to use it as a catalyst for change. And you have to take control rather than allow the crisis (or those involved in it) to control you.

In my own experience, and in watching the experiences of others and in doing research for this book, I would even go so far as to say that *rather than wait for a crisis to present itself in your life, you might actually need to engineer one* to give you that catalytic opportunity to escape your Comfort Zones.

That probably sounds completely crazy and masochistic. And yet one of the most critical steps is shaking yourself out of the lethargy and inertia of being trapped in a Comfort Zone by what is known as the 'unfreezing' process — having your complacency broken by some disruption or crisis event that will allow you to shrug off the old rules and allow you to look at things from a new perspective (like Ingrid). And if you yourself have engineered the crisis, at least you have a certain degree of control.

But why wait for a crisis to push you into a decision? You can accomplish the same thing, the same 'unfreezing', the same shift into higher levels of consciousness by a simple, conscious, rational decision to change your life and escape your Comfort Zones.

Remember, the only thing in life that is absolutely certain is change. Change is the only constant we can predict with complete assurance. So why not simply accept it and use it to your advantage? The decision is completely in your own hands!

FREEDOM OF CHOICE

It should now be clear that increasing your freedom of choice is a vital element in escaping your Comfort Zones and living a happier and more fulfilled life. It should also be clear that in order to gain increased freedom of choice you need to take control of your own life and assert your right to be who you want to be. Also, this process depends on (and in turn affects) your level of spirituality, of physical competence (ie health of the body), learning new career or hobby skills, of intellectual and psychological insight.

As Koestler explains: 'Each upward shift of attention to higher levels... is accompanied by the experience of free choice.' And '... with each step upwards to a higher level *the relative importance of the constraints decreases and the number of choices increases.*' [Italics in the original.]

It's amazing how, when you are bogged down in a Comfort Zone prison, petrified of anything that might cause the slightest crack in your security bubble, and in a state of even mild depression, every molehill seems like a mountain. And it's equally amazing how your perspective changes as you come out of that depression and paranoia, how problems and obstacles will decrease in importance as you find your journey strengthening and rejuvenating the 'inner you'. Just like learning to drive a car, where at first you are confused and terrified by all the things you have to learn (like which is the brake pedal and which the accelerator), these elements decrease in importance as you learn other things (like how to park or handle your car in a skid), ie as you progress to 'higher' levels the old constraints decrease in importance. Similarly, once you have mastered all the basic skills, you have the *freedom of choice* as to whether you want to take a trip to the country, look at the scenery, talk to your passengers, listen to the radio, or whatever. Suddenly, you have *choices*.

The same is true of being trapped in a Comfort Zone. Many people want to take the country trip or drive to the coast before they have mastered the skills of elementary driving. And yet they don't have the freedom of choice to do this until they have overcome the constraints at the lower levels.

For example, a woman may be trapped in a dependency relationship where her husband holds the purse strings and can manipulate her life at will. So she dreams of becoming financially independent in order to 'escape'. Although this is possible, it is highly unlikely that she will succeed unless she has first established and asserted her right to be independent; and until she has gained enough psychological and emotional inner strength by consciously making the decision that she wants to and is determined to escape.

And she cannot do that until she has confronted the fact that she is trapped in a Comfort Zone. Until she has spent time confronting the self-deceptions and illusions and rationalisations of that Comfort Zone. Until she has found out who she really is, and what she really wants out of life. And until she has translated all those desires and intentions into action and actually taken those first steps.

By embarking on her journey she will be strengthening and rejuvenating her psychological, emotional and spiritual inner self and empowering herself to make lucid and realistic decisions. And that doesn't necessarily mean getting divorced or 'escaping' physically to another relationship or another city — it simply means re-establishing the ground rules and her rights within the relationship. It means being true to her inner self.

When you're trapped in any Comfort Zone, you have many constraints which may seem overwhelmingly difficult to overcome. And yet a crisis (or a conscious effort to gain insight into your Comfort Zones and find the real inner you) can move you into a higher level of consciousness and make these constraints decrease in importance. As you learn to accept this and not allow the crises to throw you back into your castle dungeons and make you retreat into yourself, you will find that you suddenly have choices that you can make about your life.

And having choices in life is one of the most vital components of happiness and fulfilment and inner peace.

If you want proof of how important having choices in life is, think about what society does to punish its criminals: it throws them into prison and reduces their freedom to a tiny spectrum of choices, which can themselves be further reduced by such punishment as solitary confinement. One of the sad epilogues to this is that some of these prisoners become so 'comfortable' with the sheltered life, with not having to take decisions and accept the responsibility that comes with it, that they are reluctant to leave! And when they finally do get out, they sometimes have to learn all over again how to take responsibility for themselves and how to make their own decisions. (Doesn't that all sound chillingly similar to any one of us being in the 'prison' of a Comfort Zone?)

Freedom of choice. Cherish it, and pursue it in every way. In their book *The Inventurers* Hagberg and Leider comment:

> The basic ingredient in life and career renewal is *choice* — the choice of taking responsibility for yourself. In any situation, you have basically two options: change the situation, or change the mind set that is perceiving the situation. The choice is yours alone... Many of us are more comfortable allowing others to make the choices, until we really experience the way that self-direction mobilises us with energy and enthusiasm and ingenuity.

We've already commented on how similar the prison experience is to being trapped in a Comfort Zone, especially when we are so dependent, manipulated or security-bound that we allow someone else to control our lives and make all our decisions for us. Once we have fallen into this trap it's very difficult to 'escape' and confront the hassles/risks/responsibilities of making our own decisions.

And yet, once you have taken the leap and assumed this role, and taken control of your own life, the feeling of freedom and relief must be very similar to being released from prison.

Hagberg and Leider go on to make another important point: 'Although we talk about being in charge and taking control, it is also imperative at some point that we *let go*, give up control and try not to get in the way of our life's purpose.'

In this context, I can talk from personal experience. For many years I ran my life completely rationally. I was so completely in control that I could suppress my emotions and stay cool in the most panic-stricken or emotionally charged situations. My life was so carefully planned that I crossed bridges days, weeks, months in advance; I had worked out exactly how I would handle anything that happened to me. But, thanks mainly to a catalytic relationship with a soulmate friend, I gradually became aware that I was not living; that my life was so ordered and controlled that I was not receptive to the joy of the moment, the wonders of spontaneity, the rewards of the surprising and the unexpected. It took me a long, long time to learn to live my life in the 'now' moment, to overcome my panic at allowing myself to be vulnerable, to begin to experience the simple pleasures of just being honestly, truly me. And being genuinely alive.

For a while, in fact, my pendulum swung too far to the opposite extreme. It all seemed so strange, so scary, so unfamiliar. I then had to learn to have *balance* in my life by allowing both spontaneity and control, and maintaining a healthy interdependence between the two.

The lesson to be learned is that extremes are never the answer; that the 'middle way' is the best. Not compromises, not lukewarm 'averages', but experiencing and being receptive to the richness of the entire spectrum of life in harmonious equilibrium.

This above all: to thine own self be true.

William Shakespeare

Key points to remember from Chapter 3

1. Escaping your Comfort Zones is a natural and inevitable process. It's part of a universal law happening to everything around us. And only you can willingly (repeat, willingly) impede the process by refusing to recognise this and taking appropriate action in your own life.

2. You are being held prisoner by clinging to material and emotional security (which you could lose any day), by control/dependency relationships and obedience to figures of authority you may have long forgotten about, by Force of Habit, by denial or rationalisation, or any of the other defence mechanisms. But ultimately you are your own jailer, since you and only you can take the decision to take your life into your own hands and shrug off and overcome these things.

3. You are not alone in your Comfort Zones. Almost everybody is trapped in some uniquely constructed prison of their own. And some of the most famous and greatest figures in history have been there as well.

4. A crisis can be your best shot at escaping your Comfort Zones if you recognise it as an opportunity to change your life, and at a time when your consciousness is shifted to a higher level. But why wait for a crisis to push you into a decision? You can accomplish the same thing, the same 'unfreezing', the same shift into higher levels of consciousness by a simple, conscious, rational decision to change your life and escape your Comfort Zones. It's your choice!

5. By shifting to higher levels of self-awareness, by confronting who you are and what you truly want in life, by overcoming the lower-level constraints in your life through new insights and perspectives, you increase your freedom of choice.

6. Some of the keys to escaping your Comfort Zones seem to be a return to genuine values and eternal truths, as opposed to temporary and material symbols of success. It is also vital to learn to be truly yourself and assert that self despite pressure from figures of authority and control.

7. Escaping your Comfort Zones doesn't necessarily mean walking out of your job or your marriage or 'escaping' physically to another relationship or another city. It simply means re-establishing the ground rules and your rights within the company or the relationship or the environment. Again, it means giving yourself an increased freedom of choice — and integrating that freedom into your whole life.

4

Stage 2

Preparing Yourself For The Escape

Let's clarify something before we go on. I touched on it briefly in the last chapter, but it seems to be a serious enough misconception for me to elaborate.

When I talk about 'escaping' your Comfort Zones, I don't necessarily mean a *physical* escape. In other words, I am not necessarily advocating that you leave your job, your marriage, change partners or religions, move to another apartment or another city, or go and live on a desert island like a hippie. As you have seen, such 'external' escapes simply don't solve the problem, although they may be the catalyst for your real escape.

What I am saying is that there must be an *internal* escape from the castle walls you have built around you and the restraints that others have imposed on you. There must be a change in your attitude and perspective on life; a rebirth of a 'new you', the real you. And although a physical or 'external' change of scenery and circumstances very often follows your inner shift, this is not always the case.

For example, your partner may be receptive to sharing your journey and you can grow together into a stronger, more fulfilled relationship — or you may find that he or she resents your changes and opposes you, and you may feel that you have no alternative but to move out. Your boss may suddenly find new respect for this changed person, and promote you to a position of greater importance and salary — or he may feel threatened and make life even more difficult and unpleasant for you. You may then feel that changing jobs is the only solution. Or the regenerated you may suddenly find the strength and sense of purpose to make some changes in your neighbourhood — lead a community action, renovate the house. Or you may suddenly find your environment totally oppressive and unresponsive to your initiatives and decide that you have to move.

An external change doesn't necessarily mean that there has been — or will be — an internal change. *But where there is an internal change, some external change is certain to follow.*

Remember: your external change doesn't necessarily mean relinquishing everything that is near and dear to you. It simply means that your relationship to everything and everyone around you, and the way you experience and live your life, will change because you will be in control of the way you interpret and respond to these things. You will make your life happen instead of allowing life to happen around you. And you will be strong enough to take appropriate action if those around you can't accept the real you.

BUT ESCAPING SEEMS SO SCARY!

The most critical step in escaping your Comfort Zones is deciding that you want to and will escape, and believing that you *can* escape. And yet when you look around you at your Comfort Zone castle, the walls probably seem unscalably high, the doors solid and padlocked and chained. And beyond that there's probably also a moat filled with ravenous crocodiles. Escape seems impossible. And even if you *do* escape, what lies beyond the walls and doors and moat?

The whole wide world, that's what. A new world: a new, better, more fulfilling life. A world where you have the freedom to go wherever you want to without being restricted by walls and barriers, be they real or only in your mind.

But right now, even that feels scary, doesn't it? What is out there? Who will take care of you and protect you from the wild beasts? Where will you get food and drink and shelter? How do

77

you know which road to take? What about the friends and family you left behind? Why do you have to escape anyway?

The process of moving from one phase of life to another *is* scary. And yet you have already done it many times. Remember your first day at school — moving from the comfort and security of your home to the scary world of nasty boys and stern teachers, and no Mummy to hold your hand or comfort you when you cried? And what about going to high school? To college? Your first job? Moving from one job to another? What about your first date, when you made the transition to relating to the opposite sex? What about getting married? Or divorced?

In many cultures of the world such transitions are made easier because they are recognised and celebrated through ceremonies, where the 'Rites of Passage' from one level to another are formalised. The Jewish Barmitzvah is an obvious example — a ceremony to mark the thirteenth birthday of a boy who then assumes full religious obligations. But, for most of us, cultural and traditional roles and identities have become blurred and largely forgotten. And in the absence of these formalised Rites of Passage we never learn that the progression from one stage to another is often risky and scary and painful (think of some of the initiation rites of African tribes), but nevertheless a natural and inevitable step in life.

Joseph Campbell made a lifetime study of mythology, religion and cultures of races and nations throughout the ages. In his outstanding and authoritative work *The Hero With A Thousand Faces*, he traces the vital importance of these Rites of Passage and the ever-present stories of journeys and presents them as the basis for all our modern-day journeys. He says:

> When we turn now, with this image in mind, to consider the numerous strange rituals that have been reported from the primitive tribes and the great civilisations of the past alike, it becomes apparent that the purpose and actual effect of these was to conduct people over those difficult thresholds of transformation that demand a change in patterns not only of the conscious but also of unconscious life.

The so-called Rites of Passage, which occupy such a prominent part in the life of a primitive society (ceremonials of birth, naming, puberty, marriage, burial, etc), are distinguished by formal, and usually very severe, exercises of severance, whereby the mind is radically cut away from the attitudes, attachments and life patterns of the stage being left behind.

Then follows an interval of more or less extended retirement, during which are enacted rituals designed to introduce the life adventurer to the forms and proper feelings of his new estate, so that when, at last, the time has ripened for the return to the normal world, the initiate will be as good as reborn.

Apart from showing us that transitions from one phase of life to another are not only completely natural but also essential, that they have been going on since the dawn of time in every culture of the world, and that some form of risk and pain are inevitable components of this transition, Campbell makes an extremely important point here that I would like to emphasise: the concept of being 'reborn'. After we have left behind one phase of existence, one stage of life, and entered another, it is as if we are reborn. And before there can be rebirth, something must die.

It is this that makes most people terrified of escaping their Comfort Zones, the feeling that something in their lives will 'die'. It is something that everyone knows intuitively and instinctively, even if they are not consciously aware of it; even if they don't rationally believe it or agree with you if you were to discuss it with them.

Yet it is one of the most universal of all laws: something must die before it is reborn in another form. It is the only way a caterpillar can ever become a butterfly — and it is the only way you can ever become a 'new you'.

But this fear of 'death' that makes us so afraid to escape our emotional and intellectual and even spiritual prisons is unjustified. First, because it is an inescapable Law of the

Universe, and thus we are only impeding our growth and progress by delaying the inevitable; and secondly because by accepting the 'death' of one cycle as essential to the start of the rebirth of another, we are taking our first step towards achieving wholeness and self-fulfilment. In his book *The Fear of Freedom*, Erich Fromm points out the difference between 'freedom *from*' and 'freedom *towards*'. People are as afraid of letting go the things they cling to (even though they may be inhibiting and unpleasant) as they are of accepting the risks of freedom to act as they wish in a new, liberated context.

Once we have accepted this fact, the important thing to ask ourselves is *what* is it that will die when we escape from our Comfort Zones. And the answer is that what will die is the 'actor', the 'unreal you', the masks and the illusions, the limitations to your freedom. When we look back on change, we often find in our new insight that the things that have 'died' and that we have discarded after hanging on to them for so long, are worthless impediments and obstructions — our self-deceptions, or our illusions that we are 'victims' of fate or someone else's actions, or our delusions that we could not exist or survive independently of someone else.

Once we have confronted the honesty, once we have overcome our fears and made ourselves receptive to the Truth, once we have taken full responsibility for *our own lives*, we will realise that change is not something to be feared. Rather, change should be welcomed with open arms and encouraged — because it is only through change, through the death of a cycle, that rebirth and regeneration and rejuvenation can occur. Only through change can we be enriched, enlarged and absorbed into the fullness of life. The process of change is part of a journey of self-transformation — a never-ending journey with a final destination that can only be defined as perfect self-actualisation and spiritual integration, a destination we can only strive for but never actually reach.

So don't be afraid to take this risk of escaping. Doubts and uncertainties are only perpetuated and complicated by your failure to take action. Even if you make the wrong decision, at least you will know it *was* the wrong decision and you can eliminate it from your options. At the very least, you will have made progress from the stagnancy of indecision. Think of it as sitting on a bench at a railway station, trying to decide whether to take the train East or West. You're afraid of making the wrong decision because then you'll be even further from where you wanted to be. Yet even if this happened, at least you'd know you were going the wrong way — and you'd also know what the right decision now is. The only way we ever learn is by making our own mistakes and suffering the consequences of those mistakes — ie we have the right to exercise our own judgement and freedom of choice, but then we also have to accept the responsibility of doing so. We have to learn to accept the accountability that goes with acknowledging the consequences of our own errors of judgement, without resorting to excuses or rationalisations or other defence mechanisms.

In other words, we must be able to accept the consequences of our actions with complete honesty, both towards ourselves and others.

THE TRANSFORMATION FROM DEPENDENCY TO SELF-RESPONSIBILITY

In preparing ourselves for our escape from our Comfort Zones, we have to understand that this is a *transition* from one state to another. Joseph Campbell writes:

> One of the first functions of the puberty rites of primitive societies, and indeed of education everywhere, has always been that of switching the response systems of adolescents from dependency to responsibility — which is no easy transformation to achieve. And with the extension of the period of dependency in our own civilisation into the middle or even late twenties, the challenge is today more

threatening than ever, and our failures are increasingly apparent.

A neurotic may be defined, in this light as one who has failed to come altogether across the critical threshold of his adult 'second birth'. Stimuli that should evoke in him thoughts and acts of responsibility evoke those, instead, of flight to protection, fear of punishment, need for advice, and so on. He has continually to correct the spontaneity of his response patterns and, like a child, will tend to attribute his failures and troubles either to his parents or to that handy parent substitute, the state and the social order by which he is protected and supported. If the first requirement of an adult is that he should take to himself responsibility for his failures, for his life, and for his doing, within the context of the actual conditions of the world in which he dwells, then it is simply an elementary psychological fact that no one will ever develop to this state who is continually thinking of what a great thing he would have been had only the conditions for his life been different: his parents less indifferent to his needs; society less oppressive, or the universe otherwise arranged.

Our ideal for a society... is not that it should be a perfectly static organisation, founded in the age of the ancestors and to remain unchanging through all time. It is rather of a process moving towards a fulfilment of as yet unrealised possibilities, and in this process each is to be an initiating yet co-operative centre.

To illustrate the power of the mind to fool ourselves that we are 'right' and justify the actions of those around us, even in the face of incontrovertible evidence to the contrary, and to illustrate just how we can become ensnared in a habitual Authority-Dependency relationship, I'd like to share a personal experience with you.

Being born in South Africa in the same year the apartheid regime came into power, I had spent my entire life simply accepting its misguided justifications for what it was doing. Of course the government went to considerable lengths to manipulate us and maintain its control over us, and to continue to strengthen and justify its actions through strictly censored news. We didn't even have television until 1975.

A few years before Nelson Mandela was released, when I was group creative director of a major international advertising agency, I flew to their world conference in Bangkok. Sitting between my black co-creative director from Johannesburg, and an equally black managing director of our Zimbabwe office, I experienced one of the greatest (and strangest) compliments of my life when, after a few hours' happy conversation, they turned to me and said: '*You know, Lee, for a while there we forgot you were white.*'

And so it continued: the Thailand Trio (as we called ourselves) did everything together. We shared the oohs and aahs as our 747 skimmed the Hong Kong buildings low enough to read the labels on the clothing hanging out to dry on the rooftops, and when the chauffeur-driven Rolls Royce collected us from the airport and took us to our Kowloon hotel. We explored the river-streets of Bangkok in the long narrow water-taxis and investigated the dubious delights of Pat Pong Street. We were like any three buddies anywhere in the world.

And yet the minute we touched down again at Johannesburg's Jan Smuts airport it seemed as though we were in a castle again. The portcullis slammed down and once again we were all aware of being black and white.

Of course we were still friends. We still spent long hours together talking about everything from the political situation to mutual complaints about our lack of creative freedom in the agency. We had lunches together and dinners with our wives. And whenever our Zimbabwe man was in town, we would throw our arms around each other and discuss the good times.

But despite the camaraderie it was incredible how the *environment* changed our perspectives of each other and our respective roles within it. It was as if there was an invisible barrier between us, or some invisible jail warden lurking behind each pillar and behind every door, watching our every move.

It was incredible how we could feel so 'free' away from home, but in our own country we felt inhibited and suppressed. It only confirmed in my mind the insidious and unbelievable power that 'authority' plays in our lives and the way it affects our everyday behaviour — even intelligent, sensitive, strong-minded people at the top of our profession. No matter what our 'external' attitude and behaviour were, on a subconscious level we were always somehow aware of the 'carrots and sticks' that ruled our lives, and were influenced by those invisible, often indefinable, 'figures of authority'. And we were locked into a way of life that had become a habit because it was all we had ever known in our country.

ACHIEVING 'WHOLENESS' IN YOUR LIFE

For every success story, such as those mentioned earlier — great figures like Nostradamus or Gauguin or Dante or Eleanor Roosevelt — there are thousands, maybe millions, of untold stories of people who failed to escape their Comfort Zones. In fact, they probably never even *realised* that they were in one. Compare, for example, how Beatle Paul McCartney handled the transition from immense fame and fortune and all its turmoil and confusion and the expectations and demands of the media and millions of fans, to the inner peace and harmony of choosing to live a simple, uncomplicated family life, with the many others who apparently couldn't confront and cope with the changes: Elvis Presley, Marilyn Monroe, Jimi Hendrix — the list is tragically long.

And what about us mere mortals? You and me and all our friends and family? We all go through changes in our ordinary, everyday lives. We all become trapped in Comfort Zones and either have the courage to escape and move on, or we scurry back into our castles and continue our lives in compromise and stagnancy.

84

Clearly, material success alone is not the answer. If it were, then why are so many rich people unhappy and 'empty' and unfulfilled? Likewise, simply finding a partner to share your burdens and provide you with security is also not the solution. If it were, then why are so many married couples, with all their emotional and material 'security', simply existing and not living?

The answer is that true happiness, true inner peace and fulfilment, do not come from the pursuit of fame and fortune and security. Material possessions, if anything, are some of the biggest obstacles to growth — and some of the highest and most impenetrable walls in Comfort Zone castles. And 'security' almost inevitably means dependency and a diminishing of personal freedom.

No. The answer cannot come from any *external* source. It must come from *within*. It is a move *away* from clinging to the security of material things or people or systems, towards self-actualisation. You have to understand that it is absolutely essential to escape and move on, that you simply *have* to grow. There simply cannot be any 'rebirth' (ie of the 'new you') until there has been a death (ie of the 'old you'). You have to understand and fully accept that this process always involves risk and fear of uncertainty and pain — but the reward for accepting that risk and pain is a new, more fulfilled you. The reward is becoming truly yourself — what the Swiss psychologist Jung called 'individuation', or what Maslow called 'self-actualisation', or what Marilyn Ferguson and others refer to as 'wholeness'.

Wholeness is not about achievement, success, personality or morality. It's about becoming our true, integrated, individuated self.

Wholeness is about overcoming the tyranny of culture habits and stereotypes and expectations of who we 'should' be and how we 'should' act. It restores our true autonomy and overcomes our pain and anxiety. It integrates 'Who I am' with 'What I do'.

It's important to keep our feet on the ground here. No matter how idealistic our spiritual aspirations, we simply have to accept the fact that we are living in a real world where we have to interact with, and be sensitive to, our environment in order to survive. We have to earn a living, pay the bills, eat and drink and have shelter. So while we aspire to 'wholeness' in a personal sense, we also have to understand 'wholeness' in the sense of our interaction with the world around us. In this context, even a tribal hunter will understand the importance of interdependence in killing only enough animals or gathering only enough fruits in order to survive and to ensure the ongoing survival of his food sources.

Discussing this one day, my friend Albert Koopman pointed out how the well-known Red Indian custom of 'scalping' enemies was in fact a kindly act — an altruistic gesture to allow the enemy's spirit to escape out of the top of his head! — and how the custom amongst certain primitive tribes of keeping shrunken heads of their enemies was similarly intended as a perpetual reminder of the gravity of their actions in taking another's life. Even in these acts of apparent barbarism, there is evidence of an awareness of interdependency and integration with the world around us.

The problem of experiencing wholeness is that from our earliest years we have reduced it to a system of beliefs that become so inextricably braided into our experience that we cannot tell the culture-and-environment-influenced self from our natural, real, inner-driven self. Wholeness is about being able to recognise and separate the inhibiting or controlling external influences from those which are necessary and beneficial; and it is about asserting our inner self within that context so as not to allow ourselves to be *controlled* (eg by dependency on others).

And the irony is that whether you attempt to control others, or whether you allow others to control you, both are driven by a *fear of loss*. So, as you prepare yourself for escaping your Comfort Zones, you must understand that in order to grow and achieve wholeness, you have to have the courage to make the conscious decision actually to cross the threshold.

IT'S YOUR CHOICE: CROSS THE DRAWBRIDGE, OR GO DEEPER INSIDE YOUR CASTLE

As you are preparing to escape your Comfort Zones, you will probably find yourself feeling afraid, anxious, doubtful, wary, sceptical. And yet you know you can't remain poised on the threshold for ever — you *have* to go either backwards or forwards.

By this stage you should already be aware of the complete futility of going backwards. But what many people *aren't* aware of, is that even when we take the leap and go forward, the benefits are seldom immediately apparent.

Virtually everything in human life is a process — a completely natural integration with the processes of all else in the universe. But as you grow and discover more about these things, you'll learn that 'the way to Heaven is better than Heaven itself', that it is the *journey* that is important. And rather than expect some magical instant cure or quantum leap, it is vital to understand that the journey towards being a better, more fulfilled you — and towards escaping your Comfort Zones — is a slow, arduous, gradual *process*. Rather than being the goal at the end of the journey, the journey itself is the escape. But that journey can only begin when you actually take the first step.

Remember, only man with his thinking mind and complex emotional and psychological mechanisms has the ability to intercede and interfere in this universal process of growth and temporarily stop or delay it, allow circumstances or people around him to impose castle walls. But the bottom line is that it is inevitable, and by delaying or stopping it, we are frustrating the universal law and our own spiritual progress on an eternal scale.

So when you retreat back into your castle, it is only a temporary solution; a short-lived relieving of your anguish. You are only masking your need for change and fooling yourself, because you can be absolutely certain that the cycle will repeat itself. Before long, you will once again feel the need to approach your castle door, you will once again open it, you will once again peep through.

But your journey will only begin when you take the first step *outside* and commit yourself to crossing the drawbridge, when you are determined to ignore the crocodiles in the murky depths all around you, when you hold tightly to the hands of your guide or to your own convictions, and cross over the moat to the freedom of the green fields and the mountains and the streams of the wide world beyond. *You have to keep on going.*

In observing people in my own life, I have seen so many approach the door to their castles, open it a crack, even put a tentative toe outside — only to retreat back into the security of the castle walls the moment there was even a minor crisis, or the moment they were alone with their own fearful doubts and thoughts, or the moment they again allowed themselves to become influenced and manipulated by negative, lower spiritual environments. But each time you fail to take advantage of the opportunity of taking a quantum leap and retreat back into your familiar and 'safe' Comfort Zone, you are denying yourself the chance of growing and becoming truly yourself — as the following case study demonstrates.

Case study: Jill

Jill and Charlie have been married for twenty years. Their lives followed a pretty average pattern: meeting at college, tying the knot after graduation, and having three wonderful daughters in quick succession. Charlie moved slowly through the ranks of the local bank, was transferred three or four times to God-forsaken towns, and eventually was rewarded by being given his own major branch in the city. Because he was often away on business, his wife was left to bring up the children and take care of the home. Bit by bit they accumulated nice furniture, cars, even a swimming-pool for their comfortable middle-class home.

On the surface it seemed Jill had nothing to complain about. She was by any standards comfortable. And yet, deep inside, she felt unfulfilled. It was as if she had frittered her life away on daily chores and motherly obligations. What about her university degree that she'd never used? What about her love of drama and the theatre that she'd never pursued because Charlie wasn't interested in it? Unfortunately, most of her friends were unambitious, subdued women who were completely content to be 'just housewives', and when Jill tried to discuss her feelings with them they always talked her out of doing anything. And so the boredom continued — and Jill simply sank deeper and deeper into her secure Comfort Zone.

Then she hit a crisis. She found out that Charlie — boring, dependable Charlie! — was having an affair with his secretary. She was shattered, torn between confronting him and keeping the peace. What would the friends and neighbours and family say? What would happen to her and the daughters? Where would they live? Would she be able to find a job? How much could she earn? For months she agonised about it, withdrawing more and more from Charlie, withdrawing more from life. Instead of confronting Charlie, she simply avoided the issue and pretended it wasn't there. Eventually the secretary moved to another town (Was she pregnant? Jill often asked herself), and reportedly married a rich, local farmer.

Relative peace and stability returned. Relieved at avoiding the confrontation, Jill pushed the whole affair out of her mind until she herself wasn't sure whether it had happened at all. She threw herself into a life of boring office parties and cocktail events, making small talk with her husband's clients and their boring wives, and dedicating herself to her daughters. She was a leading light in organising community events. Overall, Jill was relatively happy, but somehow she and Charlie moved further and further apart. There was nothing to talk about; breakfasts and dinners were silent affairs; weekends were a monotonous repetition of visits to friends, family barbecues and the odd dinner party. Things were very comfortable on one level — and excruciatingly boring and stagnant on another.

As the daughters grew up and began leaving home, Jill started to feel increasingly uncomfortable. When she looked at herself in the mirror on her forty-fifth birthday, and examined the lines and crow's feet, she realised she wasn't getting any younger. The awful thoughts suddenly struck her: Where have all the years gone? What has happened to my life? Who the hell am I really? Where am I going? She felt a sense of genuine panic, and resolved to do something about it.

Next day she joined the local Drama Club. Here, at last, were people she could really talk to. People whose lives stretched beyond kitchen sinks and mortgage rates. Soon Jill was enjoying a completely new, exciting, fulfilling life. And when she went home, it was as if she was letting herself back into a prison cell.

Then one night at a Drama Club function she met David. Although half her age, he was intelligent and mature in his thinking. He stimulated her brain and made her laugh. And he loved theatre. Casual conversations turned into long, serious discussions. Serious discussions turned into occasional clandestine meetings. And, finally, occasional clandestine meetings turned into a full-blown affair using David's small downtown apartment as a base. Although plagued by guilt, Jill was happier than she could ever remember being. And then, after a wonderfully romantic Valentine's Day dinner, David asked her to marry him.

Jill went into complete trauma. She avoided his phone calls and busied herself redecorating the house. She got involved in a community group that provided meals to the disadvantaged in the inner city. She organised dinner parties and social events with a fervour that surprised even Charlie. She stopped going to Drama Club. And when she bumped into a confused and hurt David at a shopping centre one day and he confronted her, she was cold and remote, and made excuses that she simply had no time to see him any more.

Inside, she was falling apart. Here was the man of her dreams, but she was plagued by doubts and fears. He was so young. What would the neighbours/family/friends/her daughters think? How would they survive on his income? What would poor Charlie do? Balding, fat, diabetic Charlie would fall apart without her. He might even have a heart attack, and she couldn't face living with that guilt on her conscience. And David would probably dump her for a younger woman before long anyway. And so her rationalisations continued...

After months of trying to get through to her and expressing his deep love for her, David finally gave up. And Jill simply continued to get more and more involved in more and more activities to avoid confronting her own honesty. Her fear had become her jailer. And she had thrown away the keys.

How incredibly sad that Jill couldn't face the honesty of who she really was, and how she really felt inside. And the real tragedy is that she continues to build walls of rationalisations around her to convince herself that she made the right decisions in her life. I sincerely hope that when the day of truth comes, when she once again looks at herself in a mirror and peers deep into her heart and soul, that that truth will not be too devastating to handle. Even sadder, I hope that when she sees the truth, it will not be too late: remember, there is a critical point where it becomes virtually impossible to take the appropriate action and escape. (See Figure 1, page 19)

So, when you are preparing to escape your Comfort Zones and you feel that tingling of fear — or even panic — try to see it as a voice trying to coax you to take that first, all-important step. Are you going to assert yourself and take that first step? Or are you going to scurry back inside your castle?

In *The Aquarian Conspiracy*, Marilyn Ferguson uses a similar analogy to explain this reluctance to cross the threshold:

> To the individual whose gate of change is well defended the transformative process... is threatening. The new beliefs and perceptions of others challenge the 'right' reality of the unchanging person; something in himself may have to die... Indeed, each transformation is a kind of suicide, the killing of aspects of the ego to save a more fundamental self.

So, yes, it *is* frightening — but it is necessary to kill certain aspects of the ego 'to save a more fundamental self'.

For example: If your doctor told you that you had gangrene, and that to save your life it was necessary to amputate your right arm, would you hesitate? Of course not. So why are we so reluctant to 'amputate' our illusions and self-deceptions and rationalisations and denials, and all the other gangrenous aspects of our Comfort Zone lives — when this is an *essential* step to 'save' our real, inner self?

FEAR: THE GREATEST OBSTACLE TO ESCAPING YOUR COMFORT ZONES

Fear is one of the most powerful obstacles to change or growth. And fear of failure in a success-driven world is perhaps one of the greatest impediments towards achieving one's goals.

Yet, once you have overcome fear, you will feel an immense triumph and sense of growth. Winning/losing or success/failure will start fading away; goals and end-points matter less; what other people will think or say becomes irrelevant. What is important is that you are growing into a more self-assured, more contented, more serene 'you'. But make no mistake: fear is a very daunting obstacle in your quest to escape your Comfort Zones. And if you're going to overcome it, you need to understand exactly what it is.

Fear is created in our minds as a result of expectations of a possible negative outcome — and it cannot be overcome until it is *reality-tested*. The problem is, you can't escape fear until you have *actually confronted* it. Let me share a personal experience with you:

Several years ago I took my family on a white-water rafting trip through the Tugela Gorge in Zululand, South Africa. Winding through an area known as the Valley of a Thousand Hills, the Tugela becomes a mighty torrent as it thunders through an eighty-kilometre-long narrow gorge, and this particular section is regarded as the scariest of all white-water experiences in this part of the world. This opinion was confirmed by Tom, one of our guides who was from the United States and was doing a worldwide study of white-water rafting for *National Geographic* magazine.

The night before we began it started raining. Not just raining — it literally bucketed down. Unknown to us, the infamous El Nino weather system was about to cause some of the worst floods in history. We camped on the banks of a wide section of the Tugela before entering the gorge and Tom stuck a stick into the mud at the water's edge before he went to bed. The next morning, the river had risen a full metre (over three vertical feet).

Now, let's get something straight. I am not a macho man or a hero. I like adventure, but I don't like danger. Not only that, I had my wife and two young boys with me. (The tour office had dismissed my concerns and convinced me that it was quite safe for them to go.) So, it was with great trepidation that I listened to the final briefing and heard the words of our tour leader: 'You can *die* out there. Last week, one man *did* die. There are rapids here that, even normally, are Grade 5 or 6 (ie virtually unnavigable) — and Heaven knows what they'll be like with all this new water.'

There was no turning back. The trucks that had brought us had returned to base. We were on our own — and faced with a gorge that was inaccessible even to a helicopter in many places. Wearing crash helmets and two life-jackets each, our little party set out. Half a dozen puny rubber rafts against the fury of nature. Not the big rafts manned and controlled by an expert like those used on the Colorado or even on the stretch of the Zambezi through the winding gorges below the Victoria Falls in Zimbabwe. These were small, four-man rafts. And our crew was our family in its unskilled entirety.

I'll skip the rapids and the unimportant details, and move straight on to Horrible Horace. This was the name for an extended series of frightening rapids, including one monster which was deemed so dangerous that only an expert could negotiate it. And with the river in full flood, who knew what it would be like? It was hidden around a bend in the river and from afar we could hear the thunderous roar of water. But we couldn't see it.

As usual, we had stopped some distance before the rapid and walked to survey it and plan how we would get through it. Tom was right in front of me as we climbed the rocks and I could see his face clearly as he got to the top and looked down. I'll never forget the sight of the blood literally draining from his cheeks as he saw the seething mass of chocolate water boiling over and around boulders the size of houses, sweeping whole tangled trees and dead animals in a maelstrom of ruthless anger.

There was no question about it: the women and children would have to walk. When Tom addressed the small group of men his voice was a husky whisper. 'There's no way back. With all our supplies, we'll never be able to portage the rafts over these rocks. And we can't send them down unmanned because we'll never find them again. So we've got no option but to paddle them through. But each of you must know that your chances of making it alive are pretty slim. You guys can die here. I need your paddling strength, but it's up to you to do it or not. It's your choice.'

As I said, I'm not a hero or a macho man. But, like confronting escaping a Comfort Zone, I really had no choice. Go through with it, or for ever live with the fact that I didn't have the guts.

There's another thing I should mention here. At the time I was going through intense emotional trauma of my own. As a child I had never learned to give of myself emotionally; to give love and to accept it. But in my mid-thirties I had a wonderfully enriching and excruciatingly painful friendship with a true soulmate friend who was trying to teach me to confront my honesty and be true to my emotional integrity — which, of course, was the hardest possible thing for me to do. My whole life was in turmoil; my past patterns of rationally controlling my emotions for ever shattered. Yet I knew my friend was right: no matter how painful it was for me, I had no option but to continue the metamorphosis she had begun in me.

Perhaps my decision to take on Horrible Horace was because I was determined to pursue Truth and continue taking the steps, no matter how painful they were. Perhaps it was because my life in the turmoil of indecision and emotional limbo had become so meaningless that I didn't really care if I lived or died. All that was important was that there was some decision, some progress, some escape from the pain.

I can't even begin to describe the anguish and the terror and the adrenaline-saturation of that nightmarish journey. Hurtling along uncontrollably at a furious and ever-accelerating pace, threading our way past bottomless whirlpools and 'holes' behind giant submerged rocks which could suck you in, spin you around for hours, or even days, in a never-ending 'washing machine' action before spitting you out; paddling feverishly to avoid crashing into giant boulders or being ripped apart on the razor-sharp teeth of protruding rocks.

At one point we hit a standing wall of water four metres high. I was tossed out like a puppet and found myself in the water, still holding on to the paddle. Luckily, I had instinctively gulped a big breath of air, because when I opened my eyes I saw only blackness. With all the dirt in the flooded river, underwater visibility was zero. I remember only the sensation of being swept along at a great pace, feeling the momentary tug as parts of me snagged on submerged branches or rocks; crashing against boulders and tumbling, tumbling, tumbling. My two life-jackets were worthless, but I remember being thankful for the crash helmet as my head smashed heavily against something.

Afterwards Tom told me that he had started counting off the seconds as he saw me hit the water, and that he got to twenty-five before he first saw my head bob up about ten metres from the raft. A gulp of air, then another submerged rag-doll ride in the grip of the flood. I also know that by the time the river widened out and slowed down enough for me to make my way to the side and surrender myself to collapse in absolute exhaustion on the bank, I had been swept along, mainly underwater, for more than two kilometres.

Fortunately I was supremely fit, or I would never have survived the journey. Nor would I have survived the combined dose of hepatitis-B and malaria that followed the adventure. But it took me a long, long time to recover from it all. In fact, far from being the catalyst to escape from my Comfort Zone dilemma, the trauma seemed only to drive me deeper into my castle.

I am telling you all this because I think it taught me some very vital lessons about escaping from Comfort Zones. Firstly, it's *your* decision and yours alone. Secondly, if the 'escape' is forced or too sudden, or if you are not psychologically and emotionally *ready* for the escape, it can be so traumatic that it can actually drive you back further than you were before. And thirdly, if you can sustain your desire and your decision to grow, if you are *aware* of these things and have the insight, the reversal is only temporary and you will find yourself empowered with a new confidence and energy and determination to escape. My experience *did* temporarily drive me deeper into my castle. But it was also a key turning-point — because, after Horrible Horace, what could I possibly be afraid of?

I'd like to end off the story by sharing a poem about the experience that I wrote to my wife some time later, when I was trying to give her insight into what I was going through in my life. I had made the decision that I had no option but to move out on my own and be separated for some time, to be with myself and sort out the dilemmas in my life, and seek answers to the questions inside my head. It's called, appropriately, 'The Moment of Truth'.

The Moment of Truth

I recall standing on the edge of the gorge
staring in horror at the swollen Tugela
swirling and thundering and smashing against boulders as big as our house
and feeling the terror tugging at my guts.

Then, ignoring Reason's entreaties,
and with its cries of 'Fool!' still ringing in my ears,
I hid my fears lest you should fear for me
and let the roaring moment flood all out
and climbed aboard my little rubber raft.

Afterwards I was overawed by the enormity of the risk
but exhilarated by the victory over my fear
and I knew I had found another small piece
in the jigsaw of my life.

Tonight I stand before a rapid more immense and more frightening than Horrible Horace
or mighty Victoria Falls itself
and, though appalled and terrified,
I know I have no choice
but to paddle my little craft
through this barrier as well.

I only pray that when I reach the calmer water
I will not have lost my reason for being there;
and this I ask:
remember your own fears as you watched helplessly while I did the unthinkable,

how you scrambled with burning feet and burning tears
over rocks and tangled undergrowth,
not knowing if we would meet again downstream...
I cannot even ask you to trust me,
since the turbulence of Fate has its own mind
and sucks in and spits out at will.
So: once again I must hide my fear and steel myself to watch yours.

I pray with all my heart that soon the journey will be over
and we can all sit together on some warm, sandy bank
laughing and toasting future memories
in the fire of our love.

A LESSON FROM THE TUGELA

First, when rereading this poem after many years, I became aware of my own ambivalence at the time of writing it. In my trauma of confronting change I was obviously afraid, unsure, torn about my decision and the leap into the unknown. I still accepted that 'Fate has its own mind'; I still clung to the possibility that this was not a final and irrevocable break with the past and a transition into a new phase of awareness, and I still clung to the belief that somehow this was a passing phase or a mid-life crisis and that things would be 'hunky-dory' afterwards. Despite Horrible Horace, I was still anaesthetised by fear.

So, although I was on my journey, I still kept looking over my shoulder — and jumping back from the threshold of my castle.

The second lesson to be learned from this experience is that we must accept that change of any kind *always* involves risk and discomfort and inner conflict and fear and even pain — and the degree of that risk and discomfort and pain is always in direct proportion to the magnitude or the level of the goal you want to achieve. And the higher the spiritual level we are on (or even the higher the level on Maslow's hierarchy of needs), the more difficult our goal will be to attain, and the greater the degree of risk and pain we must be prepared to endure. But take courage: when you have reached those levels, you will be more prepared

97

and more able to accept that pain and risk. From my own very painful and frightening experience, I found that the more I grew, the less fearful the risks became, even when new Horrible Horaces confronted me!

So, take courage and confront your fears. Accept the worst possible scenario. And then just go for it. Because even if you get knocked back to where you began (or, it may seem, even further back), remember that although you might be in the same place, *you are now a different person.* You will have gained new insights and therefore a different perspective through your experience.

Arthur Koestler illustrates this when he talks about the Process of Evolution (remember, when you are escaping your Comfort Zones you are in a process of evolution yourself):

> The French have an expression for which I can find no English equivalent: *reculer pour mieux sauter* — draw back to take a running jump forward. In this way the artist or poet or writer or musician can tap into inspiration by a temporary regression to more primitive and uninhibited levels of ideation, followed by the creative leap forward. This *reculer pour mieux sauter* — 'draw-back-to-leap', plays a crucial part not only in creative activity, but also in the creative evolution of higher life forms.

Compare this with the view of Jean Baptiste Lamarck, a French scientist whose book *Philosophie Zoologique* in 1873 led to new perspectives on Darwinism, that *evolution is a cumulative process* and not a 'Quantum Leap'.

And so the third and main lesson from the Tugela is that a crisis can be a catalyst — and often a catapult for your growth. But instead of allowing the panic of feeling yourself being tugged back, of seeing the elastic stretching to breaking point and being terrified of where you're going, you have to try your level best simply to let yourself go with the flow. After confronting Horrible Horace, I know how terrifying that 'letting go' and the helpless feelings of complete vulnerability can be. But I also know the rewards.

THE AGONIES OF INDECISION

Overcoming fear is at the heart of making any major emotional decision — whether it's changing jobs, choosing a career, leaving home, getting married or divorced, or escaping your Comfort Zones.

And the questions people have asked me most frequently about the process of escaping Comfort Zones usually revolve around the same two things: firstly, how to make the final decision to 'take the leap' and decide one way or the other; and secondly, finding a meeting point between the idealism of theory and the practicalities of everyday living.

Let's start with decision-making. And here I must make a confession. I can speak with great authority about this subject, since I was the very worst person imaginable at making decisions. If Librans are supposed to be indecisive and always balance every aspect, then I was the most Libran of Librans. So if you find it difficult to decide, take comfort in the fact that I was worse. Yet it is possible to overcome the problem.

Firstly, let's look at exactly what is involved in making a decision. In their book *Man in Context,* authors Jordaan and Jordaan quote a definition by Fishburn:

> To decide is to make up one's mind... a decision is a deliberate act of selection, by the mind, of an alternative from a set of competing alternatives in the hope, expectation, or belief that the actions envisioned in carrying out the selected alternative will accomplish certain goals... Such a commitment to action is not necessarily irreversible. Along with *Make up one's mind* there is another familiar phrase: *Change one's mind.*

In plain English, the key points are, firstly, that we expect or hope or believe that what we decide to do will accomplish certain goals, and the second important point is that the decision is not necessarily irreversible. Elsewhere in this book you will find a reference to an analogy that has helped me a great deal when confronted by difficult decisions, but I'll repeat it here:

Imagine you're sitting on a bench at a railway station. In front of you is a train going East; behind you is a train going West. Which train do you get on? If you make the wrong choice, you could find yourself even further away from where you wanted to be. Yet even if you make the wrong choice, you'll soon know that it *was* the wrong choice − and that the right choice was the other train. And even if you have a long way to go to get back to the station, at least you have made some *progress*. At least you now *know* what the right decision was. And even if the other train isn't there when you get back to the station, it's far better than just sitting on the bench while both trains disappear into the distance and still not knowing which was right and which was wrong.

The key is to *take action*. Because any action is better than no action at all. A quote from Albert Koopman sums it up perfectly: 'It is better (and easier!) to act yourself into a better way of thinking, than to think yourself into a better way of acting.' There is no question in my mind that the easiest way − no, the only way! − to take a decision is actually to *do* something, one way or the other.

Martin Fishbein and his co-workers (also quoted in *Man in Context*) developed a *theory of reasoned action* which focuses on specific components of decision-making. 'The central theory is that of *behavioural intention*, which amounts to a *decision to act in a certain way*. A behavioral intention precedes the execution of an action, and it shows various *levels of specificity*.'

These levels of specificity are very important in making a decision. For example, you may have a vague intention of going to the movies. But if you find out that your favourite (Casablanca or Rocky Horror or E.T. or whatever) is showing at such-and-such a place next week, you will now have more than a vague intention: you will have a specific intention to see it. And the more specific the behavioural intention is, the greater the probability that this intention will be converted into actual action.

'In other words, the clearer the intention, the more certain it is that the behaviour will occur.' And, conversely, '... the inability to convert behavioural intentions into appropriate behaviour is often a result of people not distinguishing between *behavioural intentions* and *specific actions*.' (Jordaan and Jordaan)

The vital thing to remember is that even the most ambitious of intentions are absolutely worthless (and will only sink you into a quagmire of indecision) until you start taking specific action to make that intention a reality. It is *taking the first few steps on your journey*... in that way, the journey itself becomes the destination. By starting the process you have begun accomplishing your goals.

So, when trying to make a decision, try to be very specific about your goals. Then write down the specific steps you have to take towards reaching those goals. And, finally, start the process by actually taking that first step. Remember Koopman's advice: 'It is better to act yourself into a better way of thinking, than to think yourself into a better way of acting.'

LIVING IN THE REAL WORLD: IDEALISM vs REALITY

The second important point people raise is always something like: 'That all sounds wonderful, escaping my Comfort Zones and becoming myself... but what about earning a living and paying the mortgage and the rent and school fees and carrying the kids backwards and forwards...?'

I can't argue with that. We all have practical realities to confront, no matter how idealistic we may be. But let me start off with a simple analogy.

You're in the middle of an incredibly busy day. You're running late on everything, and you just don't know how you'll get through it all. Then a friend phones and invites you to lunch. You tell him or her with some annoyance that it's simply impossible.

But if that friend was someone you hadn't seen in years, someone you were once very fond of, someone who's only in town for a day? And what if it's your friend at the local TV station phoning to invite you to be a member of a panel interviewing your all-time favourite movie or music star, or to take part in a game show to win a big prize? You'd suddenly *make* time then, wouldn't you? Or what if the fire alarm went off? You'd drop everything and make a hasty escape.

The point is that it all depends on the *relative importance* of the components of your choices; how much they mean to you. If you have insight into the limitations of your Comfort Zones, and understand how much they are inhibiting you and preventing you from leading a more fulfilled life, you would *make* time to do what has to be done. Conversely, if your circumstances become so painful and intolerable, you would somehow take whatever action is necessary to escape it.

I won't expand on these points here, since this entire book is an attempt to make you understand and confront these things about yourself and your Comfort Zones; about living in the 'now' moment to help make you more aware of the joys of self-expression and self-assertiveness which in turn will give you the *motivation* to take whatever action is necessary. Once you have seriously begun your journey and its process of strengthening and rejuvenating the emotional and spiritual 'inner you', you will find to your amazement that things which previously seemed so important are now petty and irrelevant; that former mountains are now mere molehills.

Relatively speaking, other things will now be far more important to you, and you will find the time to do them. More than that, you will want to do them. Somehow, you'll find a lift scheme to help fetch and carry the kids. Somehow you'll find a way to earn extra money (or cut down on your expenses). Somehow you'll find the time to make that phone call or write that letter you promised but never had time for. When your *head* is right, the rest will follow easily.

It's also important to *think laterally*. For example, imagine you're struggling to pay the monthly bills (it's not difficult to imagine — ask me!) and because of this you have had to take an extra job at night. This, in turn, leads to tiredness and irritability, health problems, bickering with your spouse, feeling guilty because you have no time for your children, and so on. But there are alternatives.

Have you considered the 'unusual' option of *removing the source of the problem* instead of killing yourself trying to solve it? Like getting rid of that shiny new car and getting a smaller second-hand one? Like moving to a smaller apartment or house? Often a simple lateral shift in your thinking can open a whole new world of solutions. And sometimes it's better to take one step backwards in order to take two steps forward.

Finally, I'd like to suggest a very simple but effective way to manage your life and make the most of your time. Keep a daily diary. It sounds obvious, but it's the best way to determine exactly how busy and committed you really are. It's incredible how much time we all waste in our lives and how, with a little planning and prioritising, we can *create* time for ourselves to do the things that are really important. Remember Thoreau's advice: 'Life is frittered away by detail.'

WHAT TO DO WHEN YOUR ESCAPE IS BEING BLOCKED BY SOMEONE

One thing is for certain: when you start out on your journey, unless you're surrounded by some very special people, you're sure to run into some pretty strong opposition from those around you.

When this is the case, we might find it easier to capitulate to their pressure. For example, when someone close to us tries to manipulate us financially and emotionally, or when we feel we are not in control of our own destinies and are not prepared to assert ourselves against that control. Probably we will rationalise the reasons why we couldn't or didn't change, perhaps blame this book as being a dumb idea anyway, and simply settle back into our Comfort Zones once more. Yet when we do this, we are simply placing the responsibility for our lives into someone else's hands — blaming them (consciously or subconsciously) for the fact that we 'can't' or 'don't want to' escape.

In many cases we fail to recognise that we are being influenced by our own emotional baggage (resentment, anger, blame), or manipulated by someone — a spouse, a boss, a parent — as a result of their own selfish and egocentric motives. It *suits* them to keep you in your Comfort Zones because by maintaining your dependency on them, they have control over you. And for this reason they will often vigorously *resist* your attempts to escape.

First, they know that they will lose control over you when you become your own, individuated self. Secondly, you will inevitably expose their selfishness and spiritual immaturity. Few people are fortunate enough to be in a relationship where the partner has the maturity to let you be who you truly want to be — someone who will willingly open the door of your cage and set you free to fly, in the full knowledge that you may never return.

This theme of the threat of the emerging 'new you' to your existing 'old' relationships was very eloquently outlined in Marilyn Ferguson's *The Aquarian Conspiracy*, and I would like to take the liberty of quoting this section fairly extensively:

> Personal transformation has a greater impact on relation-
> ships than on any other realm of life. It may be fairly said
> that the first impact is on relationships: they improve or
> deteriorate but rarely stay the same.
>
> In some cases the changes are welcomed. More often
> they are threatening. The game-playing inherent in most
> relationships cannot withstand the departure of one player.
> Just as the larger cultural trance is shattered in transforma-
> tion, so is the trance of our miniculture, the relationship.
> We see that its habits and its fences may have kept us from
> richer, more creative lives, from being ourselves. If one
> partner now feels that vocation and day-to-day living
> [*Author: ie personal transformation and growth*] are more
> urgent than long-range goals, the partner who still
> supports the old agenda may feel angry and abandoned.

'Gus is gone, and he's not coming back,' one woman said of her husband's new world. Their inability to share the transformative journey had created an ever-widening chasm, and she felt she could not find a bridge.

Ferguson goes on to say:

> Reassurances help very little. The threatened partner may show open disapproval, either through anger, mockery or argument. People want us to change, but to meet their needs, not ours. And the partner who feels threatened cannot see why the other does not just change back ('If you loved me...') − or hopes that this is a passing phase like adolescent rebellion or mid-life crisis. But you can't leave a new reality the way you resign from a job... Yet trying to argue someone into a paradigm shift, telling him to disregard old cynicism or limiting beliefs, is as futile as telling someone blinded by cataracts to open his eyes wider.
>
> Whatever the cost in personal relationships, we discover that our highest responsibility, finally, unavoidably is the stewardship of our own potential − being all we can be. We betray this trust at the peril of mental and physical health.

And so we can understand why there is such opposition from an unenlightened partner. They may feel threatened and angry because they fear the *loss* of the relationship. They may mock and deride you and accuse you of being selfish and egoistic − and worse. They may try to induce guilt through emotional manipulation. They may try to manipulate you financially if they can, or even threaten you physically. And this is the great sadness you will feel: as Ferguson says, 'not only for the loss of what might have been a shared journey, but more intensely for what the companion seems to be rejecting: freedom, fulfilment, hope.'

One of my hopes in writing this book is that once you have started on your own journey of escaping from your Comfort Zones, you might share it with your partner or family or friends; anyone who shares a meaningful relationship with you, in the hope that it will in turn stimulate their journey and enlightenment as well.

Even more wonderful than a transformed self is a *transformed relationship*, that is, a relationship between two people who are equally aware, equally receptive to change with all its risks and pain, equally respectful of the other's individuality and right to be truly him- or herself, equally acknowledging the other's freedom. In short, people who are on the same spiritual level; people who can truly communicate with each other. Such relationships are synergistic in the true sense where one plus one equals more than two. Such relationships are true connectivity with the Cosmos. Such love embraces eternity, the ecstasy described in words of awe by the world's greatest poets.

I offer no apology for making such expansive statements. I am an eternal Romantic. And I do believe in the eternity of love, and I do believe that Love is the greatest and most noble thing man is capable of, and that in its purest form it justifies almost anything. And, since we have seen that your journey will inevitably affect your relationships, and knowing how important those relationships are to you (and thus may be perceived as being insurmountable walls in your Comfort Zone castle), I would like to digress for a moment to reflect on what real love is. Perhaps these insights and quotations will help you assess your own relationships; perhaps they will help your partners to understand and thus improve those relationships — and make your journey a little easier. And, after all, the one thing that Love and Comfort Zones have in common is that they are both manifested primarily through *relationships*.

Think of this as a resting place on your journey: a shady spot beside the road where you can stop and relax and listen to the babbling stream while you regenerate your batteries and prepare yourself for the rest of your journey.

LOVE

'The only thing in the world as strong as love, is truth.' Compare this with a wonderful description of love in the Bible:

> I may be able to speak the languages of men and even of angels, but if I have no love, my speech is no more than a noisy gong or a clanging bell. I may have the gift of inspired preaching; I may have all knowledge and understand all secrets; I may have all the faith needed to move mountains − but if I have no love, I am nothing. I may give away everything I have, and even give up my body to be burnt − but if I have no love, this does me no good.
>
> Love is patient and kind; it is not jealous or conceited or proud; love is not ill-mannered or selfish or irritable; love does not keep a record of wrongs; love is not happy with evil, but is happy with the truth. Love never gives up; and its faith, hope and patience never fail. Love is eternal.
>
> Faith, hope and love; and the greatest of these is love.

(I Corinthians 13 and 14)

After reading that, whether or not you are a Christian, I think you'll be pretty convinced of how incredibly important love is in your life. Not selfish, egocentric or frivolous love, but love in its most mature and altruistic context; a deep enduring love that embraces every aspect of your life and the way you act and behave. One might even conclude that without love, there is nothing.

As Dr Harry S Overstreet said: *The greatest cause of mental illness is lovelessness.* And when we compare this to the statement of another psychologist that *Lack of self-love is one of the most important causes of mental illness*, we realise that you cannot love another, or be receptive to another's love, if you don't love yourself.

Self-love is not selfish love or arrogance or egocentricism. As Dr Robert Felix of the National Institute of Mental Health in Washington DC writes about self-love:

> One has a feeling of dignity, of belonging, or worthwhile-ness, feeling of adequacy — yet a healthy sense of humility.

The same principles of lack of arrogance and egocentricism characterise a proper love relationship with another human being. Dr Overstreet also writes:

> The love of a person does not imply the possession of that person... it means granting him, gladly, the full right to his unique humanhood. One does not truly love yet seek to enslave by bonds of dependence or possessiveness.

And Dr Erich Fromm amplifies this:

> To love a person implies caring for and feeling responsible for his life, for the growth and development of all his human powers.

I believe that such love comes only with spiritual insight and self-actualisation to the point where your own ego is subsumed into a gestalt that transcends the here and now — where it operates from a level way above the primal 'pleasure principle' level of human development. At this level,

> Love is being prepared to give keys without getting angry if the other does not use them to unlock the door. Love is sowing seeds without expecting to share in the harvest. Love is being prepared to be completely honest even if that honesty risks the wrath of the other; love is having the courage to sometimes be cruel to be kind.

You've probably seen the one that eventually found its way in several garbled forms on to bumper stickers all over the world: *Love is being prepared to set your favourite canary free; willingly opening the door to the cage without expecting, or demanding, that it will return.* Please don't misunderstand this as meaning that you must encourage the people you love to leave you — it means respecting their independence and freedom of choice enough to be prepared to let them 'fly away' if they want to.

The concept of love has become romanticised and diminished by generations of picture stories, soap operas, movies and popular songs, to the point where especially young people often have idealised expectations of love and an inadequate understanding of what it really is. As Dr Erich Fromm wrote: *While every human being has a capacity for love, its realisation is one of the most difficult achievements.* The more readily and completely one can express his real self to another person, the more deeply he can love. So love is essentially *communication* at its very deepest level.

This is the essence of a true relationship. *Love is the passionate and abiding desire on the part of two or more people to produce together conditions under which each can be, and spontaneously express, his real self; to produce together an intellectual soil and an emotional climate and a spiritual receptiveness in which each can flourish, far superior to what either could achieve alone.*

In a mutually dynamic and receptive relationship, one plus one can equal three — or three thousand. Love is also much more than admiration or physical attraction. For example, a man may love a woman (or a woman a man) because she (or he) is beautiful, talented, competent, hardworking, successful. This is not love. It is *approval*. Love depends not on the attributes of the love object, but upon the individual's ability to love. This ability does not come naturally — it must be cultivated. And the only way to teach love is by example. By cultivating our own capacity to love, we teach others around us to love. Children must receive love in order (later) to be able to give it.

Sculptor Sir Hubert von Herkomer must have been given lots of love as a child. Because later in life he obviously understood that love is doing something for its own sake, without the expectation of reward or recognition. The story goes that his father who lived with him was getting old, and used to go to bed depressed because his skills had faded and his wood carvings were frequently clumsy. Sir Hubert would steal downstairs after his father had fallen asleep and apply a few deft strokes of the chisel. The next morning his father would be rejuvenated and encouraged. He would look at the work and exclaim: 'Yes... yes, it's not so bad after all ... I can make something of this yet!'

Love manifests itself in a wonderfully rich spectrum of ways. At any given time, a single person can experience love for (and from) a parent, a sibling, a child, a pet, a lover, a friend, a God, a cousin, a grandparent or grandchild; a love of nature, of music, of gardening — the list is endless. But no form of love has been more celebrated in the world's literature and arts than romantic love. Romance is one of the most important elements of enduring love between a man and a woman (or, in some cases, between members of the same sex). I believe that no form of love between humans is more intense, passionate and all-consuming, and more able to elevate the human spirit into a state that transcends all the problems and cares of the world — indeed, transcends time itself.

Poet Robert Bridges wrote: *Love is a fire in whose devouring flames all earthly ills are consumed.* And all who have loved and been loved recognise the great enduring truths in classical love poetry. (If you doubt that, read Byron and Browning, for starters!)

The great Romantic poet John Keats, dying of tuberculosis, wrote: *I am certain of nothing but the holiness of the heart's affections, and the truth of imagination.*

Eighteenth-century essayist William Hazlitt felt the pain of unrequited love for a common lodging-house girl called Sarah. Though she accepted Hazlitt's gifts and poems and love letters, Sarah mocked and deceived. When she finally left him for another, his wound was deep and bitter. Yet he could write to a friend: 'When I am dead, who will love her as I have loved her? When she is old, who will look in her face and bless her?'

Romance is absolutely antecedent to love. Its death diminishes each of us, and society suffers. And only romantic love could inspire a thought like: *Perfect love has this advantage: it leaves the possessor of it nothing further to desire.*

There is also a wonderful, mysterious difference between *loving* and *being in love*. We may think we are in love because of the way another person makes us feel, but love is not delight in *Me*; it is self-realisation together in *Us*. Self-realisation together includes the right of each partner to pursue individual interests. It often takes people years to discover that 'we do everything together' is sentimentality, not love. Love is self-discovery and self-fulfilment through healthy growth with and for the other person.

Where immature love is blocked, it turns to anger or hate. Mature love is eternally forgiving, understanding, compassionate. And eternal in itself. Love is *giving*. To think that nothing must be given up, is to suppose that love costs nothing. And something that costs nothing, is worth nothing.

Love's development is like that of a tree; it grows irregularly through rains and droughts and winters and summers . . . the art of love is patience until the spring comes.

Real love will grow as the years go by. The very expression of loving will lead to the discovery of how to love better. What we have really loved can never be taken away or lost. Its influence on our personality is always with us, and perhaps even death cannot take it away. Heartbreak comes and goes, wisdom lingers.

True love is not blind — it sees faults as well as virtues. And in a true love relationship, each can accept these unpleasant truths knowing that they are expressed from a point of view of love and altruism and for the other person. True love is being *honest*. And, finally, *The most delicate and critical element of a deep relationship is trust.*

What is love? Sociologist Robert Winch, after an extensive eight-year study of couples:

> The love of man for woman and woman for man is basically self-serving; its primary purpose is to benefit the lover, not the beloved. Each of us tends to fall in love with

someone whose personality is the complement of our own and through whom we can relieve our own frustrations and vicariously live out our impossible wishes. This dovetailing of psychological needs is the essential reason for love and a far stronger force than sexual desire, beauty, similarity of tastes, etc.

And if we believe the words of the old song about love and marriage going together like a horse and carriage, where does marriage fit into all this?

Marriage is a state freely and consciously and joyfully sought by men and women... It is an elective state. Only within the self-sought marriage bond can two people create for themselves the security of peace and solitude and time − lifetime − by which they can accomplish that which is pivotal and central to all else... namely, total communication.

Rabbi B R Brickner commented: *Success in marriage is much more than finding the right person − it is being the right person.*

What do women want in the men they marry? Tenderness. Courtesy. Sociability. Understanding. Fairness. Loyalty. Honesty. Integrity. Gentleness. Patience. Forgiveness. Unselfishness. Commitment. Sensitivity. Sexuality and sensuality. Romance. Humility. Kindness. Compassion. Wisdom. Communication. (And I hear my male readers commenting, Yes, yes! That's also what men want in the women they marry!)

I could go on for ever. But the point I want to make is how incredibly important love is in anybody's life; in the process of finding true happiness and fulfilment and inner peace. No matter where you go on your journeys, make sure love is your constant companion and goal − because it will be your comfort, your guide, your inspiration.

A final sobering note on love (or an inspiring note, whichever way you want to see it) is supplied by Krishnamurti and quoted by Marilyn Ferguson in *The Aquarian Conspiracy*: *When you ask what love is, you may be too frightened to see the answer... You may have to shatter the house that you have built, you may never go back to the temple.*

Because this section on love and relationships has to do with escaping Comfort Zones, I would also like to quote a story from Gail Sheehy's book *Passages* about top designer Aaron Webb. When he reached the pinnacle of his success at an exhibition of his designs in Paris, he heard a voice whispering inside himself and he suddenly realised his success was all worthless because he had always used work as a substitute for solving problems in his life. The voice said, 'You have to be ready to give it all up.'

A year later, after he had gone through the pain of transition and growth, he was able to say:

> What I've discovered over the past year is how much of what is inadmissible to myself I have suppressed. Feelings that I've always refused to admit are surfacing in a way that *I am no longer willing to prevent.* I'm willing to accept the responsibility for what I really feel. I don't have to pretend these feelings don't exist in order to accommodate a model of what the world thinks I should be. I'm amazed at the incredible energy we all spend suppressing them and not admitting growth.

Asked at that stage if he could invent his concept of what 'love' should be, he replied that 'I think that would require an acknowledgement of my own dependencies. And from there, just possibly, we could move on to a sense of concern that has nothing to do with dependency... where both people want to see the other grow and mature whether there's any advantage in it for themselves or not.'

And on a more sobering note he added, 'It's something that occurs so much more often in deep relationships than in marriages.'

Finally, although it is a natural instinct for you to share your insights and try to encourage those in your relationships to share the journey with you, this is not always possible. Remember that a true relationship is one of *freedom of choice* — and although you may give a person a thousand keys, only they can unlock the door. You can sow seeds, but cannot demand to share in the harvest.

As Albert Schweitzer said: 'Impart as much as you can of your spiritual being to those who are on the road with you, and accept as something precious whatever comes back to you from them.'

So, although you may feel a great sadness and frustration when someone who is dear to you refuses to understand what you are saying, and will not share your journey, you cannot force the issue. This was one of the most difficult lessons I myself had to learn as I tried to help people in my life see what to me was so obvious. Also, at that time I did not yet understand that escaping your Comfort Zones is a *process* — a long, arduous, gradual process — and consequently I was trying to find the mechanisms for a 'quantum leap': a kind of magical 'quick fix' that would transform the person overnight.

The turning point in my clumsiness came when I found a faded photostat copy of this story pinned to the wall of a secretary's office at a company I was consulting for. Try as I might, I have not been able to find out who the author was, but I repeat it here because it best illustrates the necessity of the process of gradual strengthening rather than making a sudden quantum leap. Though untitled, I call it *The Lesson of the Butterfly*.

The Lesson of the Butterfly

A compassionate person, seeing a butterfly struggling to free itself from its cocoon, and wanting to help, very gently loosened the filaments to form an opening. The butterfly was freed, emerged from the cocoon, and fluttered about, but could not fly.

What the compassionate person did not know was that only through the birth struggle can the wings grow strong enough for flight.

And so this butterfly was doomed to spend its life on the ground. It would never know freedom; it would never really live.

Since reading that, I have tried to be compassionate without intruding or imposing myself on others' lives. If you force the issue, you are merely taking away their freedom of choice. All you can do is *enlighten* them; give them the keys to insight and freedom. The rest is entirely up to them. It's also dangerous to keep doing things for people, no matter how compassionate you are. By giving someone a crutch, you may be denying him the chance to learn to walk by himself; by giving him water-wings, you are denying him the decision to sink or swim. If that sounds terribly callous and uncaring, think about it: it really is the greatest expression of your love and caring to see the bigger picture, to feel the agony of watching another's pain without interceding, knowing that it is the only way he will truly grow.

Of course, you can easily extrapolate this principle and start thinking about things like artificially prolonging life, and comparing it to Thoreau's insights into dying leaves ('One wonders if the time will ever come when men, with their boasted faith in immortality, will lie down as gracefully and as ripe.'), or comparing it to the practice amongst Bushman and Red Indian tribes of leaving behind their sick and old when they move on, simply allowing them to die naturally. But perhaps such insight and mature acceptance of the process of living and dying is a little too painful for most of us to accept at this stage.

Hey, let's get back to our journey!

OK, you've had enough of a break. It's time to leave the babbling stream and the shady trees behind, gather up your lessons and get ready to continue the journey.

OVERCOMING YOUR FEAR OF ESCAPING

Before we move on, let's look at our map and remember where we've come from — to make sure we're on the right track. You already know what some of the risks are when you are preparing to escape your Comfort Zones. But, of course, knowing the enemy is half-way towards overcoming him. And you are already motivated by the knowledge that all you have to lose is self-deception, old illusions, limitations, suppressions... and that the 'old you' must die before the 'new you' can be reborn.

Comfort Zones are tender and seductive traps. So you don't have to feel guilty about being in one, because everyone is caught in his or her own uniquely constructed Comfort Zones. The key is to be able to recognise them and continuously be in a process of escaping them. Let's remind ourselves again about one of the most common — the Material Comfort Zone — and what it will mean if you escape it.

In a success-driven world, financial achievements are driven by non-financial needs — eg the need to feel important. This is why status symbols, such as the badges associated with certain luxury cars, designer labels, a house in the right suburb, and many others, are so important to some people. They are the 'badges' that the *nouveau riche* wear to show the world how important they have become and how successful they are. It often works in reverse as well. Sometimes 'old moneyed' people resort to reverse snobbery as a form of protest against these 'badges' and display contempt for the *nouveau riche*, or as an inverted attempt at self-importance in placing themselves 'above' the rest of the 'rabble'.

But far from impressing enlightened people, both of these actions invariably indicate that there has been very little spiritual growth or maturity despite all the material needs being satisfied. As I've said before, if money and possessions are so important, then how come so many rich people are desperately unhappy and unfulfilled and hollow human beings?

On the other hand, those who are spiritually more mature, or have genuinely reached the highest level on Maslow's hierarchy of needs, will no longer have the desire or the need to prove anything to the world. Such people have progressed beyond the need to accumulate material wealth as a statement of who they are, and have realised that material success has nothing whatsoever to do with true success or fulfilment in life; that in

116

fact it is the antithesis of success and can be the single biggest impediment to real growth of the inner you.

Also, when there is no longer a need to feel important, or when you are assured of who you are and feel happy with that, there is no longer a need to get acknowledgement from others to confirm this.

You no longer need 'stroking' in order to feel good. Nor can petty gossip or ingratitude or malicious criticism or jealousy harm you. Your reaction, instead of indignation and hurt, will be tolerance and understanding and empathy. Instead of these acts inspiring feelings of revenge or resentment, you will genuinely feel the desire to help the person/s gain insight into themselves and will be prepared to help them in turn to attain a higher level of maturity and spirituality. You will know the serenity of 'turning the other cheek'.

Of course, reaching higher levels of spirituality and maturity in life does not mean you can sit back and rest on your laurels, secure in the knowledge that you have overcome all its problems. In fact, the challenges only become more difficult, the obstacles higher, the risks greater, the pain more scary and intense. But at least you will have the knowledge that the journey is more important than the destination; that you should in fact welcome the risks and pain, for they are the very mechanisms that will allow you to reach the next level or phase.

Morris West expressed it beautifully in *The Shoes of the Fisherman*. (Please read it again, very carefully, and think about each line. Yes, I know I've used it before, but I'm repeating it here for a good reason: to prove to you that you are making progress on your journey. When you read it this time, I'm sure you'll find you have some new perspectives on some of the thoughts.)

It costs so much to be a full human being that there are very few who have the enlightenment or the courage to pay the price... one has to abandon altogether the search for security and reach out to the risk of living with both arms.
One has to embrace the world like a lover.

117

One has to accept pain as a condition of existence.

One has to court doubts and darkness as the cost of knowing.

One needs a will stubborn in conflict but apt always to total acceptance of every consequence of living and dying.

It all comes down once again to that simple truism: that pain and decay and death are essential and inevitable steps in the universal cosmic process of change, and therefore of progress and movement forward. Without them, there can be no rebirth. Without them, there can be no progress — only stagnancy and non-growth. Like most clichés, 'no pain, no gain' encapsulates a deep wisdom.

Now that we've grown, aren't we just great?

Attaining higher levels of spirituality doesn't mean that you are 'superior' in any way. (In fact, the higher you go, the more truly humble you inevitably become.) It merely means that, through insight and courage, you have progressed in some small aspects of your life. Levels of spirituality or maturity should also not be seen as the rungs of a ladder: this analogy is too simplistic and two-dimensional.

I believe that we should rather see each individual as having many, many ladders in his or her own multi-dimensional cosmic school. At any given moment, or in any given life, each one of us is positioned on some rung of each of our ladders — in some instances higher than someone else, but then simultaneously possibly lower on some other ladder in some other aspects of life.

It is possible that in the greater scheme of things some individual whom you compare yourself with, or whose life you want to influence in some way (even with the most noble and altruistic of intentions), does not feel the need or desire to progress, or is not ready to progress at that specific moment. At best, you can share your own insights and experience with them, but you can never expect them to respond or take your advice or even express gratitude or appreciation.

In fact, you'll find that if they are not ready to escape their Comfort Zones they will most likely express the exact opposite of gratitude in the form of resentment and antagonism. But remember that you can only sow the seeds, secure in the knowledge that they will germinate and bear fruit one day, but you should never have the egocentric demand or expectation of sharing in the harvest.

The same is true of this book. Some people whose opinions I asked during its development labelled me arrogant, misguided, even a little touched in the head. Some said I had no right to encourage people to shatter their illusions and confront their own honesty: who was I to tell people what they should do with their lives?

I accept all these criticisms with absolute humility and understanding. I am not trying to dictate anyone's life. I am only trying to give them insight and freedom of choice to be truly themselves. Through my own experiences and my readings and discussions with many wise and enlightened people, I believe I have learned some very important lessons about the art of and the reason for living, and would merely like to share them with whoever chooses to listen.

I would also like to emphasise again that I am not trying to force anybody to do what they don't want to do. I am merely showing you the peak of Everest, and giving you climbing equipment, and a guide, and warning you about the crevices and the slippery ice and the cold and the lack of oxygen near the summit.

It's entirely up to you to decide whether you want to make it to the top and experience the exhilaration of the conquest, or remain in your cosy little camp in the foothills. At the very least, I want to make you aware that there is a massive, magnificent peak right in your backyard and that, sooner or later, you will inevitably turn from enjoying the view below you and confront the challenge that lies ahead.

A spiritual journey is a very private experience. And only you can decide when to take it, and how far you want to go.

HOLD ON HERE...
I Thought This Book Was About Escaping My Comfort Zones!
So What's All This About Inner Values And Spiritual Journeys?

If you've been getting the uncomfortable feeling that perhaps this book is after all just a sneaky way to force some cranky religious or New Age philosophical principles down your throat, you're absolutely wrong.

It's just that inner values and spiritual journeys are exactly what separates this book from many other similar 'self-help' books which concentrate primarily on 'external' growth and self-empowerment in a material sense. (They are, in fact, diametrically opposed.) Understanding the difference between the two, and accepting the necessity of *inner* growth, is as important to your journey as getting your automobile serviced before you take a long trip. Or getting your passport and visas in order before you take a trip overseas. Without inner growth and enlightenment, your journey is worthless.

And whatever your own religious convictions, you needn't worry or feel threatened by these concepts of inner values and spiritual levels. If you are religious, they will fit into whatever you already believe: that there is a Higher Power (whatever you call Him or Her or It) who is Perfection Itself, and who has given mankind rules or commandments for living which will prepare you for entering His or Her or Its Kingdom after your physical death. And if you aren't religious, these concepts of inner values and spiritual levels will come to mean to you what in essence they already are: essential tools for living life to its full, for attaining true inner peace and harmony and happiness.

And they are some of the most vital keys to escaping your Comfort Zones.

I say it won't threaten your religious convictions simply because every religion has its symbols of spiritual levels. Joseph Campbell again:

When Cortez and his Catholic Spaniards arrived in Aztec Mexico, they immediately recognised in the local religion so many parallels to their own True Faith that they were hard put to explain the fact. There were towering pyramidical temples, representing, stage by stage, like Dante's Mountain of Purgatory, degrees of elevation of the spirit.

The world is so full of such symbolic representations of ascending spiritual levels that I have no doubt whatsoever about the universality of their relevance to the human journey.

Campbell also quotes psychologist Carl G Jung in connecting the two, and goes on to say: 'Through a dialogue conducted with these inward forces through our dreams and through a study of myths, we can learn to know and come to terms with the greater horizon of our own deeper and wiser, inner self.'

In Campbell's view, even one of the most important elements of Christianity — Christ dying on the cross to redeem all mankind — can be seen as a symbolic acceptance by Christ of the pain that is necessary for that ultimate transition from earthly life through death to eternal life.

LEVELS

Few people nowadays know what man is.
Many feel it intuitively and die more easily for that reason.
Hermann Hesse: Demian

Nobody can deny the existence of different levels in life. All organisations and societies and businesses are based on a hierarchic system, from the lowest to the highest. Indeed, almost every system in the world has its own hierarchic order, be it the food chain or the complex society of an antheap.

But there are other, more invisible but no less important, hierarchies. And all involve progression from the lowest to the highest. A great number of legends and myths are based on this progression, on this journey, on this quest for something higher and greater. We'll get to these later in this chapter.

But let's start with Maslow. We've already made mention of psychologist Abraham Maslow's hierarchy of needs, which he used to describe man's innate progression from the lowest levels of pure survival to the higher search for meaning and transcendence in life. For those who aren't familiar with it, here it is.

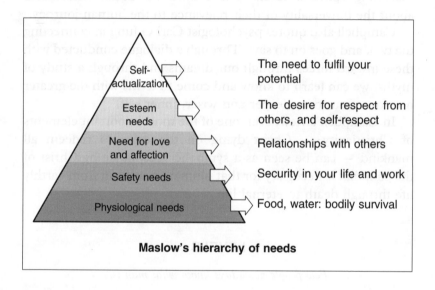

Maslow's hierarchy of needs

Self actualisation needs

The need for self-fulfilment and individuation. The freedom to fulfil your full potential.

Esteem needs

The need for a healthy and stable self-evaluation. The need for self-esteem and self-respect, and the respect of others.

Social needs

The need to have satisfying relationships with other individuals and have a recognised place as a member of groups, and being fully accepted by your peers.

Safety needs

The need to have a generally safe and stable environment and live an ordered existence which is relatively free of threats to your safety.

Physiological needs

These are the most basic needs of survival, such as food, shelter, water and sleep. They also include the purely physical, animalistic aspects of sex.

As can be seen from the above, we all have needs — ranging from the most basic for our physical survival, to the more complex emotional and psychological and spiritual needs.

Maslow identified that these needs are hierarchic — ie when man's physiological needs are satisfied and his safety and security are reasonably well assured, his social needs begin to motivate him. These are needs for affectionate relationships with other individuals and the need for acceptance by others (especially your peers), a sense of belonging, and the giving and receiving of friendship and affection. Thereafter come esteem needs: a need for a stable, firmly based self-evaluation; the need for self-respect, self-esteem, and the esteem of others. And the difference between higher and lower needs is that the higher needs are never fully satisfied.

Once the lower needs have been reasonably satisfied, man can progress to yet higher needs — self-actualisation, altruism, spirituality, self-fulfilment.

We can see it all around us every day. Those unfortunate individuals living in ghettos and squatter camps are primarily concerned with basic survival. They will steal to survive — or to ensure their family's survival — ignoring the 'higher' concepts of honesty and obedience to the law, or justifying their actions as being more important than the law.

We see it in the *nouveau riche*. An an individual acquires a good job or makes some money, his first priorities are the accumulation of 'badges of success'. The big house in the right suburb. The luxury German limousine or the snappy Italian sports car. The designer clothes. (I'm not belittling them. I've been there myself!) These things are not 'wrong' but rather are predictable and essential aspects of the learning processes of this phase or level.

But some people — in this crazy, materialistic world of ours, it seems like *most* people! — cling to this level far too long. It is a wonderfully comfortable Comfort Zone, and wonderful food for the ego. Of course, they might make the token concessions to altruism through donations to charities (often making sure that others know about it); serve on committees; participate in (usually) very public fund-raising drives, and so on. And usually they try to build their social self-esteem by becoming social climbers, often forming essentially parasitic relationships with people who can help them become 'accepted' into a higher social stratum; sending their children to private schools or ballet classes or violin lessons; being seen at classical concerts and the theatre and the opera; buying original art which they often don't understand or appreciate or even like.

As I said, these things are simply natural and predictable ways of learning important lessons related to this level. But they are also bricks in the very seductive Materialistic Comfort Zones that have become so prevalent in our age. People at this level can only progress to the higher *spiritual* levels when they learn to see these things in their true perspective; when they learn to develop beyond these lower level needs; to subjugate them and relegate them to their true roles; when they learn to confront their own insignificance in the greater scheme of things and learn real humility.

124

It's a paradox: in order truly to be yourself, you need first to disintegrate yourself. You need to realise the futility and ephemerality of material possessions, and understand the vital importance of basing your life on eternal truths and genuinely altruistic inner values. Only then can you begin the journey towards true self-actualisation — and beyond.

MY PROBLEM WITH MASLOW

In my opinion, Maslow's hierarchy, as widely accepted as it has become and as valid as it is in its context, is incomplete. It is too simplistic and, well, too *hierarchic*.

As I have explained, I see man as existing on a *multi-dimensional* plane at all times, and in this context there is always an integration of all the levels of Maslow's hierarchy to a lesser or greater extent in any given individual at any given time. And, just as I introduced the further dimension of the *infra-ego* to Freud's psychoanalytical theory of id-ego-superego, so I believe that Maslow's hierarchy must always be seen in conjunction with, and in juxtaposition to, a broad *inner-driven level of values*. I believe it is this awareness of and commitment to growth to ever-higher spiritual levels that, more than any other single element, is the key to escaping your Comfort Zones and attaining true inner peace and fulfilment in life.

Almost all cultures and religions and spiritual teachings have their own equivalent of Maslow's hierarchy. For example, the Indian *Chakras* — which describe spiritual levels in very much the same way, starting from primal and elementary physical urges and needs, and ending on full self-actualisation and spiritual awareness.

So, whichever culture we turn to, we find a recurrence of these themes — a confirmation that people are on different spiritual or developmental levels. It seems we cannot help what level we are on when we come into this world. We are simply born that way. Some people will consequently be innately on a higher level as well as more receptive to spiritual matters. I believe, though, that our spiritual environment and the level of education and maturity of those closest to us also plays a major role in this context. While nobody can feel 'guilty' or 'inferior' about the level they find themselves on (conversely, neither can they feel 'superior'!), it is up to each one of us to strive continuously to grow our spirit or 'soul'. To many, this is the answer they would give when asked what is the *meaning of life*.

This is equally valid whether you believe your entire existence (and the growth of your spiritual self) takes place in this one life here on earth, or whether you see the process as eternal and never-ending in the context of reincarnation where every life is a kind of 'classroom' where we are destined to learn different lessons to enrich our spiritual self and progress towards perfection. It is also equally valid whether you are religious or not, and equally valid for any religion you choose to practise. No matter what level we are on, our greatest life task is to grow spiritually towards Perfection.

And if the purpose of life is growth, then in the final analysis each life is a *spiritual journey*. Writer Joseph Campbell made an extremely valuable and significant contribution in this context with his great work *The Hero with a Thousand Faces* which traces, through the mythologies of the world, the 'hero' who embarks on this great journey. The story is repeated a thousand times in a thousand different ways, but it is always basically the same.

There is the 'hero' who sets out to confront a daunting task. There are always the dangers that lie ahead, be they in the form of a dragon or a perilous task, and there is always the guide or mentor who helps him on his way. To quote:

... the Wise Old Man of the myths and fairy tales whose words assist the hero through the trials and terrors of the weird adventure. He is the one who appears at the moment of greatest confusion, of terror, of crisis; and who points to the magic shining sword that we will kill the dragon with, tells of the waiting bride and the castle of many treasures, applies healing balm to the almost fatal wounds, and finally dismisses the conqueror, back into the world of normal life, following the great adventure into the enchanted night.

When I first read Campbell (for this I have to thank Texan psychologist Dr Sherrill Kendrick who gave me his own personal copy of *The Hero with a Thousand Faces* when we were fellow passengers on the world-famous Blue Train), I was filled with excitement at his revelations and insights, and with the parallels between the mythological journeys and the ordinary, but no less daunting, journeys of mere mortals such as myself. I saw in these stories the elements of escaping Comfort Zones, the mechanisms for achieving change or quantum leaps.

I was interested in his opinion that religions have their origins in myths, and the ability of man to comprehend and contemplate his own being and origins leads inevitably to the recognition that he is going to die one day. That it is this recognition of mortality and the great desire to transcend it that leads to mythology — to the need for something that transcends our mortality. As Voltaire said: 'If God did not exist, he would have to be invented.'

Campbell also goes on to point out a major shift in human evolution: the rise of the individual as a result of increasing scientific knowledge and the questioning of apparently immutable truths and historical facts. The world, too, has 'shrunk' and geographical, cultural and religious boundaries have faded or disappeared. We have thus started taking the social order for granted, or it has become too unstable itself to serve as a Comfort Zone and we have started to rely on ourselves as individuals — not as an organ of 'the state', but as an end and entity within ourselves.

I also found very interesting Campbell's interpretation of the Garden of Eden as being an analogy of our own interior self — the truth, the immortal life within that we are excluded from. (In truth, we exclude ourselves!) As he says:

> In the Buddhist view, that is to say, what is keeping us out of the Garden is not the jealousy or wrath of any god, but

our own instinctive attachment to what we take to be our lives. Our senses, outwardly-directed to the world of space and time, have attached us to that world and to our mortal bodies within it.

We are loath to give up what we take to be the goods and pleasures of this physical life, and this attachment is the great fact, the great circumstance or barrier, that is keeping us out of the garden.

I would say this is a perfect description and example of a Comfort Zone — and our fear of shattering the illusionary and rationalised lives we have built around us to confront the inner journey by acknowledging the truth, confronting it, and accepting the risk and pain of the shattering of our illusions and the long, hard journey towards Truth.

In talking about the archetypal and ubiquitous symbols of mythology, Campbell also talks of the figure of the 'tyrant-monster' whose havoc is universal and whose inflated ego is a curse to the world and to himself — no matter how his affairs may seem to prosper:

> ... self-terrorised, fear-haunted, alert at every hand to meet and battle back the anticipated aggressions of his environment (which are primarily the reflections of his own uncontrollable impulses to acquisition), the giant of self-achieved independence is the world's messenger of disaster, even though, in his mind, he may entertain himself with humane intentions.
>
> Wherever he sets his hand there is a cry (if not from the rooftops then — more miserably — from within every heart): a cry for the redeeming hero, the carrier of the shining blade, whose blow, whose torch, whose existence, will liberate the land.
>
> The hero is a man of self-achieved submission.

When I compare these images to the individuals on Maslow's hierarchy, and to certain people I have met in my own life, and judge them by the principles of man's progression to higher levels of spirituality and awareness, I see the opposing forces of the 'self-achieved independent' and the 'self-achieved submissive'. In other words, those on a low spiritual level who have empowered themselves and are increasingly puffed-up with their own self-importance, as opposed to those who have advanced to a higher spiritual level by recognising their own significance and subjugating their ego.

I personally found this very interesting because it reflected my own experiences and journey, and my eventual realisation that the most important thing I have learned is that I know nothing. My true learning in life began when I stopped trying egoistically to attain perfection (my colleagues used to call me 'the young Jesus') and submitted myself to acknowledging totally my insignificance in the Universe and accepting the humbleness of who I am. It was truly one of the most important turning points in my life.

But to get back to Campbell. I became very excited when I read all those mythological confirmations of my own beliefs and discoveries and experiences — for example, the universality of the 'journey', or that 'death can only be conquered by birth, not of the old thing again, but of something new'.

The more I read, the more I encountered striking similarities in such diverse areas as religion, mythology, psychology, quantum physics, literature, metaphysics and nature; and the more I realised the need for a holistic approach, a weaving together of all the threads of experience into one great tapestry of life.

When studying my final year of psychology at university I had become cynical of the science, particularly when I found out that the rate of cure for many psychological maladies was virtually the same whether the therapist used Freudian or Jungian or whatever-ian techniques, or whether he was simply a family doctor or a kind and wise old friend. Consequently, I began exploring the field of parapsychology, and the possibility of incorporating things like hypnosis and telepathy and telekinesis

(PK) and astral travelling into the science. (Of course, hypnosis has been used for a long time, but in limited applications.)

Unfortunately the university was particularly conservative and Christian-Nationalistic in its orientation, and my papers were often red-lined and I was branded as something of a heretic. I'll never forget one scrawled comment by a particularly dogmatic lecturer: *'Dit is die duiwel se werk hierdie!'* ('This is the devil's work!')

Of course, I should have treated this with the contempt it deserved. But since I was studying part-time at night and couldn't afford to go anywhere else, my reaction at the time was to simply change my mind about pursuing a career in psychology.

But to return to my recent research and my excitement about discovering the many similarities in the findings of many writers from different cultures and disciplines and backgrounds. For example, reading Toynbee's terms 'detachment' and 'transfiguration' to describe the crisis by which the higher spiritual dimension is attained that makes possible the resumption of the work of creation.

The first step, detachment or withdrawal, consists in a radical transference of emphasis from the external to the internal world, macro- to microcosm, a retreat from the desperations of the waste land to the peace of the everlasting realm that is within. [Our unconscious.]

In a word: the first work of the hero is to retreat from the world scene of secondary effects to those causal zones of the psyche where the difficulty really resides, and there to clarify the difficulties, eradicate them in his own case, and break through to the undistorted, direct experience and assimilation of what Jung called 'the archetypal images'. [This process is known in Buddhist and Hindu philosophy as *viveka* — 'discrimination'.]

The hero has died as a modern man; but as external man — perfected, unspecific, universal — he has been reborn.

Man's second task, therefore (as Toynbee declares and as all of mankind's mythologies indicate), is to return to the world of unenlightened people, transfigured, and teach the lesson he has learned of life renewed.

Journeys, enlightenment, spiritual levels. They seem to crop up everywhere. During my own journey and exploration of escaping my Comfort Zones I wrote reams of letters to myself and diary entries and poetry. I often referred to levels, and used analogies such as 'a pearl trapped in an oyster' or 'a diamond lost in a coalyard' to describe people who refused to recognise who they really were by confronting their inner honesty, and who allowed themselves to be subdued and suppressed and imprisoned in Comfort Zones.

At first, I was hurt by their reactions: Who was I to be so arrogant as to say that they or their friends or partners were on 'lower' spiritual levels? How could I be so arrogant as to assume that I or anyone else was on a higher level? But in retrospect, their criticisms were justified. Perhaps I had not yet learned how to express myself adequately about something I was only just beginning to understand myself.

It may have taken me a while, but eventually I learned to dispel my doubts and became confident and self-assured about all these things. I also accepted that each man or woman is on his or her own unique quest of learning in life, and that each lesson and each experience is uniquely important to that individual's personal quest and journey.

As Hermann Hesse writes in his Prologue to his novel *Demian*:

> But every man is not only himself; he is also the unique, particular, always significant and remarkable point where the phenomena of the world intersect once and for all and never again. That is why every man's story is important, eternal, sacred; and why every man while he lives and fulfils the will of nature is a wonderful creature, deserving the utmost attention.

Materialism provides us with no solutions to these problems — only temporal comforts and diversions. The only answer to eternal questions is to explore eternal principles on a spiritual level. And I believe that we can only judge other people (as potential friends, trustworthy business colleagues, formal representatives and so on) on this basis — that is, to what degree their behaviour reflects deep, eternal, spiritual values. Thus, when I talk of levels in the context of two individuals and their relationship to each other, and their relationships to others around them, it is not arrogant or judgemental or subjective to designate them as existing on specific levels. It is merely observed fact.

Like Thoreau contemplating Walden Pond and likening it to man's character, '... perhaps we need only to know how his shores trend and his adjacent country or circumstances, to infer his depth and concealed bottom.' You can tell what spiritual level someone is on by studying his behaviour; his actions and reactions. Not the behaviour or image he might consciously project or wear like a gilded mask for the world to see, but rather his intuitive behaviour, his instinctive actions and reactions, the things he does when his guard is down or when he thinks the world isn't watching and he believes he can get away with it.

Case study: Jules

Jules is an extremely successful businessman who, after many years of struggling and failed ventures, started his own publishing company and quickly built it into a thriving concern. He is always impeccably dressed; always drives the latest model Italian sports car; and recently married an ex-beauty queen half his age. (We'll call her Amanda.) At every social event he is the centre of attraction; he is forever in the social columns of newspapers and magazines (especially his own!), shaking the hand of some dignitary or giving money to some deserving charity. He has become so adept at all this that he honestly believes in the image his public relations company has built for him.

And yet an entirely different side of Jules is revealed by some of his employees, like the secretary whose life he made a misery and who eventually resigned from her job because she refused to have a sexual liaison with him. Like his brother, who ekes out an existence as a printer, and who gets no work from his own kin because he refuses to play along with his devious and corrupt schemes. Like his ex-wife, who stood by him through the hard years, even selling her family jewellery to provide collateral for starting his business, and who was unceremoniously dumped when he felt he needed a more glamorous companion at social events. Like his ex-partner, who used all his contacts from his previous publishing job to give Jules the big breaks and acquire the first big contracts which set his business irrevocably on the road to success — and who was systematically forced out and left virtually penniless because of Jules's greed and desire to take decisions unhampered by ethics or morality. But even when some of these stories have leaked out, Jules and his 'image machine' have always managed to gloss over them or cast doubt on their veracity.

And for a long time his wife Amanda bought into it all. When confronted with unpalatable facts about his business practices or like his supplying potential clients with cocaine when they visited, or hearing the stories other people told about him, Amanda would rationalise it all away by saying that even if they were true, they were all in the past, and that he was a changed man since she had married him. And then one day she found out from a disgruntled employee who had just been fired that her husband had been tapping her phone and listening to her private conversations. Afraid to confront Jules, she confided in her best friend, who was horrified. But Amanda tried to justify it by saying that he probably had to do it for company security. Then she found out how he had bribed his ex-partner to take the rap for him in a tax evasion inquiry, and for the first time she started examining the facts realistically. After several other similar incidents and reports and rumours, she eventually took her friend's advice and set a trap. [*Author: Without knowing it, she was 'engineering a crisis'.*] She made some ambiguous and rather provocative entries in her private diary which Jules knew she kept, and one night told him she was going to see her mother and left her diary in its usual place locked in her bedside drawer. When she got home Jules was waiting for her, high as a kite and lividly waving her diary. He screamed at her and beat her so badly that her jaw and wrist were fractured and she had to have four stitches above her eye.

Even though she could no longer deny the reality of who her husband really was deep down, Amanda still refused to report him to the police and even lied to the hospital authorities about the cause of her injuries. This was probably because the physical injuries were

133

insignificant compared with the pain of her inner confrontation of what a fool she had been for so long. She became totally remote from Jules and oblivious to his smooth excuses and entreaties that she should stay, and within a month had moved out and went back to live with her mother. And while one might question the ethics of Amanda's ploy, there can be no question about the ethics of Jules's behaviour or the fact that despite his carefully manicured image, he simply confirmed what Nobel Prize-winning novelist and philosopher Hermann Hesse described in the Prologue to *Demian*: 'Each man to the end of his days carries round with him vestiges of his birth — the slime and egg-shells of the primeval world. There are many who never become human; they remain frogs, lizards, ants. Many men are human beings above and fish below.' No matter how rich he might have been in a material sense, Jules was a pauper in spiritual terms.

THE AGONIES AND ECSTASIES OF SELF-EXPLORATION

Let's look at how Sigmund Freud described the process of exploring our inner selves:

The unconscious sends all sorts of vapours, odd beings, terrors and deluding images up into the mind — whether in dream, broad daylight, or insanity; for the material kingdom, beneath the floor of the comparatively neat little dwelling that we call our consciousness, goes down into the unexplored Aladdin cave.

There, not only jewels but also dangerous jinn abide: the inconvenient or resisted psychological powers that we have not thought or dared to integrate into our lives. And they may remain unexplored, or on the other hand, some chance word, the smell of a landscape, the taste of a cup of tea, or the glance of any eye may touch a magic spring, and then dangerous messengers begin to appear in the brain.

These are 'dangerous' because they threaten the fabric of the security into which we have built ourselves and our family.

But they are fiendishly fascinating too, for they carry keys that open the whole realm of the desired and feared adventure of the discovery of the self.

Destruction of the world that we have built and in which we live, and of ourselves within it; but then a wonderful reconstruction, of the bolder, cleaner, more spacious and fully human life — that is the lure, the promise and the terror, of these disturbing night visitants from the mythological realm that we carry within.

So let's just accept once and for all that fear and uncertainty are absolutely natural and also absolutely inescapable. They are also the price we have to pay for growth, for gaining access to this wonderfully enriching world beyond. There is no ecstasy without some agony. No pain, no gain. It's a principle for everything we do, whether it's getting fit, losing weight, learning a new skill, getting a better job, getting an education, learning to ride a bicycle or fly a plane, or taking a parachute jump or running a marathon.

For years my wife Lorraine talked about doing a parachute jump. What a wonderful feeling it must be, she said, to float slowly down with the world beneath one's feet! So, on her thirty-fifth birthday she woke up to find a box attached to the ceiling with a piece of string hanging from it and a tag instructing her to 'Pull'. When she did, a tiny parachute floated down with my present attached to it: a parachute jump.

The next weekend we were out at the airport and, with a small band of macho nineteen-year-olds who eyed her with supreme scepticism, Lorraine went through the training. It wasn't easy. I know — I was watching! The big jump was to be the following week and, though she said nothing, I knew she was going through agonies of indecision. Yet she has enormous spunk and, being the only woman in the family, has endured innumerable hiking and fishing and canoeing and white-water rafting expeditions with me and our two boys.

Came the big moment, she was there. And her jump was absolutely perfect: she landed right in the circle. Like me, the macho nineteen-year-olds suddenly looked at her with awe and respect. Afterwards, she talked of her absolute terror as she climbed out on to the wing, felt the wind tugging at every flap of clothing, and experiencing the Black Hole in her stomach sucking in every ounce of reason and bravado. And then the ecstasy of the weightless freedom of temporary flight, with the whole world stretched beneath her feet just as she had imagined it for all those years.

What a wonderful moment — to actually experience something you've dreamed about for so long. To have the courage to overcome your fear, to take the action required, and to reap the rewards. The gain was worth the pain; the ecstasy well worth the agony. Once you've accepted that, it's much easier to take the first steps towards confronting the truth of yourself and everything around you.

Facing reality is a powerful stimulus for change. But you need to truly *confront* reality by being completely honest and receptive to whatever risks/pain/discomfort that reality implies. You must have the courage to internalise whatever insights you gain and be prepared to make changes accordingly. But you can only change when you are *ready* for that change and *want* it; and when you are *free* to make such changes — ie when outside stimuli/external factors/manipulative influences are not so strong as to overwhelm you.

'Enough already with the agonies!' I hear you saying. 'Tell me about the ecstasies!'

There *are* ecstasies waiting for you — ecstasies of a sense of freedom from the shackles of manipulation and capitulation and dependency and control, freedom from the skeletons of your past; the ecstasy of being in control of your own life, of self-fulfilment and true inner peace, of overcoming your ego. Right now, they probably seem vague and far away — especially in this world where instant gratification is the norm.

Don't despair. You're about to find out how some of the stages of your journey can bring you joy and freedom and more 'immediate' ecstasies.

But remember that although these immediate pleasures are only stepping-stones in your journey, they are also part of the greater *process*, the strengthening and regeneration of your emotional and psychological inner self. As Thomas Kühn writes of Paradigm Shifts in *The Structure of Scientific Revolutions*: 'All previous minor questions and doubts fall away and take on a new perspective; it revolutionises the individual's life and causes a kind of quantum leap in awareness and outlook on the world. It is an enlargement of life itself; a second chance at finding meaning.'

Isn't that something to look forward to − an 'enlargement of life itself'? Kühn goes on to say that

... the transformative process, however alien it may seem at first, soon feels irrevocably right. Whatever the initial misgivings, there is no question of commitment once we have touched something we thought forever lost: our true journey to our true destination.

Let's end this section by referring to Maslow again. As he observed, once the individual has experienced the satisfaction of his higher needs, they often become more important to him than his lower needs, to the point where he might be willing to forgo satisfaction of those lower needs for a time. In fact, in the highest spiritual beings on earth, some (like the Buddhist monks who stare at the sun, or eat one grain of rice a day, or choose complete seclusion and physical deprivation as an act of faith) are willing to dedicate their entire lives and completely forgo all other lower needs for this higher quest.

That's one of the dangers in escaping your Comfort Zones and reaching a higher level of awareness and consciousness and spirituality: that those around you will find it very difficult to understand why you are more interested in your eternal journey and less interested in mundane, day-to-day activities; why you are less concerned about chasing a buck than you are about pursuing eternal truths or the incredible transcendental experience of a 'now' moment. It really is very difficult to explain to them that you have achieved a serenity and inner peace that makes material things relatively unimportant. Or how wonderfully serene it is when, through insight and a new perspective, the previous constraints, the previous mountains, have now become insignificant molehills.

I have experienced this sadness and frustration at people's refusals to confront the truth and be receptive to my insight and honesty when I was trying to give them sound advice from a completely altruistic point of view. But sometimes it was as if I were trying to explain quantum mechanics to a pre-school child, or describe the call of the fish eagle to a deaf-mute. As they say, there is none so blind as he who will not see.

Why is it that people have become so wary and suspicious of each other? Perhaps it is because each one of us has experienced the pain of being manipulated and used and betrayed so often that we will not allow ourselves to become vulnerable again. What a sad indictment it is of the world and of mankind that through bitter experience we have all had to learn to be distrustful of people. Perhaps this is one of the most tantalising aspects of our concept of 'Heaven', that everyone there will be on a spiritual level where such things as deceit and manipulation and hidden agendas are unheard of and inconceivable.

And yet it doesn't help to be idealistic about it, or to think that if we're good and honest others will be good and honest in return. We have all been betrayed, even by people we trusted; and we have all in turn (myself included) in some way betrayed people who trusted us. We're all only human, after all. But the key is not simply to accept your 'being human' as an excuse to continue doing wrong. We need to accept that we have to be wary of people, but we can also make a commitment to try to improve ourselves constantly in terms of being more trustworthy and spiritually stronger. Thus, even when we are sorely tempted selfishly to take care of our own interests or protect our egos, we can be true to ourselves and therefore true to everyone else around us as well.

It is only when we take full responsibility for our own lives, and for everything we do, that we will understand that we have the freedom to do anything we like in life *as long as it does not harm anyone else or impinge on their freedom in any way.* It is only then that we will understand that every action has a reaction; that, somehow, somewhere, we are *accountable* for everything we do. Whether we shift that accountability to a Higher Power and recognise that we will one day be judged by Him, or whether we internalise that accountability and recognise that we are only harming ourselves by harming others, it comes down to the same thing.

As you progress on your journey, you will begin to *internalise* these values and standards more and more, to the point where your actions and reactions will be automatically determined by your inner self. There will be an *integration* of 'Who I am' and 'What I do' when you allow your infra-ego to be integrated into your everyday life.

Again, I must remind you that by this I am not implying or advocating that you yourself become 'God'; on the contrary, this internalising of values and eternal truths and making them inextricably part of the very fabric of who you are can only strengthen your faith and bring you closer to whatever God you worship. It is, in essence, 'letting your faith shine through'. It is proclaiming that faith by being a living testament to it. And it is the key to the future peace and prosperity of our world, and to the very survival of all mankind.

If we want to stop wars and misery and corruption and all the other dreadful things brought about by ourselves, then we have to bring about a major *internal change* in ourselves. It is the dawning of the 'Age of Aquarius' that Marilyn Ferguson and others talk about, that will begin a new day of hope and peace for all of us.

Unfortunately, it seems that people prefer to wait for the catalyst of the Second Coming of Christ, or the crisis caused by the disasters predicted in the Bible's book of Revelations and the writings of Nostradamus, or any of the other predictions in any other faith, rather than take responsibility for their own lives and start to lay the foundations for Heaven or Nirvana on earth right now.

Key points to remember from Chapter 4

1. You've already made several successful 'escapes' in your life: starting school, leaving home, changing jobs. Escaping your current Comfort Zones is just as scary and turbulent, but just as natural and inevitable. And the rewards are far greater.

2. Escaping doesn't necessarily mean forsaking all that is near and dear to you; they could well become even nearer and dearer. Alternatively, your whole concept of what is near and dear could change so much that losing all or some of them is inevitable — but it will be more of a relinquishing than a losing.

3. Your journey is described in all the cultures and religions and mythologies of the world, and recognised by thousands of writers and poets and scientists. Although in the modern world the 'Rites of Passage' have largely become blurred or have disappeared entirely, these transitions from one stage of life to another, from a lower to a higher level of existence, are inevitable.

4. Before there can be rebirth, something must die. And before you can become the 'new' you, you must accept that some aspects of the 'old' you must die. But all that 'dies' when you escape your Comfort Zones are the masks and illusions and self-deceptions, and the suppressions and limitations to the freedom of being the real you.

5. It's your choice and your choice alone to cross the drawbridge to a better life, or to retreat deeper within the walls of your castle.

6. Don't expect a 'quantum leap', which could knock you even further back unless you are prepared for it (which most of us aren't). Your escape is a process. And the escape is not the destination, but the journey itself. You learn with each step.

7. Fear is one of the greatest obstacles to escaping your Comfort Zone prison. But you can overcome that fear by confronting it head-on, or you can overcome that fear by simply starting off on your journey and gaining strength and courage with each step along the way — until the old constraints lose their power, and former mountains become molehills.

8. You can expect resistance from those close to you, especially when they want to perpetuate control/dependency relationships. If you can get them to share your journey, the resulting transformative relationship will be what poets write about. But you cannot demand that they go along with you. At best, you can give them keys knowing that only they can open their own padlocked doors. Remember the Lesson of the Butterfly.

9. Understanding the real meaning of 'love', and internalising it and living it, is one of the best motivations for escaping your Comfort Zones.

10. Accepting yourself on (or aspiring to) a higher spiritual level is not selfish or arrogant. It is a matter of fact, of insight, of enlightenment. Moving from a lower to a higher level is natural and inevitable, and the only thing stopping man is the narrowness of his mind. And remember: you can never be true to anybody unless you are true to yourself.

11. The integration of your inner self with your actions in your exterior world, of your values with your behaviour, is a vital part of self-actualisation and wholeness. As you progress on your journey, you will begin to internalise these values and standards more and more, to the point where your actions and reactions will be automatically determined by your inner self. There will be an integration of 'Who I am' and 'What I do'.

12. Confronting and overcoming your fears and doubts and taking a leap into the unknown is difficult and painful. But the ecstasy is well worth the agony; the gain well worth the pain. And your reward is 'an enlargement of life itself'.

5

Stage 3

Taking Time Out To Get To Know Yourself

By now I can hear you thinking, 'Enough already! I know about as much about what Comfort Zones are as any human being can assimilate. I *know* I'm trapped; I *want* to escape; and I'm prepared to accept the risks and pain that go with it. But when am I going to find out *how* to escape?'

Almost without being aware of it, you've already taken a whole lot of steps on your journey simply by *starting the process*. But so many people, when they knew I was writing this book, said 'I hope you'll put in some exercises to do, like a do-it-yourself manual.' Personally, I have always disliked such things in books. They made me feel like I was back in school. Yet when I actually tried them, I found they helped me a great deal. So, with a little help from my friend Albert Koopman (I'm the dreamer and romantic theorist; he's the pragmatist!), I've included some simple and quick exercises that will help you feel you're actually starting to take some practical, conscious steps towards escaping your Comfort Zones.

You begin by really getting to know yourself. Your true, inner self; the self that you talk to in your most private moments. The self that wants to live your life according to what you *want* rather than what you *need*; what you *desire* rather than what you *have to do*.

To do that, you'll need to take *some time out for yourself*. If you can afford to go away all by yourself (can you afford not to?), that's the best way to do it — even a few days will do, away from all constraints and obligations and worries and influences of others around you. But if you really can't afford that, then find a way to isolate yourself completely. If that's not possible in your own home, then go to a park, a museum, a library, an art gallery, a church, a friend's house. Make a commitment to go frequently — every day, if you can. But however you do it, find a way to take time out and do the exercises on the following pages.

They are designed to help you discover who you really are, and what you really want out of life. What the obstacles are to your becoming that person, and having those things you truly want. It's important to be completely, brutally honest when you do these exercises. Nobody else will see your answers — and if you lie, you're only fooling yourself and making your escape impossible or futile. Somehow you must find the courage to confront the truth: as Sigmund Freud said, 'Honesty is not an ethic for weaklings.' But at the same time you must be aware of what psychotherapist Dr Albert Ellis claims: 'Failures in self-honesty are at the root of almost every psychological and emotional disturbance.'

It is also important that in answering these questions you not only write down what you *think* but, more importantly, what you *feel*. *Needs* must be differentiated from *wants* or *desires* which are not motivated by specific needs. Because at the end of the day, you can only achieve your goals — even the satisfaction of your most basic needs, let alone escaping your Comfort Zones — if you sincerely want to.

Think of a person crippled in a car accident, who lapses into a quagmire of despair, depression and inactivity. He will only begin his journey and be able to rebuild his life if he has the desire to do it — and that usually implies first confronting his situation and then being determined to change it.

So, to progress in life, we first need to *want* to do something. And then we need to translate that 'want' into positive action.

This is partly an intellectual decision but, more importantly, it is also an emotional decision. We must be inspired and motivated by genuine feelings. Moreover, those feelings must be in harmony with our reasoning if we want to generate the power from within to achieve our goals.

Self-inspired action thus only comes about as a result of a stimulus (ie a deep desire to gratify a need), which is evidenced and supported by feelings and emotions.

SELF-AWARENESS – WHY?

In a time of accelerated change, where the only certainty is the uncertainty of change, the time available for responding is becoming relatively shorter. Everyone is under pressure to respond faster and more often to more and more changes. This requires new skills and new methods of dealing with situations, as the old ways of handling relationships show themselves to be inadequate in the new, changing environment. People are finding that they need new ways to cope, to relate and to respond.

In asking ourselves what we need to do to enable ourselves to cope better in a world of accelerated change, the first step may simply be to acquire self-awareness. We must answer the questions 'Who am I?', 'How did I become this kind of person?', 'Who do I want to be?', 'Where do I want to go?'

Without a clear understanding of who you are now, and how you got to be that person, there is absolutely no possibility of growth, modification or change — because you cannot modify or change anything unless you know what it looks like, and you cannot know what it looks like unless you take the time to examine it from all angles. The process of looking at yourself and deciding what about yourself you would like to keep and strengthen, and what you would like to change or modify or even discard, is the process of self-awareness.

Self-knowledge has been part of Western civilisation's rhetoric for centuries, but there are few mechanisms for actually putting this into practice. We've all heard the advice of great teachers and philosophers: 'Know thyself'; 'The unexamined life is not worth living'; 'To know oneself is man's greatest achievement'.

144

But, in fact, in both our formal and informal education, we are taught very little about ourselves as human beings, about our feelings, our needs, our sexuality, about how to relate, how to achieve goals, and so on.

Before beginning the process of attaining self-awareness and self-actualisation one might (and should) ask: What is the attainment of self-awareness going to give me?

This can be answered in very simple terms: If we understand what it is that is holding us back, we can then attempt to remove these barriers and make use of all our potential for success and achievement — indeed, all our potential for living a successful, happy and fulfilled life.

When people rationalise their present unfulfilled lives by hiding behind emotional and psychological security blankets and other aspects of their Comfort Zones by saying 'That's my fate!' or 'That's just the way I am', or 'I can't help myself; I've always been that way!', or 'It's my personality', or 'I blame that person', they are just running away from the problem. They are avoiding or delaying a process that is absolutely inevitable.

The sooner we have the courage to confront realities and accept the risks and fears and discomforts inherent in change, the sooner we can discard the negatives and the painful baggage of the past. The sooner we stop blaming people or events and accept that the problem was *our reaction* to those people or events, and the fact that we are still allowing them to be a negative influence in our lives, the sooner we can begin to progress in life.

The great Swiss psychologist Carl C Jung makes the point (quoted by Joseph Campbell) that 'in the living of our lives every one of us is required by his society to play some specific social role'. In order to function in the world we are all continually acting parts, and these parts Jung calls personae (from the Latin persona, meaning 'mask, false face'). Many of the masks are playful, opportunistic, superficial, expedient, manipulative. Others, however, go deep, very deep, much deeper than we know.

145

Campbell goes on to say that

> To become — in Jung's terms — individuated, to live as a
> released individual, one has to know how and when to put
> on and to put off these masks of one's various life roles. But
> this, finally, is not easy, since some of the masks cut deep.
> They include judgement and moral values. They include
> one's pride, ambition, achievement, fears, guilt, obligations
> to social norms and parental expectations. They include
> one's infatuations, and one's defense mechanisms such as
> denial, rationalisations and sublimations.

Now do you understand the need to strip away the masks and
illusions and find out who you really are, deep down inside? It's
called 'unfreezing' or 'disassembling' yourself, and begins with
self-confrontation of anything that shakes up the old understanding of the world; or forces self-confrontation; or bursts our
bubble of rationalised defence mechanisms, expedient half-truths
and self-deception; or removes our security blanket and lowers the
drawbridge to allow us to escape our Comfort Zone prison.

*Because — and here's the most important point — we cannot
escape unless we know that we are prisoners.* We cannot leave the
trap of our glass cage limitation unless we know that we are in it.

And in order to become aware of the need to escape, we have
to feel pain or discomfort or disequilibrium.

We have to explore and question and evaluate ourselves and
our situation with total honesty and receptiveness to whatever we
may find — unpleasant though it might be.

The very first step, thus, in growing and becoming a whole,
fulfilled human being, is to confront the fact that we have
deceived ourselves into coping with unpleasant facts by avoiding
the truth — and thus forfeiting our awareness of the present
moment and forfeiting the freedom of spontaneity... and the
very essence of living.

IT'S TIME TO TAKE THE FIRST CONSCIOUS, PRACTICAL STEPS

OK. So now you've taken some time out. You're all alone and private. You've sharpened your pencil. And you're determined to be completely honest with yourself.

Now answer the following questions in the space provided (use your own sheets of paper if you want to keep them absolutely private, or if you need more space for your answers). Nobody's going to see your answers (unless you choose to share them with a trusted friend or soulmate), so try to really pour out your soul and be absolutely true to the inner you.

Remember, above all else, you have to be completely honest with yourself. After all, who are you going to impress by writing what you think the answers should be, or what other people would expect of you? You'd only be deceiving yourself. And throwing away the chance of being who you truly want to be.

Question One: Who do I want to be?

[Before you answer, read this!

In our early life stages this question crops up frequently — we ask it of ourselves and our parents/teachers/friends ask us 'What do you want to be one day?' Our normal responses are either fantasy-driven (eg a fireman/movie star/ballet dancer/doctor/ sports hero), or motivated by the expectations of those asking the question, especially if they are important in our lives at the time. For example, if you know your father expects you to become a doctor, you would inevitably answer in such a way as to fulfil that expectation and gain acceptance and approval.

But now that we are free agents, let us answer that question for ourselves and play a 'what if?' game. What if money was no object? What if you had all the connections and the knowledge and skills to achieve your dream? If all these things were there, there were no obstacles whatsoever, then what would your dream be?

Write it down in one sentence — an all-embracing statement as to what that dream would be and how you would fit into it. There is no right or wrong answer here. You probably won't be sure what exactly you want, and what you want today may be different from what you want tomorrow. Or, once you've written down your answer, you may (as my eighteen-year-old son Rowan did when he read my manuscript for this book) start questioning and analysing your answer and saying 'Yes, but if I achieved that, maybe I'd find it wouldn't be exactly what I wanted after all.'

That's OK. What we are looking for here is just a starting point. So write whatever you feel, no matter how impractical it may seem. Don't think or rethink too much. Let it come straight from your heart. My own statement here was about twenty lines long when I did this exercise. Don't be afraid to delve deep into your emotions and feelings and put your dreams down on paper.]

If I had no limitations whatsoever, I would be:

_____

_____

_____

_____

_____

_____

_____

_____

_____

_____

_____

_____

Question Two: Why do I desire this dream of the ideal me?

In other words, if the above dream could come true, what would be in it for you apart from any material benefits? What is the underpinning subconscious need driving it? What deep-rooted value system made you choose this particular dream? (Recognition? Self-fulfilment? Authenticity? Being of service to others?) Try to identify these rewards and write them down here.

Apart from any material benefits, I would gain:

_____

_____

_____

_____

_____

_____

_____

_____

_____

_____

_____

_____

_____

_____

_____

_____

_____

_____

Question Three: What do I need to do (or undo) in order to become more like the person I want to be?

When we ask ourselves 'What do I want to be?', we should rather be asking ourselves 'Who am I, and what do I need to help me become more completely who and what I want to be?'

Having said that, try to identify what you perceive as your single biggest limitation which has stopped you/is stopping you from achieving your desire of being who and what you want to be. Only once you've identified the *main* reason should you go on and identify others that have added to the problem.

For example, lack of confidence, money, lack of communication skills, inability to relate to others, time, peer pressure, fear of failure, procrastination, uncertainty, etc. Be honest with yourself and write down these limitations and obstacles here.

To become who I really want to be, I need to overcome:

Question Four: Why haven't I yet overcome the obstacles mentioned above?

You've written down your dream, you understand the value systems underpinning it, and you've identified some perceived obstacles standing in the way of achieving it.

Now comes the most crucial, soul-searching question of all: What is/are the reason/s why you have not yet implemented remedial action to overcome these obstacles that stand in the way of your dream?

Be very honest with yourself. Your answer could very well be the beginning of your new life journey. It is thus in itself a vital mini-goal that is an essential step towards achieving your greater goal and vision.

I haven't yet overcome the obstacles mentioned above because:

_____

_____

_____

_____

_____

_____

_____

_____

_____

_____

_____

_____

151

HOW DO I KNOW THESE EXERCISES WILL WORK?
I'VE DONE SO MANY BEFORE...

Before we go on to actually use the information you have written down on the past few pages, allow me to digress a little. Look upon it as being another 'resting place' on your journey. The relevance will soon be clear.

The above exercises come from a course called *Goal Source* which was developed by my friend Albert Koopman when he was managing director of a building material chain called Cashbuild, and was used to enlighten and educate his staff.

At the time, South Africa was in the deepest throes of apartheid, and Albert was in the process of introducing what in those days was a dirty word in that country: participative management.

Not too surprisingly, his initiative was viewed with great suspicion by many of the right-wing proponents of apartheid, and welcomed with relish and appreciation by the more liberal elements of the country's society.

To cut a long story short, his efforts led to record-breaking profits and worker support even through the worst strike and boycott actions ever experienced in South Africa. The exercise is chronicled in his excellent book *The Corporate Crusaders* which is today prescribed in business courses in colleges worldwide.

But to return to its relevance to this book. Albert and I were in the same class at Bloemfontein's well-known Grey College, but after school our paths took us on different journeys. We met up again many years later in Johannesburg and resumed our friendship. To the chagrin of our wives, we spent many late nights, fuelled by frosted Castle lagers (Albert's) and glasses of Port (mine), discussing our philosophies and discovering how much we had in common. Though my journey had been mainly personal and psychological, and Albert's mainly corporate, the principles were largely the same.

What was most exciting to me was finding out about his Goal Source exercise (which had remained hidden under a bushel for many years) and I wondered whether, in fact, the whole participative management success had been made possible *because* of Goal Source. I believed that by putting his staff members through this 'self-discovery' exercise he had made them more receptive to the next stage of his plans. It ensured, as it were, that the later seeds would be planted in fertile soil. It had, in fact, *shifted them on to a higher level of consciousness and awareness.*

The point is that it *works*. So, don't worry about 'right' or 'wrong' or even 'final' or 'complete' answers. It's the process of answering the questions and examining yourself that does the trick. And each one is a step on your journey — even though you don't perhaps realise it yet.

'Goal Source'

I have condensed Albert's original course into what I consider to be the most valuable components. [It's also important to note here that Koopman acknowledged in Goal Source that he drew widely on many reference sources, including and especially on Hagberg and Leider's excellent book *The Inventurers*.]

Thinking about the exercises you have completed on the previous pages, look at Albert's summarised stages of activities required to move you towards 'Individuation' and true 'Interdependence' in relationships, and gaining the insights into your true self which he refers to as 'Innovision'.

Individuation ————	Interdependence ————	Innovision

Developing my vision

Thinking about who I want to be, what would my specific personal goals be if I became that person? What do I want to do with my life? What is my vision?

_____

_____

_____

_____

_____

_____

_____

_____

Recognising my potential

Thinking about what I would gain if these things came true (apart from material benefits), what are my talents, my skills, my strengths, my abilities, that I can use to help me achieve this — and what are my weaknesses?

_____

_____

_____

_____

_____

_____

_____

_____

_____

_____

Structuring my activity

Could you eat a whole elephant at one sitting? Of course not. But you can — easily! — if you take it one forkful at a time, one meal at a time, one day at a time.

So... thinking about what obstacles stand in the way of achieving my goals, and knowing why I haven't yet overcome them, where should I focus? What can I start going Right Now (however small) to start making actual progress?

_____

_____

_____

_____

_____

_____

Committing my resources

Knowing that if I want to travel the highway I have to be prepared to pay the toll, am I prepared to take the risks necessary to achieve my goals? What will it cost and am I prepared to pay the price? What skills must I commit myself to, and what action must I take, in order to achieve my goals?

_____

_____

_____

_____

_____

_____

_____

Adapting to change

If I recognise and accept the risks entailed, how should I adapt my current lifestyle to accommodate my goals? What sacrifices will be needed, if any?

_____

_____

_____

_____

_____

_____

_____

Involving other people

If I look at the people in my life, who of these are on a lower spiritual level than I am, and who are on a higher level? Am I being dragged down or lifted up? Is my environment continuously elevating me, or am I a diamond lost in a coalyard?

Which people will help me towards achieving my goal? Who has the wisdom, the insight and the desire to do this? Who can I really trust to guide me?

_____

_____

_____

_____

_____

_____

_____

_____

Making it happen

Even the greatest intentions and plans are worthless unless you put them into action. *Have I systematically listed all the actions needed to achieve my goals? Have I got target dates with expected outcomes?*

This is what I need to do:	Date by when it must be done:
_____	_____
_____	_____
_____	_____
_____	_____
_____	_____
_____	_____
_____	_____
_____	_____
_____	_____
_____	_____
_____	_____
_____	_____
_____	_____
_____	_____
_____	_____
_____	_____
_____	_____
_____	_____
_____	_____
_____	_____
_____	_____

WHAT HAPPENS WHEN YOU DON'T ACHIEVE YOUR GOALS?

I believe the questions on the preceding pages are all good 'trigger questions' to ask yourself at this stage. Albert then goes on to explain that when a person is blocked from achieving a desired goal, or comes up against a barrier, frustration is experienced, the degree of which is directly related to the strength or magnitude of the desired goal and/or the need that is being thwarted.

And when a person is frustrated, he can act in one of two ways:

1. *Adaptive response*

   The person may find some new or acceptable way of reducing the need — ie an acceptable substitute goal which is attainable.

2. *Maladaptive response*

   The person may continue trying to reach the unattainable goal, or may give up trying to reach any goal whatsoever, and even lapse into withdrawal and a state of non-activity and lethargy, often coupled with depression and resentment and a feeling of lack of self-worth. Often, however, the frustration leads inevitably to aggression, which may, of course, be directed towards himself. In fact, Yale University studies by Dollard *et al.* found that the existence of frustration always leads to some form of aggression.

MECHANISMS FOR ACHIEVING GOALS

Albert used several self-empowerment techniques to help his staff go about actually achieving their goals. These included auto-suggestion as a means of eliminating old entrenched negative feelings/beliefs/emotions, and turning them into more positive 'new you' feelings; 'affirmations' and other ongoing self-programming and reinforcement techniques, such as 'imaging' — ie imagining yourself as already having achieved your goal.

I think it's important for me to preface any further discussion with a few words of caution about the dangers of self-empowerment, and the need for humility and complete altruism. I should also add that auto-suggestion as such is not necessarily a bad thing, but it must never be used consciously to enrich oneself materially, or egocentrically gain power or status, or manipulate other people's lives in any way. That would be an abuse of cosmic energy, and will be punished kharmically on a universal plane.

Unless you are guided by someone of unquestionable integrity and high spiritual values, I myself would hesitate to recommend these techniques, or even meditation techniques, to most people. Perhaps as a result of many years' study of paranormal phenomena, which obviously embraced many elements of the occult, I have grave reservations about the uninitiated tapping into these immensely powerful energies. It's like giving a child a loaded .44 Magnum to play with, or putting a Ouija board in the hands of giggling schoolgirls at a pyjama party. If you want to know more, read *Dark Secrets of the New Age* by Texe Marrs, or any of Colin Wilson's excellent books on the occult.

Yet there is no denying the incredible power of the human mind. As I have pointed out earlier, it can be used negatively or positively to influence one's life. Only you can choose which will dominate your own. Each positive thought in your head will displace or cancel out a negative one. And if your head is constantly brimming with positive thoughts, that has to be a recipe for success and happiness.

THE VITAL IMPORTANCE OF SELF-ESTEEM

So much depends on the way we feel about ourselves. It is our *attitude* more than anything else which governs the way we act and react in our day-to-day lives — and our happiness and fulfilment. It colours our behaviour, our actions, our thoughts and interpretations, our social interactions, the way other people respond to us and feel about us.

There is great wisdom in the maxim *you are what you think.* But, more importantly, *we are what we feel.*

Remember that we are motivated primarily by *feelings and emotions* and that although these need to be in agreement with our rational decisions if we want to achieve our goals and feel happy about it, our feeling mind is not moved by logic.

In fact, emotions very often overrule logic. (Examples: a persuasive salesman who knows how to manipulate your emotions by stimulating your inner fears and needs and guilts; a stirring political speech; a seductive man or woman.) Also, despite our strongest logical and rational attempts to change feelings of depression or emotional trauma, these things often operate on a purely subconscious level of which we are not aware and which may only be uncovered and confronted through psychotherapy. These may have their roots in some long-forgotten incident or remark at a very young age, yet they can influence and colour your entire life until you *confront* them and *gain insight* into them and come to terms with them.

Yet we can use the principles to help us achieve our goals, become happier, and so on — for example, by affirmations or auto-suggestion which will influence our feeling minds in much the same way as our minds and thoughts can influence our physical bodies and make us feel ill or well. Remember that 'a suggestion is a message to the mind which affects our behaviour by *making a direct appeal to the imagination*'. However, if we derive our pleasure from imagining or dreaming, instead of from doing what we have previously imagined, then we are on the wrong track and must change if we want a successful and happy life.

SUGGESTION AND AUTO-SUGGESTION: 'IMAGINING' AND SELF-ASSERTIVENESS TECHNIQUES: AFFIRMATIONS

Our central feeling about ourselves in terms of 'superiority' or 'inferiority' or 'cleverness' or 'stupidity' or 'attractive' or 'ugly' — or whatever it may be — often depends largely upon what we imagine other people think of us.

Our bodies, our whole physical being and presence, our attitude and the impression we make on others, become what we imagine them to be. René Descartes said: 'I think, therefore I am.' This is a powerful concept in itself, but there is much more implied in the extrapolation of this thought — ie 'We are what we think'. The whole question of suggestion and auto-suggestion can be simplified if we think of it as an activity of our imagination.

A suggestion is a message to the mind which affects our behaviour by making a direct appeal to our imagination.

Every act is preceded by 'imagination'. For example, if we want to sign our name on a piece of paper, the act of doing this follows a mental picture that we have formed of behaving in this way.

When people say they have no imagination, what they are saying is that they do not use their imagination as a way of creating energy and incentive for future activities. They take life as it comes, relying rather on the impulse of the moment to dictate their behaviour.

We always tend to behave in obedience to our feelings. And by the exercise of deliberate imagination, we prepare the channel along which our feelings will run when it comes to the moment of action. Consequently, by the correct use of imagination, we can make all the difference in the world to our future behaviour, no matter what kind of event we might be involved or participating in.

Research has shown that there are two distinct ways in which we can use our imagination:

- to prepare us for activity, or
- to enable us to find pleasure without engaging in activity.

Because we all take a certain amount of pleasure in the exercise of our imagination, there is a tendency in us as we grow up to continue to use it for purposes of 'make believe' as we did when we were children. We day-dream and build castles in the air. If we want an excuse for not taking an active and energetic part in life, we can get into the way of enjoying these airy fancies so much that the pleasure we derive from them becomes a substitute for the real thing. This can lead to neurosis, where a person confuses dreams with reality. The game of 'let's pretend' becomes so real to the dreamer that it takes the place of his interest in the actual world, where disappointments, difficulties and failures must be met and overcome by steady work and sincere determination.

The correct way to use the imagination deliberately is the *opposite* of this. It consists in allowing this wonderful faculty to arouse our interest in the things we actually intend to do.

We build castles in the air, but we build them of a size and material that we can rarely find in the real world around us. Our day-dreams do not act as substitutes for activity. Their effects, then, are to stoke up the fires of our energy, prepare our bodies and minds with strength for the tasks we intend to undertake, and give us courage and perseverance to perform them.

The easiest way to find out for yourself if you are using your imagination in the wrong way, is to ask yourself if you derive your pleasure more out of the *imagining* itself rather than out of the actual *doing* of what you have previously imagined. If this is so, then you must change your tack. The world of dreams is no place for a normal man or woman to live in.

Correct use of *deliberate imagining* can help us change our habits or behaviour; help us alter our faulty convictions; help us improve our body tone; help us become masters of our moods. With its aid, we can enlist all the energies of our lives for the fulfilment of our constructive purposes. But the conditions must first be obeyed. The most important condition is: *We cannot successfully suggest to ourselves (or attain) anything that we do not want to imagine will come true.*

Thus, no matter what you want to suggest to yourself, first examine the proposal in the light of this rule to learn whether you will have any real prospect of carrying out your intention. You have to actually imagine yourself feeling happier about yourself after having achieved your objective/proposal (and honestly believe that you will be), otherwise the suggestion won't work. You have to imagine yourself actually adopting the plan and feeling pleased about it.

Where the will and the imagination are in conflict, the imagination always wins.

FIVE STEPS TO SUCCESSFUL AUTO-SUGGESTION

1. Get a clear picture in your mind's eye of exactly what you want to do or achieve or become. Frame the simplest possible, and most positive, sentence that expresses that desire, then write it down. This is a very important step and needs a great deal of time and thought devoted to getting it exactly right. Don't be satisfied until what you write down says precisely and completely what you want to bring about.

2. Carefully consider the reasons why you have not until now done what you intend (ie what you have written down). What are the habitual feelings that are holding you back, or have kept you on some course of action different from the one you are now proposing? In what way has your imagination been at work — ie have you derived pleasure from the imagination of doing or achieving this, rather than from the actual action of doing what you now propose to do?

    This self-examination can be quite difficult and complex. For example, you may find it difficult to admit or understand that you have derived satisfaction from some bad behaviour; nevertheless, if you are truly honest with yourself you will inevitably find that this is the case. Putting someone else down may have given you a feeling of power or superiority and thus prevented you from acknowledging your feelings of weakness or inadequacy or selfishness or the need for self-importance. It is important that you fully understand how and why your behaviour has been satisfying you before you can change that behaviour and substitute more fulfilling, more real behaviour. The most vital element in this step is total honesty. You must be brutal with yourself and resist resorting to rationalisations or old, entrenched excuses and explanations for your previous beliefs and behaviour.

Force yourself to be completely objective; try to see yourself from the outside, as if you were another person (eg a trusted friend or a psychologist) examining you.

3. Now ask yourself sincerely whether the satisfaction of the course you want to pursue in the future can compare, in your imagination, with the satisfaction given by the older habit.

4. If not, keep turning over in your mind and imagination all the possibilities of interest, pleasure and self-esteem that you can see in your new plan of action. Picture yourself in all sorts of different circumstances, in all sorts of moods, behaving in the new way. Keep on doing so until you are satisfied that you can feel *more happiness* in doing what you intend to suggest to yourself, rather than by continuing to do what you have hitherto done.

Only when you are absolutely sure of this — and not before — can you safely begin to adopt a definite plan of suggestion. If you cannot do this, then drop your present proposal and find another which does fulfil the above conditions.

5. By the time you have undertaken all this, you may find that you have had to revise the written form of suggestion that you originally prepared. That's fine. Go over it again, and if necessary revise it again, until you have got it exactly right. Now crystallise it as a positive and personal affirmation in a simple sentence beginning '*I can and will do . . .*'

Once you have reached this step, it is important that you put this affirmation into practical application to make it a part of your life so that it can positively change your behaviour and achieve what you wanted to achieve. But remember what I said before: it is very important that your affirmation is not designed to influence another person's life in any way. Just as no other person has a right to manipulate your life, so you have no right to manipulate theirs.

PUTTING YOUR AUTO-SUGGESTION TO WORK FOR YOU

- Find yourself a quiet place — a 'retreat' — where you will not be disturbed for at least thirty minutes.

- Relax. Loosen restrictive clothing. Get comfortable.

- Breathe deeply and evenly, drawing up each breath and slowly filling your lungs, holding it there for a moment or two, and then letting it escape just as slowly. Breathe normally for a few breaths, and then repeat.

- Put your mind into a state of peace and tranquillity. Think about being somewhere where you always feel happy and at peace. It could be the mountains, or a country stream, or anywhere peaceful and quiet, like a deserted beach. Imagine yourself strolling next to the gently lapping waves, or lying on the warm, soft sand with the sun giving you strength; smell the sea breeze, feel it blowing softly through your hair; listen to the sound of the waves; taste the salt on your lips.

- Relax, using the best way you know how to. Here are some ways you might try. Imagine a restful person — a Mexican having a siesta beneath his sombrero. Imitate an old sock — all limp. Play the children's game of 'make yourself heavy' — imagine your whole body being subjected to five times the earth's normal gravity. Consciously relax each part of your body starting from, say, the big toe on your right foot. (It often helps to flex or stretch that part as hard as you can for a few moments, and then relax it totally.) Now work your way from there to your other toes; then your foot, your ankle, your lower leg, your knee, your thigh muscles; and so on. When you have relaxed your entire body, repeat your affirmation several times out loud in a clear, positive and determined way, with absolute conviction, imagining at the same time all the good things that will happen to you once you have achieved your objective. See your new self in day-to-day situations: at home, at work, in social situations. Enjoy these moments.

- Relax and let the peace and tranquillity of your place of retreat wash over you, knowing that you can return here any time when you are feeling stressed, out of sorts, negative or unhappy.

- Repeat this procedure every day without fail, morning and evening, until you have achieved exactly what you want.

Apart from the affirmations and auto-suggestions, this is also a wonderful way to relax and give yourself 'islands' in your life — private and secluded moments away from the worries and cares of the world. Moments when you can fill your head with beauty and peace and positive thoughts.

Those thoughts might be reflecting on some of the quotations about Love given in an earlier chapter.

You might use this time to pray, or to forgive your enemies, or to wish someone strength and happiness.

You might want to dig deep into your memories and recall moments when you were truly happy. Relive those moments; think about how you *felt* at the time and try to relive those *feelings*.

Perhaps you could listen to calming music — perhaps one of your favourite classics, or popular songs that recall moments of happiness. Try to relive those moments and see the people and environment around you once more. Or, as you listen to the classics, try to understand the *emotions* in them, what the composer was trying to express through his music.

Finally, you might want to read these thoughts from Og Mandino's book *The Greatest Salesman in the World*, which one of my friends maintains was the book that had the greatest influence on his life when he read it as a teenager.

Og Mandino's 'Ten Ancient Scrolls'

1. *Today I begin a new life.*
   'I will form good habits and become their slave.'

2. *I will greet this day with love in my heart.*
   'When I am tempted to criticise I will bite on my tongue; when I am tempted to praise, I will shout it from the rooftops.'

3. *I will persist until I succeed.*
   'Each obstacle I will consider as a mere detour to my goal and a challenge to my profession.'
   'Never will I allow any day to end in a failure.'

4. *I am nature's greatest miracle.*
   'I am unique. There is, never has been, never will be, anyone exactly like me.'

5. *I will live this day as if it is my last.*
   'I will waste not a moment mourning yesterday's misfortunes, yesterday's defeats, yesterday's aches of the heart, for why should I throw good after bad?'

6. *Today I will be master of my emotions.*
   'Weak is he who permits his thoughts to control his actions; strong is he who forces his actions to control his thoughts.'

7. *I will laugh at the world.*
   'Never will I become so important, so wise, so powerful, so dignified, that I forget how to laugh at myself and my world.'

8. *Today I will multiply my value a hundredfold.*
   'I will set goals for the day, the week, the month, the year, my life.'
   'It is better to aim your spear at the moon and strike only an eagle, than to aim at the eagle and strike only a rock.'

9. *My dreams are worthless, my plans are dust, my goals are impossible... All are of no value unless they are followed by action. I will act now.*
   'This is the time. This is the place. I am the man.' [*Author: Or the woman!*]

10. *I will pray to God for guidance.*
    'Who is of so little faith that in a moment of great disaster or heartbreak has not called on his God?'
    'Never will I pray for the material things of the world. Only for guidance will I pray, that I may be shown the way to acquire what I need and want. And my prayer will always be answered.'

When I have felt depressed or disillusioned with life, I have found that reading these words first thing in the morning, before going to work, and thinking about them very carefully, often helped to make a big difference to my day.

'LIFESTYLE ODYSSEY II'

An important part of Albert's Goal Source course for his staff was recognising that our happiness is closely linked to the people around us. And so in this section he asked the question: How do I function and how do I fit in with other humans?

> Generally speaking, our journey through life is determined by our external striving to improve ourselves and grow.
> Individual needs constantly require fulfilment or expression, and these two aspects constitute the most powerful motivational forces that we have to contend with.
> It therefore stands to reason that if we can identify people's needs, values, attitudes and behaviours around us, we will be in a superior position to achieve our own goals... not by ourselves but through other people.
> No person has achieved his/her goals 'going it alone'. We all need people, but before we are able to develop people around us and help them to be what they can be, we need to know who we ourselves are and how we function.

There is no doubt that this is true. Other people are an essential and vital component of every aspect of our lives – not only for companionship, but also to enable us to learn more about ourselves. For this is the greatest value of a relationship: we always learn more about ourselves than we do about the other person. We always gain more from a relationship than we give. And if we are lucky enough to find a mentor, someone who can truly guide us and teach us unselfishly, we can grow in quantum leaps.

So, unless you are a monk or a nun dedicated to shutting yourself off from the world for the sole purpose of prayer and transcendent meditation in an attempt to attain the closest possible association with your God, you need people.

Man is a social animal. There have been numerous experiments conducted to show the effects of social deprivation, and we all know the pain of loneliness in life. So, before we get on to Albert's questionnaire in this context, I'd like to share some thoughts I've selected from a well-worn book in my library. It's called *How to Live with Life* and it was compiled by the Reader's Digest. The particular section I have borrowed from here is called *Reaching Out*.

- Make friends. Loneliness is one of the greatest causes of depression.

- Get involved in projects that allow you to meet people; altruism is a great healer (forget about yourself!). Join projects that cut across colour/socio-economic lines. Take a trip/drive/bus into a part of town you never visit. See how the other half lives. You'll realise just how fortunate you are — no matter how important or rich or talented you are, there is always someone who is richer, more talented . . . and the converse is also true.

- Pay a sincere compliment. Try to make someone smile. Smile yourself and see how others respond. It will make you feel better about yourself not only because of the physical catalyst you are supplying, but also by the response of the world around you. Find something good to say or think about everyone. Turn a criticism or cynicism or judgementalism into an instant compliment — 'cancel out' or 'make neutral' or 'balance the Kharma'. Compliment-givers become compliment-receivers.

- 'Never accept flattery as though it were a compliment; and never treat a compliment as though it were merely flattery.' (Russell Lynes)

- Give little gifts. A fresh flower picked at the side of the road, a card, a chocolate. We feel joy when we are giving because we are satisfying a basic human desire — the act of giving is an act of self-fulfilment. If you give for selfish or egocentric reasons, it's better not to give at all.

- 'I shall pass through this world but once; any good thing, therefore, that I can do, or any goodness that I can show to any fellow creature, let me do it now, for I shall not pass this way again.' [This was my school motto when I was a small child in Johannesburg. I still remember every word. Someone in his or her wisdom had the insight to inculcate such a noble thought into a child's education.]

But let's get back to our self-discovery exercises. Let's accept that we can't achieve most of our goals by going it alone. We all need people, but before we are able to develop people around us and help them to be what they can be, we need to know who we ourselves are and how we function. This part of Albert's course endeavours to achieve this. So, with your new knowledge and revelations about yourself, do the following exercises.

Goals

Which aspects of my personal style must I focus on to improve my adaptability as a human?

_____

_____

_____

_____

_____

_____

_____

_____

Values

Why do I believe that these items listed as 'Goals' are important to achieve, improve, overcome? What do I feel about them?

_____

_____

_____

_____

_____

_____

_____

_____

Obstacles

Probe your past and see whether you can list the perceived obstacles which block you from achieving those goals (upbringing, parents, friends, circumstances, self-image, etc).

_____

_____

_____

_____

_____

_____

_____

_____

_____

_____

_____

_____

Action

What plans must I implement and what must I do to overcome these obstacles so that I can achieve my goals? (Note: It helps if you organise these plans into Step 1, Step 2, Step 3, etc to give structure to your plan, and then also fill in a Target Date behind each step to give you a deadline and a way of measuring your progress.)

My goals are:

_____

_____

_____

_____

_____

_____

_____

Step 1: _____

_____

                                    Target Date: _____
Step 2: _____

_____

                                    Target Date: _____
Step 3: _____

_____

                                    Target Date: _____

Rewards

If I complete the above action steps, what would I stand to gain?

_____

_____

_____

_____

_____

Your Lifestyle 'Review'

Upon reviewing your personal lifestyle you have probably remembered or become re-aware of some specific strengths you have. For example, on certain occasions you can probably recall how these strengths stood you in good stead and helped you overcome some potentially difficult situations.

What were those strengths? Review the past and declare the positive outcomes affirmatively.

Did some of these successes come from your particular leadership style? From your conflict-handling abilities? If so, try to remember exactly when, how, in what circumstances, with or against whom? How did you feel under these circumstances? In other words, what were the rewards?

Make a list below, reinforcing all your strong points. Feel good about yourself!

_____

_____

_____

_____

_____

_____

ALBERT'S LIFESTYLE ODYSSEY III

(with a few additions of my own!)

Finding your life course

In this session you have gained some insight into what the 'blockages' are in your life that have prevented you from achieving your goals, and where they come from. It is important to realise that in order to achieve your goals and ambitions, you have to bring together idealism and realism.

The exercise you are about to do is to explore your inner emotional processes further in the privacy of your own home.

If Positive Thinking is the 'magical' solution, then why doesn't it always work? The answer is simple.

'Thinking' is a superficial intellectual exercise. Thinking cannot overcome the control that our emotions (particularly our unconscious emotions) have over our thoughts and our daily actions and responses.

We may be able to suppress or repress our feelings and emotions, but they still dictate success or failure in our lives. It is easy to become frustrated or confused when we find we cannot satisfy our desires and ambitions — especially if we don't know why — and until we can recognise our underlying emotional agenda, there can never be relief from anxiety. (Anxiety is nothing more than the result of our conscious self working overtime in trying to deal with the unconscious inner fears and concerns, and building emotional roadblocks in our conscious minds.)

When emotional agendas overwhelm our positive thoughts, they become destructive roadblocks which inhibit growth and goal achievement. The sad part is that our hidden unconscious self is very creative and can trick us into believing what we want to believe so that in the end we follow our hidden agendas.

The converse is also — happily! — true. The very creativity of our unconscious is just as powerful to enable you to believe that you can achieve your goals and desires, whatever they are.

Therefore, to release our natural constructive instincts and creativity, we have to bring to the surface and acknowledge any ingrained destructive inner emotions, and then confront and address them.

Remember: *taking charge over a destructive inner self requires you to rethink what you think.* You must realise that what you think has nothing to do with what will happen. The only *real* thing is your worry and anxiety.

THE 'HOW-DID-I-GET-HERE?' GRAPH

Before we get on to Albert's specific questions, I would like you to do an exercise to help put your life into perspective. It's not a new technique (I can remember doing it when I was a foreign exchange student at Detroit's Grosse Pointe High School), but it really works in giving you a 'helicopter view' of your life.

I call it the 'How-did-I-get-here?' graph.

Take a big sheet of paper and draw a horizontal line across the middle. Mark your birth at the left side with a large dot positioned on the line and write in 'BORN'.

Now mark your current age at the other end (the right-hand side) and write in 'ME NOW AT AGE XX'. This 'where-I-am-now' dot should be positioned according to how you feel about yourself and your life right now. If you are feeling positive and happy, position it somewhere *above* the horizontal line. If you feel your life is a mess, that you are unhappy and unfulfilled, then position it somewhere *below* the line.

Now divide the horizontal line into equal segments of five or ten years between birth and your current age. Thinking back, try to remember all the key incidents and events that have had an important effect on your life — both positive and negative. Mark these at the age when they happened, using a large dot and writing next to them exactly what that event or incident was. For example, 'FATHER DIED AND LEFT US DESTITUTE' or 'I WAS SEXUALLY MOLESTED' or 'JOINED XYZ COMPANY' or 'MET ABC'.

175

If the event was positive, put it above the line. If it was very positive, put it high above the line. If the incident was negative, put it below the line according to how negatively it influenced your life. (The more negative it was, the lower it should be.)

Now join the dots with straight lines, starting from birth and ending with where you are now. This will give you a graphic illustration of your own life — your own personal 'How-did-I-get-here?' graph, and you will more clearly be able to see *why* you are in your present position or mental or emotional state.

You can also use this graph to gain perspective on the events in your life, which will help you to plan your future better. Ask yourself why you positioned certain things above the line as positive experiences. How did they make you feel? If they made you feel good, how can you feel that way again? Have you neglected or discarded some of these things, and can you regain them realistically or repeat them in a new way?

Similarly, you can examine the negative aspects in better perspective. Remember that it is not the events or people or incidents themselves that are important, but rather how you *reacted or responded to them*. Re-examine them honestly and see how you can turn these things into positive learning experiences rather than allow them to continue burdening your life with anger or regret or resentment. Ask yourself if, in retrospect, you reacted wrongly or unfairly, or interpreted events too hastily or unrealistically. Did you perhaps blame someone else when it really wasn't his fault, when the fault perhaps lay with you? If so, can you correct it? Perhaps apologise? Perhaps even reverse it? What can you learn from it?

Nothing can change the past. But you *can* change the *future* by 'unbundling' your life in this way. Here are some examples of how people have used this 'how-did-I-get-here?' graph to change their lives.

176

After several failed relationships, Sue did the exercise and noticed that the four lowest points on her graph were all related to men: the period early in her childhood when her father had sexually molested her, her two unsuccessful marriages, and the death of her stepfather. There was only one high point − when her mother had got divorced and remarried, which heralded a time of blissful emotional and material security, until her stepfather had suddenly died of a brain tumour.

For the first time she realised that she had chosen men primarily on the basis of providing her with material security, and also that her relationships had failed because she had not been able to come to terms with her childhood molestation trauma. She had not been able to fully participate sexually or emotionally in her marriages, with the result that both men ended up having affairs and leaving her for the 'other' women − which left her feeling even more suspicious and more resentful of men. And less able to give of herself emotionally.

On the other hand, she realised that her need for material security had made her grab the first qualified prospect who came along; that she had married both men primarily for their money. Inevitably these marriages became dependency relationships which, together with her emotional and sexual inadequacies, led to her feeling out of control, used and emotionally unfulfilled.

Armed with these insights, Sue has started seeing a therapist to help her get over her childhood trauma and learn to trust men. She has also resolved to pursue her career more aggressively, has started taking a computer programming course at night school in the hope that this will give her the financial independence to enable her to enter into relationships on an equal, non-dependency basis.

Reading this as a summarised case study, you may wonder why Sue didn't see the obvious before. But because of her emotional cocooning she had never really discussed anything about her real self with anybody. She simply wouldn't allow herself the vulnerability of pure honesty − not even with herself.

It was only when she reached a valley of depression in her life − a crisis point − that she resolved to do something about it. She started reading self-help books and asking questions. It was an old family doctor who had finally suggested that she draw her 'how-did-I-get-here?' graph, and put her on the road to healing herself.

Case study: Chuck

Chuck's highest point on the graph was a time in his early twenties when he was a successful rock singer – and from there the graph went steadily down. As a recording artiste with many adoring fans, he had high self-esteem, money and creative fulfilment.

Then one day while on tour Chuck's band was involved in an accident and three of the members died in the flaming van. Seeing the event as an omen, Chuck's wife made him give up singing and made him move back to the small country town where her family lived. Because of his music success he had dropped out of high school and was consequently not qualified for anything else. His father-in-law insisted that he should get a 'real' job and took him into the family hardware business as an assistant manager of one of the stores. Gone was the glory and excitement, and in its place was a home life dominated by endless family visits and small-town boredom, and an ever-increasing burden of children which Chuck saw as an attempt by his wife to tie him down irrevocably. After the fifth, he stopped having sex with her. He tried to 'escape' his situation by giving singing lessons and playing solo night gigs in the city nearby, but something was dead inside him and he found he wasn't enjoying it. [*Author: 'External' escapes never work unless there's been an internal change.*] Also, his wife was suspicious and jealous and soon stopped even those minimal enjoyments.

Chuck became more and more despondent and started drinking heavily. [*Author: Another attempt at 'escaping' the wrong way.*] He put on weight and took less and less interest in his appearance. He started taking out his resentment on the business, spending little time and attention on his job, until his father-in-law eventually let him go. Unable to find a job, he used the skills learned in the hardware business to do home repairs. His wife continually nagged about money and put him down, removing even the little self-esteem he still had left. When confronted about his life, Chuck admitted that his marriage was doomed, but he had discussed it with his wife and they were both determined to wait for all their children to graduate from high school before they ended it.

After years of allowing himself to be trapped in this downward spiral of unchallenging jobs and social boredom, and finding relief from his dead-end marriage by engaging in numerous reactive affairs and increasing alcohol abuse, Chuck one night had a head-on collision while under the influence and landed in hospital. Unable to handle it any more, his wife ran off with another man and he was faced with a divorce and an empty apartment. He was fifty, fat and a failure.

Confronted with this crisis, Chuck listened to the advice of a hospital counsellor. She told him he could now only sink or swim. There were no options in between. When he got out of hospital, he booked himself into a clinic where, apart from being weaned off alcohol, he drew his 'how-did-I-get-here?' graph.

Suddenly he saw the crisis not as a disaster but as an opportunity to turn his life around. The graph told him that creativity, music and the social acceptance it had brought were important to him. He stopped drinking, got himself into shape physically, and moved to the city where he could earn a living and pursue his creative interests simultaneously by singing at a country bar at night while resuming his studies to complete school during the day. In his spare time he even started building customised electric guitars which were snapped up by a music dealer in the city.

Again, it seems pretty obvious that Chuck should have realised these things many years before. He should have taken control of his life, he should have asserted himself, he should have done lots of things. But he didn't.

Instead, he allowed himself to get caught up in a complex series of Comfort Zones. If he had not had the accident, if his wife had not added to his life crisis by running off with another man, Chuck would probably still be trapped in a stifling marriage with a wife who continually put him down and stopped him from being his real self. He would still have been living in the glories of the past while his real life passed him by.

By drawing his 'how-did-I-get-here?' graph he was able to identify what made him happy in life and pursue it. For the first time, he had 'helicopter vision' perspective on his life.

QUESTIONS TO HELP YOU FIND YOUR LIFE COURSE

Read the following and after thinking carefully about each statement, rate how important this is to you in your life on a scale of 1 to 10. (Rate as 1 anything that is not at all important, rate it 10 if it is extremely important.) This is not an examination; it's not to impress anyone; in fact, nobody else will even see it. So don't 'cheat' on yourself. Be absolutely, completely honest.

Score

1. Being good at something meaningful to me (expertise). [ ]

2. Contributing to the satisfaction of others (service orientation). [ ]

3. To have influence and authority over other people (leadership). [ ]

4. Money — plenty of money for the things I want. [ ]

5. Fun, enjoyment and satisfaction from pleasure. [ ]

6. Wisdom — a keen insight and understanding of the world around me. [ ]

7. Having a keen, active mind — being mentally active. [ ]

8. Security — having a stable and secure life. [ ]

9. Authenticity — being frank and genuine yourself. [ ]

10. Excitement, risk opportunities and adventure. [ ]

11. Achievement — sense of accomplishment and promotion. [ ]

12. Giving and receiving a lot of attention. Caring for others. [ ]

13. Meaningful work — relevant and purposeful job. [ ]

14. Happy family — contented living situation. [ ]

15. Physical health — attractiveness and health. [ ]

16. Self-growth — exploring inner self in order to develop. [ ]

17. Spirituality — meaning to life, religious beliefs. [ ]

18. Personal freedom — independence, making own choices. [ ]

19. Emotional health — ability to handle inner feelings and
    control them. [ ]

20. Recognition — being well known and praised/respected/
    recognised. [ ]

List any other things that are very important in your life and were
not covered in the above questions, and then rate them on the 1-10
scale.

Score

_____

_____

_____

_____

_____

_____

_____

_____

_____

_____

_____

_____

_____

_____

_____

_____

_____

_____

HOW TO USE THIS INFORMATION ABOUT YOURSELF

Look through your scores and circle the five highest ones.

Now think about your current life: your career, hobbies, interests, family, general lifestyle. Compare each with the statements to which you gave your five highest scores and see to what extent you are currently pursuing the things that are most important to you in your life.

If there is a high correlation, chances are you're on the right track. But if you find little correlation between your current lifestyle and the things that are most important to you, you need to re-examine where you're going. And accept the fact that you're probably trapped in a Comfort Zone or two.

If this is the case, you need to think carefully about the reasons why there is a low correlation. Ask yourself whether you are being blocked from doing the things that are important to you; or whether you've just drifted into a habitual behaviour set by simply allowing life to 'happen' to you instead of having a real direction and exercising your freedom of choice.

I think you'll find the following passage from *The Inventurers* by Janet Hagberg and Richard Leider very interesting in this regard:

> The basic ingredient in life and career renewal is *choice* — the choice of taking responsibility for yourself. In any situation, you have basically two options: change the situation, or change the mind set that is perceiving the situation. The choice is yours alone.
>
> Many of us are more comfortable allowing others to make the choices, until we really experience the way that self-direction mobilises us with energy and enthusiasm and ingenuity.
>
> Although we talk about being in charge and taking control, it is also imperative at some point that we *let go*, give up control, and try not to get in the way of our life's purpose.

Hagberg and Leider also talk of the fundamental truth:

It is the thought patterns and expectations in our heads that make us unhappy, not the people and conditions outside ourselves (where we usually put the blame!). We have learned to live according to the arbitrary expectations set up by the people and conditions in our lives (the arbitrary 'they') rather than growing according to our own expectations.

The answer, of course, is to escape from your Comfort Zones by taking control of your own life and not allowing others to dominate or manipulate or negatively influence you. And the only way you'll ever know if you are being suppressed or dominated or manipulated, is *when you know who the 'real' you is*.

Until you know that, and until you assert that 'real you' and live the kind of life you really want to, you'll remain stuck in a rut. And, as someone once said, 'The only difference between a rut and a grave is the depth of the excavation.'

In doing research for this book, it was amazing how many times I found the same situation described in different terms. Hagberg and Leider, for example, speak of the 'postponed life'. We keep making excuses for not doing something by convincing ourselves that the time is not right. We say things like 'When I find the right man (woman/job/etc), then I'll do X'. Or, the most common of all, 'When I have enough money, then I'll do so-and-so'. And what about 'When the kids are old enough (have finished school/college/etc), then I'll do Y'.

In other words, you are postponing living your life the way you want to, and being happy, until something happens. But if you want to be really honest with yourself, the real reason why you haven't done these things is that you are *afraid of confronting the risk and discomfort that always accompanies change*. The easiest thing in the world is finding excuses not to do something. And so there *never* is a 'perfect' time to do anything, except *right now*.

In other words, it is more comfortable to stay where you are right now than face the realities of doing what you really want. Your Comfort Zones are no more than little bubbles of security.

But, as you have seen, those fragile soap-bubble walls soon harden into stone blocks, high and impenetrable castle battlements which imprison you and prevent you from becoming who you really want to be.

Hagberg and Leider's *The Inventurers*, an excellent book about life and career renewal, also includes an interesting analysis of the stages we pass through in adult growth. I have taken the liberty of adding to it in certain places to make it clearer to the readers of this book how it also describes the processes of getting trapped in, and escaping from, Comfort Zones:

STAGES OF ADULT GROWTH PROCESS

1. *Stage 1 — Life Cycle Plateau* (eg the Postponed Life)
   Things aren't too bad; our lives are going along OK. We are existing but not living... but there's no real need to change, no stimulus to make us confront it all. [*Author: So our Comfort Zone is an OK place to be.*]

2. *Stage 2 — Triggering Events*
   Suddenly things change — voluntarily or involuntarily. We are knocked off balance and are forced to confront ourselves. These 'awakening events' can act as catalysts for renewal or change. [*Author: A crisis — minor or major — happens in your life, and you have the option either to cross the drawbridge or to retreat into your castle.*]

3. *Stage 3 — Limbo*
   To insulate ourselves against the shock of abrupt change, we often go into a state of shock, a suspended animation, a limbo. [*Author: We retreat back inside our castle.*] We withdraw emotionally. Limbo is a feeling of knowing what your life *isn't* going to be in the future, but not having any notion of what it *is* going to be. Being in limbo is being immobilised, trapped, without options, not knowing in which direction to

turn. In time, limbo becomes boring or frustrating. We must do something — act, do anything to escape from our dilemma.

4. *Stage 4 — Seeking the Solution*
   We explore solutions — counselling, a personal growth workshop, a new relationship, a book, a job change, travel, new friends, ideas, a geographic move. We know the answer is out there somewhere; we just have to find it. But *nothing will happen while our orientation remains external* — ie centred on such options. The only way we can change is to change inside. You have to move from expecting to find a magical solution (no matter how hard you seek, you won't find it!), to making the solution come from *within*. The question should not be 'What do we want?' but rather 'Who am I, and what do I need to help me become more completely who I am?'

5. *Stage 5 — A Decision*
   Eventually the quest for external solutions loses its allure, and we seek resolution. Often we stop our frenetic search and return to the stability of taking care of the things we have been neglecting in our lives. It may not be a perfect solution, but we can at least start from there. [*Author: But the danger is that we have simply retreated to our Comfort Zone. We still have to escape if we are to move on. But at least we are now more aware. As poet T S Eliot said, 'We shall not cease from exploration and the end of all our exploring will be to arrive where we started and to know the place for the first time.' But whether we use our new knowledge and insight and awareness and move ahead, or whether we simply remain in our Comfort Zone, depends on what form our decision takes.*] These decisions could be one of the following:

   (i) *'Play it again, Sam'*
       We decide to stay put and make the best of things. We scurry back to the security of the 'old familiar'. But, of course, nothing has changed. We have just returned to where we were before. And so — not surprisingly — we find we are chronically unhappy, constantly complain-

ing, constantly feeling unfulfilled. And no matter how much we rationalise our decision and try to fool ourselves that things are different, they aren't.

(ii) *'Masquerades and masks'*

We make a life or career change 'according to the book' and go through all the outward motions. But *inside* nothing has changed. No new self-assessment has occurred. There has been no *real* renewal, and we are once again stuck where we were before.

(iii) *'Renewal'*

We recognise that the 'magic' solution simply doesn't exist, that life is a series of changes, each one moving us further forward. It's a *process,* a never-ending journey. We now move ahead with our decisions, more confident of our own worth and confident about the future. We have learned to take responsibility for our own lives. We have learned not to be dependent on anybody or anything but ourselves. We have learned not to seek the answers in external or material solutions; we have learned that the question should not be 'What do I want?' but rather 'Who am I, and what do I need to help me become more completely who I am?'

6. *Stage 6 — The Inventurous Life*

We see more clearly the purpose and meaning of our lives — and this is often blindingly obvious. We understand that it is not enough to understand the mechanisms, but that we have to implement and internalise them into our life — moment by moment, day by day, in a never-ending journey forward. *[Author: Doesn't that exactly describe escaping your Comfort Zones?]*

MORE QUESTIONS TO HELP YOU FIND OUT
WHO YOU REALLY ARE

Since finding out who you really are, and what you really want in your life, are such vitally important questions in the process of escaping your Comfort Zones, I have included 52 more questions which you can use to examine every aspect of your life.

Don't worry if some are repetitions of previous questions. Think about them again and you may find your perspective has already been changed by the few steps you've taken on your journey so far. To tell the truth, your answers are not nearly as important as the fact that you are spending time assessing your life and finding out who you really are inside.

Remember: be absolutely honest with yourself. *Feel* rather than merely *think*.

1. *Who is the real me?*

2. *Who is in control of my life?*

3. *If it's not me, why not?*

4. *What skills and abilities do I have? (Also, what am I qualified to do?)*

_____

_____

_____

_____

5. *What do I most enjoy doing?*

_____

_____

6. *Can I combine these skills/abilities/qualifications with what I really enjoy? How?*

_____

_____

_____

_____

7. *How can I use these skills and likes to escape my Comfort Zones?*

_____

_____

_____

_____

8. *Do I need to acquire new skills? If so, which? And how?*

_____

_____

_____

_____

9. *What changes do I need to make in my life?*

_____

_____

_____

_____

10. *What is holding me back from making these changes?*

_____

_____

_____

_____

[More questions, to help you think more specifically about who and where you are now, how you got there, and who you are within your current circumstances.]

11. *In what ways am I different today from five years ago?*

_____

_____

_____

_____

12. *Am I a better or worse person than I was five years ago?*

_____

_____

_____

_____

13. *What has caused these changes in me?*

_____

_____

_____

14. *In what ways would I like to change in the next five years?*

_____

_____

_____

15. *How can I start now? Where would I begin?*

_____

_____

_____

_____

16. *What is stopping me or holding me back?*

_____

_____

_____

17. *How can I remove these obstacles?*

_____

_____

_____

_____

18. *The most important thing to me at this stage of my life is:*

_____

_____

_____

19. *The most important thing to me at this stage of my career is:*

_____

_____

_____

20. *The three people who have had the greatest influence on my life to date are:*

_____

_____

_____

21. *Were these influences positive or negative?*

_____

_____

_____

22. *Are they still influencing my life?* _____

If positively, am I encouraging the relationship? _____

What am I doing to maintain a relationship with, and bind myself with hoops of steel to these people?

_____

_____

_____

23. *If negatively, have I (or can I) cut them out of my life? Can I truly forgive and forget and walk away from it all? How can I remove their influence?*

_____

_____

_____

_____

24. *The key turning points in my life have been:*

_____

_____

_____

25. *If they have pointed me in the wrong direction, how can I turn around?*

_____

_____

_____

_____

26. *A major issue in my life that I am currently facing is:*

_____

_____

_____

_____

27. *How will this affect my life?*

_____

_____

_____

_____

28. *If it is negative, how can I make it a positive learning experience? Can I 'turn a lemon into lemonade'?*

_____

_____

_____

_____

[More questions, which you can perhaps explore with the help of a trusted friend or soulmate to help you know yourself better with the help of an objective and sympathetic listener — someone who will be totally honest with you without predatory self-interest, who will let you make the decisions based on your self-knowledge]:

29. *Five words that describe me and my personality best are:*

_____

_____

_____

_____

_____

30. *Two feelings I never allow myself to express to others are:*

_____

_____

_____

31. *My best points are:*

_____

_____

_____

32. *My worst points are:*

_____

_____

_____

33. *How do other people perceive me?*

_____

_____

_____

_____

34. *Are their perceptions accurate?*

_____

_____

_____

35. *If not, why not?*

_____

_____

_____

36. *How can I correct this?*

_____

_____

_____

37. *If a cheque equivalent to a month's salary suddenly arrived in the mail, I would:*

_____

_____

_____

38. *Looking at my previous answer, did I spend it on something I need or something I want?*

_____

Did I spend it on myself or someone else?

_____

39. *If on someone else, what is my real motivation?*

_____

_____

_____

40. *A place I can imagine myself living in is:*

_____

_____

_____

41. *What is stopping me from living there?*

_____
_____
_____

42. *The person I most admire is (contemporary or historical, you don't have to know him or her):*

_____
_____
_____

43. *What do I most admire about him/her?*

_____
_____
_____

44. *How can I become more like him/her?*

_____
_____
_____

45. *Five things I'd like to do before I die are:*

_____
_____

46. *My best childhood memory is:*

_____
_____
_____

47. *My worst childhood memory is:*

_____

_____

_____

48. *How has this affected my life?*

_____

_____

_____

_____

49. *The type of people I like best are:*

_____

_____

_____

50. *The age I would like to be is:*_____*Why?*

_____

_____

51. *Three occupations I can fantasise myself doing are:*

_____

_____

_____

52. *If I were to choose something else to describe me, this would be:*
    (i) *What animal?*_____
    (ii) *What bird?*_____
    (iii) *What car?*_____
    (iv) *What movie star?*_____
    (v) *What famous person — past or present?*_____
    (vi) *What song?*_____
    (vii) *What book?*_____ .

(viii) *What movie?*_____

(ix) *What TV programme?*_____

(x) *What singer?*_____

Now try to describe the walls of your Comfort Zones castle.
What things or people or circumstances are trapping you and
preventing you from having the total freedom to be who you
want to be?

_____

_____

_____

_____

_____

_____

_____

_____

_____

_____

_____

_____

_____

_____

_____

_____

_____

_____

_____

_____

A valuable guide — keep a daily diary

A good way to prove to yourself how much — or how little — in control of your own life you are, is to keep a daily diary. (Most people in full-time jobs can't live without one.) Now start *planning* your life instead of letting events determine it. Decide what you want to do for *you*, and block off some time every week, starting today, for *yourself*. You may want to go and sit in the park, go to lunch with a friend, go to a movie, the library, art gallery, or whatever.

After a week or two you can look back and see if you've kept these appointments with yourself, or whether you've allowed other things to intrude. Of course, there are genuine emergencies, so they don't count. But if you are habitually breaking or changing dates, the chances are you are allowing other people to dictate your life for you. The key is to start *taking control* and asserting your right to your own time.

Another important thing you can learn from keeping a daily diary is just how much real time you actually spend being totally productive, and how much is 'frittered away on detail'. It's the easiest escape on earth to say glibly 'I'm too busy' or 'I haven't got the time'. If you carry your diary around with you and write down every single thing you do, you'll be able to look back at the end of a day or a week and assess exactly what you have done with your life.

I can guarantee that you will be amazed at just how much of your day is spent on petty, time-wasting things.

I tried this once in one of my companies when I asked every employee to keep an accurate job sheet, noting down actual time spent on every job. They didn't have to put their names on the sheets, so there was no way they could be 'found out' and therefore they didn't need to cheat or 'manufacture' hours. The results were incredible. Not one single employee worked fully productively for more than sixty-five per cent of his or her total day. And the average was an unbelievable thirty-five per cent! Remember — this was a highly successful and profitable company, and for three years running we had the lowest ratio of employees to income in the industry. Frightening!

You'll find the same phenomenon everywhere. The people who most easily say 'I haven't got the time' are usually those with the most time to spare. But when you look at the lives of top executives, you find that they seem to fit in 150 per cent of what most people do in a day. You must have heard the saying: 'If you want something done, ask the person who's the busiest' — and this is inevitably the case. The really busy people are the most productive; they plan their day to make sure they accommodate everything that needs to be done.

For example, when I left school I worked a full-time six-day week in order to put myself through college at night. After class I would go to band practice (we rehearsed every night and did gigs virtually every Friday and Saturday night), then finally went home and had supper well after midnight. Then I still had to do homework and assignments, and preparation for the next evening or for examinations. Yet I managed to pass both degrees cum laude and win the university's academic medal.

It's amazing what you can do when you want to. So before you say 'I'm too busy earning a living and carting the kids around and doing X and Y and Z to spend the time living in the now moment, reading and talking to my mentor and finding myself and escaping my Comfort Zones', take stock of your life. Plan your activities. No matter how full your present life is, with a little planning and organising and prioritising what's really important to you, and taking control of your own life, you'll probably find the time to do whatever you always dreamed of doing. Taking extra classes, a second job, a hobby, gym, learning a new skill, spending time with a special friend or mentor, or whatever — and escaping your Comfort Zones in the process.

Once again, it's in *your* hands. If something is important enough, you will find the time to do it. And when you put your mind to it and prioritise, almost anything is possible. Don't just take my word for it. Try it.

What to do with all this information

After you've answered all the questions in this book, keep all the answers in a safe and secret place. Refer to them frequently to remind yourself who you are and who you would really like to be; to see whether you're making any progress or whether you're still wandering aimlessly around the courtyard of your castle.

If necessary, write down the key points on a small card and keep it with you at all times to remind yourself who you want to be. And then go out and start *being* that person — hour by hour, day by day, week by week, for the rest of your life. But remember: even if you do nothing with your answers, you will still have *gone through the process* of thinking about yourself and discovering who you really are and what you want in life; and taking stock of your life. And that's what is most important and has permanent value in changing your life for the better.

REMEMBER: ESCAPING IS A QUANTUM PROCESS!

Just in case you've forgotten, I'd like to remind you that finding your true self and taking the steps outside your castle and escaping your Comfort Zones doesn't happen overnight.

For many years I searched for mechanisms which would allow us to take a 'quantum leap' in self-development. Like the phenomenon in physics where subatomic particles leap from one orbit to another and change the fundamental elemental structure, I wanted to find magical ways for humans to emulate that feat.

But the more I searched, the more I realised that the so-called quantum leap is almost always a tiny, final step at the end of a long and arduous journey. *The journey is the quantum leap in process form.* As the old adage puts it, 'There is only one way to eat an elephant — one bite at a time.'

I believe that true quantum leaps are possible, but that they are extremely rare. Also, most people simply cannot cope with the psychological and emotional trauma of such a major and sudden change in their lives. It is thus important to understand that this long and gradual orientation which conditions us to face the changes, is necessary to strengthen and regenerate our spiritual and emotional and psychological inner selves.

After having thought about this question for a long time, I became more and more convinced that it is probably not possible for most people to make a quantum leap from one spiritual level to another within one lifetime.* Rather, it seemed more probable that one is born on to a particular spiritual level and that it is up to one to use one's life to accomplish the tasks and learn the lessons related to that spiritual level. However, this is always difficult and painful, and the higher the level you're on, the more difficult and painful it gets! Many people rather retreat to *lower level behaviour* because it's easier and less painful.

It's like going to a new class in a new school, say Grade 2. You feel afraid and uncomfortable. Here are strange new faces, a new teacher, and the lessons are difficult. So you slip out of the door and escape back to your old school and your old Grade 1 class. It feels so *comfortable* being there and, rather than face the scary prospect of doing what you should be doing and learning the higher-grade lessons you should be learning, you simply continue to waste your time by repeating old, useless lessons.

True, you've done them before and gained insight and experience since you first encountered them. So, even though you might experience the 'same' experiences, you now have deeper insights and thus gain new perspectives on even the old lessons — so your time isn't entirely wasted. It's all part of the process.

Perhaps it wasn't even your own choice to return to the lower grade, or a result of your fear or discomfort. Perhaps an old classmate, stuck in the lower grade and jealous of you, persuades

* Perhaps this transition happens only in the spiritual 'limbo' period [wrong word: it's not a limbo — ie lack of dynamic action, but rather a kind of processing period or debriefing], where you reflect on the lessons learned and unlearned, and then set about structuring a new life or incarnation which will give you another chance of learning unlearned lessons.

or coerces or bribes you to return. Perhaps a selfish teacher or mother, afraid that your growth is alienating you from them, makes you return to the lower grade. They might force you to stay by threats or removal of privileges, or try a little bribery by giving you material or emotional rewards for staying with them. In both these cases, you will have to have a great deal of courage to assert yourself and be true to your own inner honesty and follow the path of personal growth.

This is a very simplistic analogy, but its relevance to life is obvious. I see examples of it every day in people around me. I see people terrified of learning lessons, and wasting away in the safe sanctuary of a lower-grade spiritual level Comfort Zone. I see people emotionally blackmailed or otherwise manipulated by selfish and spiritually inferior partners and friends and family members who don't *want* their partners to grow. Why can't they see the *obvious*? That growth is absolutely inevitable, and that they are just delaying the process? I can only believe it's because they don't *want* to see, that they can't handle admitting that they are allowing themselves to stagnate. Like the mother who thinks her soldier son is the only one in step at the parade, these people are using psychological defence mechanisms to protect their ego, instead of simply confronting the truth.

So: a vital aspect of the quantum *process* of escaping your Comfort Zones is finding out exactly who you are and who you want to be, with absolute honesty, and then *asserting* your right to be that person, no matter what anyone else has to say about it.

I'd like to end off this section with a few anecdotes that illustrate the point.

First, a case study reported by Dr R D Laing in his book *The Politics of Experience* about former Royal Navy commodore Jesse Watkins's ten-day schizophrenic experience during which he suffered terrible anguish and turmoil on some deep psychological plane and during which he underwent an inner journey that (in his own words) 'left everything so much more real than they had been before... I could see everything more clearly... I could see the bad things and the good things and all that . . . I was much more aware'.

Says Dr Laing, commenting on this whole experience: 'Can we not see that this voyage is not what we need to be cured of, but that it is itself a natural way of healing our own appalling state of alienation called normality?'

Isn't that a frightening indictment of being trapped in a Comfort Zone — where our world can become 'an appalling state of alienation called normality'? Where we fool ourselves by rationalisations and denials and subservience to what others expect us to be?

How often do we find that people reject the obvious reality in favour of their own desired interpretation of how things 'should' be? Just think about the madness of the characters in the story of The Emperor's New Clothes and the innocent honesty of the little child who shows them all up! But my favourite illustration of this point is the story told by Kahlil Gibran:

> There was a small kingdom where the only source of water was a single well in the middle of the town. Everybody was very happy, and they all liked and respected the kind and wise king. But one day an evil person poisoned the well so that everyone who drank there would go mad. The next day everyone drank from the poisoned well — everyone except the king, who wasn't thirsty.
>
> And the next morning all the people in the kingdom huddled round, talking in worried whispers about the king who had suddenly gone mad . . .

So the moral for your own life is: *Be yourself.* Your own deep, honest, inner self. The person you want to be. And if others don't like it, that's their problem — not yours. Because you *can* be right even if everyone else thinks you're wrong.

My final story to illustrate this point comes from that wonderful children's book *The Velveteen Rabbit* by Margery Williams. The scene takes place in the nursery where the toys talk to each other. One day the young rabbit asks the Skin Horse, who has been around for a long time, 'What is real? And does it *hurt?*' This is how the Skin Horse answered:

'Sometimes,' said the Skin Horse, for he was always truthful. 'But when you are REAL you don't mind being hurt.'

The rabbit then asked: 'Does it happen all at once, like being wound up? Or bit by bit?'

'It doesn't happen all at once,' said the Skin Horse. 'You *become*. It takes a long time. That's why it doesn't often happen to people who break easily, or who have sharp edges, or who have to be carefully kept.

'Generally, by the time you are REAL, most of your hair has been loved off, and your eyes drop out and you get loose in the joints and very shabby.

'But these things don't matter at all, because once you are REAL you can't be ugly, except to people who don't understand.'

Key points to remember from Chapter 5

1. Take time out to get to know who you really are and what you genuinely want out of life. And before you make excuses as to why you can't afford the time off, ask yourself if you can afford *not* to. It could be the most valuable investment of your entire life.

2. Be absolutely, brutally honest with yourself. If you aren't, the person you'll become still won't be the real you.

3. Concentrate on *feelings* rather than merely thoughts.

4. Without a clear understanding of who you are now, and how you got to be that person, there is absolutely no possibility of growth, modification or change — because you cannot modify or change anything unless you know what it looks like, and you cannot know what it looks like unless you take the time to really examine it from all angles.

5. Stop blaming other people or circumstances for who you are or what has happened in your life. It's your *reactions* to these things that really count. Take full responsibility for your own life. Take control, and stay in control.

6. Throw off your masks and show the world your true face.

7. What must you do to become the real you and live your life the way you want to? And why haven't you started yet?

8. You are what you think. So make sure your head is filled with positive thoughts and recognition of your self-esteem. (An appreciation of who you are, not an arrogance!) Each positive thought displaces a negative one. And emotions overrule logic — so you are what you *feel* as well.

9. Use auto-suggestion and affirmation techniques only with great caution. Be very sure that your motives aren't selfish or manipulative or materialistic.

10. Read Og Mandino's 'Ten Ancient Scrolls' first thing in the morning. The wisdoms will help you cope and put things in perspective. (Of course, reading the Bible or your own particular religious book will do the same — or you may want to compile your own list of wisdoms from all these sources and more.) The point is to fill your mind with positive messages.

11. Remember that you are constantly in *relationships* with people, organisations, environments. You can't simply ignore them. So learn how to integrate them into your own life's purpose.

12. Identify how people and incidents in your past have influenced — and continue to influence — your life. Remember that it was not these people or the incidents that affected you, but rather *your response to them*. And this you can change by forgiving and forgetting, and casting off the burdens of anger and resentment.

13. Stop living a 'postponed life'. Life is *now*. And only you can decide whether you are going to perpetuate the mistakes and regrets and unhappiness of the past, or whether you are going to make sure the rest of your years are happy and fulfilling.

14. Escaping your Comfort Zones is an quantum *process*. Have patience. You've already started getting there. Persevere!

15. Saying you're 'too busy' is just an excuse and an escape. If something is important enough to you, you will find the time to do it. It's all a question of priorities.

16. *Be yourself.* You own, deep, honest, inner, true self. The person you want to be. Don't succumb to the madness of trying to be who others think you should be.

6

Stage 4

Stimulating The Motivation And Readiness For Change

The last chapter was a very long one, so I'm going to balance it out with a very short one. (Being a Libran, I believe everything should be in balance and harmony!)

This is to give you a chance to absorb and digest and internalise what you have learned up to now. And to refresh your memory of some of the things that have happened on your journey so far.

As I have mentioned earlier, in doing research for this book I came across many echoes of my own thoughts and experiences and they often helped me to get a better perspective on myself. One of the most enlightening and valuable was a book called *Passages* by Gail Sheehy. She describes how she saw a boy's face blown away while she was talking to him when on assignment as a journalist in Northern Ireland, and how this was a triggering event for a sustained period of rootlessness, depression, lack of direction and commitment in her life. Then she 'woke up':

> Some intruder shook me by the psyche and shouted: Take stock! Half your life has been spent. What about the part of you that wants a home and talks about a second child? What about the side of you that wants to contribute to the world? You have been a performer, not a full participant. And now you are 35.

Sheehy talks about some of her own fears and insights gained as a result of confronting her life. 'The major task of midlife is to give up all our imagined safety providers and stand naked in the world, as the rehearsal for assuming full authority over ourselves. The fear is: What if I can't stand on my own two feet?'

While Sheehy concentrates mainly on the 'passages' of midlife (see how similar this is to Campbell's 'Rites of Passage' and my own analogies of journeys?), her insights and advice are valid for *all* transitions and transformations − including (and especially) your escape from your Comfort Zones.

> A person's life at any given time incorporates both external and internal aspects. The external system is composed of our memberships in the culture: our jobs, social class, family and social roles, how we present ourselves to and participate in the world.
>
> The interior realm concerns the meanings this participation has for each of us. In what ways are our values, goals, and aspirations being invigorated or violated by our present life system? How many parts of our personality can we live out, and what parts are we suppressing? How do we *feel* about our way of living in the world at any given time?
>
> The inner realm is where the crucial shifts in bedrock begin to throw a person off balance, signalling the necessity to change and move onto a new footing in the next stage of development.

Sheehy also talks about the two sides of people as the 'Merger Self' and the 'Seeker Self'. Namely, 'The Seeker Self is driven by the (opposite) wish to become separate, independent, to explore our capacities and become master of our own destinies.'

She goes on to talk about the process of confronting such realities which do not necessarily fit into the beliefs and images that we have grown up, and grown comfortable with. She talks about this process of coming to terms with realities as 'the search for authenticity', and states that this is achieved by moving through a 'disassembling to a renewal' − ie 'disassembling the narrow self we have thus far put together in a form tailored to please the culture and other people . . . The shock of this turning point (ie confronting realities) is to discover that the promise was an illusion.'

[*Author's note: This 'promise' could be the expectation you have built up of what life should be and how the world should treat you. But as psychologist Mavis Derman once asked me: 'Whoever said that life is fair?', and her other favourite piece of advice with regard to my idealism about people: 'Potential doesn't count. What you see is what you get!' — which the eternal optimist in me still refuses to accept despite many painful experiences that seem to prove her right!*]

Sheehy goes on to say:

> That narrow, innocent self is indeed dying, *must* die, in order to make room for the fully expanded self who will take in all our parts, the selfish, scared and cruel along with the expansive and tender — the 'bad' along with the 'good'.
>
> It is not *either* disassembling or renewal. It is *both*. By allowing this disintegration... each of us prepares at gut level for the reintegration of an identity that is truly our own. We are free to seek the truth about ourselves more vigorously and thus to see the world in truer perspective.

Towards the end of her book, Sheehy ponders all this and adds her own reflections:

> How many can look into their own dark? I thought. And those who do, and give themselves permission to let go? Who make this leap of bold faith towards a new beginning? Perhaps ideas of the opposite come together and lose their oppositeness, and a new writing begins. Perhaps at the farthest outpost of our explorations, we come back to knowing ourselves for the first time.

And in her Afterword, after four and a half years of research involving some sixty thousand people for her sequel book *Pathfinders*, she has this to say:

> So many people slip backwards at these crossroads, blame others, attempt some frantic escape, or simply give up and

join the walking dead. The unanswered question was: What allows certain people to see at the crossroads the path to a new beginning — not just a set of obstacles, but the opportunity to make themselves more?

The greatest surprise of all was to find that in every group studied, whether men or women, the most satisfying stages in their lives were the later ones. Simply, older is better.

The people I came to call Pathfinders had all met at a crossroads — either one of the predictable passages or stages in life, or an unpredictable life accident/crisis/trauma — and had taken the risk of change. Faced with failure, divorce, physical setbacks, financial reverses, losses of love, and traps of all kinds, these men and women dared to take the less-travelled road. By creating new dreams, they have opened up new paths. As a result, they enjoy an outlook on life that goes beyond happiness — a sustained background tone of equanimity beyond the more intense contrasts of daily moods, behind even periods of uncertainty or unhappiness. Call it well-being.

Now, isn't that the most incredible motivation for escaping your Comfort Zones?

Note that Sheehy's 'Pathfinders' all needed a *crisis moment* in their lives to motivate their leap, their escape from their Comfort Zones. And though it was a scary process, all discovered a wonderfully fulfilling new life beyond the threshold.

So, yes, *you* can do it as well. And all it takes is to follow the path, the guidelines in this book, and to have the courage to pursue your dreams. You can learn how to only if you truly want to. As Sheehy concludes:

When I looked into their lives at an important crossroads — although they had often not recognised it as such at the time — I found that the same set of qualities had helped most of them to make those brilliant new beginnings or to make comebacks. The qualities they have learned. One can work on them. Which means we all have the capacity

209

(if not the inclination) to become Pathfinders. *We just have to learn how to do it.*

In this world of immediate gratification and the need for tangible rewards, it's often hard to be motivated by something as vague as 'self-actualisation' and 'spiritual maturity'. But as you grow and are more and more filled with the sense of liberation and freedom and insight, you will look back and wish you could express in words the wonder of it all.

In *The Developing Adult* Lily Gerdes quotes Abraham Maslow's analysis of self-actualised people, both living and historical personalities, where he found them to have

> ... a *spontaneous zest for life* which many people lose with childhood. It is a spontaneity characterised by a freshness of experience unfettered by convention. It is childlike, but not childish. It is the ability to enjoy each experience afresh instead of the blasé feeling of having seen and heard it all before. Maslow also comments on the quality of individuality and strength which characterise the self-actualiser. The self-actualised person can thoroughly enjoy a wide range of experiences and is open to 'peak experiences', that is, euphoric experiences of a peculiar intensity, insight and revelation.

So when you're feeling a little unmotivated, just think about what you are going to gain on your journey. Ask yourself if you'd like to be inner-driven, have the freedom to be and do what you truly feel inside, be able to experience the 'euphoric experiences of a peculiar intensity, insight and revelation', and have true inner peace and self-fulfilment. If those aren't big enough or juicy enough carrots, you're a hell of a hard person to please!

LOCUS OF CONTROL

When my psychologist friend Mavis Derman read the first draft of the manuscript for this book, she suggested that I include a section on 'locus of control'. (*Locus* from the Latin meaning 'place' or 'location'.)

The term 'locus of control' was coined by Rotter and refers simply to determining where a person's 'control' is coming from — internally or externally. In other words, are you controlling your own life, or are you allowing external forces (including people) to do it for you?

Numerous studies have shown that an extremely important factor in your development and adjustment to life — especially as you approach old age — is your perception of *your ability to influence the course and outcome of your life*. When you perceive yourself to be in control of your own life, you will inevitably be happier, better adjusted, and experience a greater degree of fulfilment and life satisfaction. Obviously this is helped considerably by such factors as reasonable financial independence, good health, good personal relationships, including those on an intimate level — but *how you feel about yourself inside* is a vitally important element of happiness.

On the other hand, when you experience a feeling of 'helplessness' and not being in control of your own life — whether as a result of a control/dependency relationship, ill health, financial setbacks, compulsory retirement from your source of income or the social and intellectual stimulation you are used to, the death of a spouse and friends and an increased awareness of your own mortality — you will tend to experience life as threatening, depressing, unhappy, tedious. You will increasingly feel you are a 'victim' in the inevitable drama of your own demise.

As I have explained many times in earlier chapters, this same mechanism is vital to your happiness at every age in life. Let me give you a personal example:

Although in retrospect I value the discipline imposed on me at school, I can remember hating it with a passion while I was being subjected to it. And so I could easily understand when my sons Rowan (with his fierce individuality and interrogative mind) and Kyle (with his yearning to get close to nature and experience the freedom of the African bush), reacted against petty discipline

211

at school. They had very little *freedom of choice* about the matter. They had to play by the rules, or leave.

Later, it was wonderful to see the upliftment of spirit as Rowan made the transition from the petty discipline and oppression and obligations of high school to the self-motivated freedom of university life — when he had his own car (freedom of movement) and could make his own decisions about his life.

I saw the same transition in the black peoples of South Africa as they made the transition from the oppression of apartheid to the freedom of independence in South Africa's first ever democratic elections. It manifested itself in the very fabric of their being. I'll never forget standing in a kilometre-long queue waiting to vote... whites, blacks, coloureds, Asians, all together, bonded on that unique day by the universal desire for peace and harmony. I vividly remember feeling the incredible spirit of goodwill that sustained each one of us through those long, long hours in the hot sun, as we all patiently waited to make our crosses and initiate a proud new dawn in our country's sometimes shameful history. It was as though, on a national scale, South Africa was escaping some gigantic Comfort Zone and taking a quantum leap into a new, better life for all.

Of course, independence means *assuming responsibility and accountability* for all your actions instead of blaming it on 'fate' or 'circumstances' or the 'powers that be'. And that's just as true of my sons as it is of the people of a new nation. The point I want to make is that the process of individuation, of attaining wholeness, of being true to the real you, is a wonderfully liberating and fulfilling experience that will bear fruit as long as you live.

So, what's stopping you from doing it? If it's indecision, or the fear of making the wrong decision, take courage. Consider the example of a research study of a hundred chief executives in the United States (as I remember reading) whose major corporate decisions over a period of time were re-examined a couple of years later and found to be *wrong* in more than fifty per cent of cases. But the important thing was that they had actually *made* a decision at the critical time and the company/division/

individuals concerned could carry on with business. *The inertia of the Comfort Zones had been broken.*

To relate this back to Albert's *Goal Source*: I believe that it was not some magic key that changed the people in his company's lives, but rather that it was *the process that was the mechanism* for people actually to do something, to get up and focus their attention on some kind of *progress* and *growth*. It got them to take their first few steps. And just as a house can't magically appear unless you lay thousands of bricks one by one, so you can't hope to achieve your goal or personal transformation in one quantum leap. It's the *process*. It's each brick you lay. It's each step you take. It's each page you read in this book.

Albert's programme was in essence the process that made his staff *receptive* to the next phase — ie introducing the new, scary, unfamiliar concept of participative management — in that after the Goal Source self-awareness exercise they were more open to suggestion and in 'Growth Mode'.

Once again, it is the readiness to progress that is the key. The individuals concerned were all convinced that something better lay ahead, and that Albert and his Goal Source programme was the way to achieve this. Through his leadership and enthusiasm and mechanisms such as this, he was the catalyst for upliftment. But only the catalyst. Each staff member had to do it for himself.

I also believe that one of the key success elements of Goal Source was in making each person look inside himself instead of waiting for 'the Company' to magically transform his life (which of course was about to happen anyway in management driving the new parameters from the top down). There was a *personal transformation* that was such an essential preparation for the *external transformation* that was about to be introduced to them — and which made them more receptive to it.*

Receptiveness — ensuring the soil is fertile in readiness for the sowing of the seeds.

---

* Albert and I have subsequently formalised these simultaneous processes into what we believe is a new paradigm in management and transformative re-engineering called *InfraManagement*.

That is one of the most important keys after the first step of realising that you want to or need to change. That is, after becoming aware of your discomfort in the Comfort Zone or the futility of staying in a state of inertia and non-growth, or the realisation that you can have a better and more fulfilled life.

A quote from Ayn Rand's *Atlas Shrugged* is appropriate here: 'Every man is free to rise as far as he is able or willing, but it is only the degree to which he thinks that determines the degree to which he will rise.'

It begins and ends with what's in your mind. Whether your castle walls are real, or whether they are illusions (like the shadows on the cave wall were to the people who had never seen reality), it's your *interpretation* of circumstances and events that become your reality. It's not so much the events themselves that cause unhappiness, but how much you *allow* them to make you unhappy.

So, to get back to Gail Sheehy's 'unanswered question' as to why many people slip backwards at these crossroads, blame others, attempt some frantic escape, or simply give up and join the walking dead. What allows certain people to see at the crossroads the path to a new beginning — not just a set of obstacles, but the opportunity to make themselves more? The answer, I believe, is *insight* into the absolute futility of remaining in your Comfort Zones — the insight I hope you will gain by reading this book. Once you have the insight, you need only the *courage* to make the decision and start your journey.

Translate that rational decision into *feelings*. Believe in yourself. Be convinced that you can and will escape your Comfort Zones. Understand that it is this internal change, this new perspective, this new receptiveness to truth, this shrugging off of past ego-protective illusions and excuses and constraints, this acceptance of the turbulence of change, that makes it possible for you to escape your Comfort Zones.

But, most of all, don't delay any longer what is absolutely inevitable. Don't wait to think yourself into a better way of acting. Act yourself into a better way of thinking. And do it now.

Key points to remember from Chapter 6

1. 'Take stock! Half your life has been spent!' What about the part of you that wants...? Time is running out — no matter how young or how old you are.

2. 'The major task now is to give up all our imagined safety providers and stand naked in the world, as the rehearsal for assuming full authority over ourselves.'

3. 'That narrow, innocent self is indeed dying, *must* die, in order to make room for the fully expanded self... It is not *either* disassembling or renewal. It is *both*. By allowing this disintegration... each of us prepares at gut level for the reintegration of an identity that is truly our own.'

4. 'So many people slip backwards at these crossroads, blame others, attempt some frantic escape, or simply give up and join the walking dead. The unanswered question was: What allows certain people to see at the crossroads the path to a new beginning — not just a set of obstacles, but the opportunity to make themselves more?' And the answer is to use the insight you have gained and translate it into some form of action, no matter how small, as the first step in 'acting yourself into a better way of thinking'.

5. 'The greatest surprise of all was to find that... whether men or women, the most satisfying stages in their lives were the later ones. Simply, older is better.' (That is, unless you *haven't* escaped your Comfort Zones!)

6. Break the inertia of indecision and *just do it*. The journey and the destination are one. The process of *seeking* the solution *becomes* the solution.

7. Shift your external locus of control to an *internal* locus. Take control of your own life. Exercise your right to have freedom of choice. And then assert that right.

8. Be receptive and stay receptive... 'Open your mind and be wise.'

7

Stage 5

Getting In Touch With Yourself By Living In The 'Now' Moment

By the time I have finished writing this sentence about thirty seconds of my life will have passed by. For ever. But at least I have spent that time doing something that is very meaningful to me. In my opinion (which is all that counts here!), I have used those thirty seconds well.

Next time you get into a lift or a bus or a train or an aeroplane, or when you look around at people waiting at a corner for the light to change, or when you look at your colleagues at the office, study their faces. You'll be appalled at the flatness and lifelessness you'll inevitably see.

These people aren't living. They're merely existing. Going through life as a mere habit. 'Measuring out their lives in coffee spoons', as T S Eliot observed in his poem *The Love Song of J. Alfred Prufrock*. Worrying about yesterday. Worrying about tomorrow. Worrying about worrying. And, meantime, their lives are passing them by.

Be honest with yourself. How much of your precious, precious life do you actually spend *living*? A few hours a day? Most people couldn't even count a few minutes a day of real living.

Isn't that incredibly tragic? When the deaf, dumb and blind Helen Keller was once asked what she thought was the worst calamity that could befall a person, she replied: 'To have eyes and fail to see.'

This reminds me of an incident related by Jean Houston in Caroline Jones's book *The Search for Meaning*. Jean speaks of herself as a 'geologian', or a theologian of the earth. With a double doctorate in psychology and philosophy in religion, her mission in life is exploring human loneliness and wounding and the vital purpose of these experiences.

She talks of meeting the deaf, dumb and blind Helen Keller.

[Miss Keller] talked to us with that awesome voice of someone who has never heard speech. And I remember being so moved. I knew I had to ask her something, I didn't know what it was, but I knew I had to. So I went up to her and presented my mouth to be read. She did not put the tips of her fingers to my lips, she put her whole hand on my face so that with the centre of her hand she read my lips, but with the rest of the hand, the fingers, she read my whole face. So you see, she was reading character as well . . . and I blurted out 'Why are you so happy?' And she laughed and laughed and she said . . . and this is what she sounded like (haltingly) . . . 'My child, it is because I live each day as if it were my last. And life in all its moments is so full of glory.'

Jean Houston, humbled by the inner peace of this so-called cripple, concludes that we as so-called 'normal people '. . . are barely living out who and what we are'.

How incredibly sad. And how incredibly true. Isn't it time you learned that the more vividly you learn to see, the more alive you are?

Photographer Ernst Haas used a 'framing' technique to shield out the world at large and thus be able to look more closely at the details at hand. For example, to look at the 'micro world' such as exists deep inside a lily, or the starburst centre of an ice cube, or by using a magnifying glass to look and see for the first time what wet sand on a beach *really* looks like, with each grain surrounded by its own mantle of water. Think about the child who says, 'Look, Mommy, there's a rainbow in the gutter!' And when

217

Mommy looks all she sees is a dirty oil slick floating in the rain water.

The more vividly you learn to see, the more alive you are.

I remember using this as a teacher, to try to get the girls in my English class at Greenhill Convent in Bloemfontein to expand their minds and see things in fresh perspective, in the hope that this would be a catalyst for stimulating their insight into poetry. I took them out into the veld below the hockey fields and made them sit down. *Feel* the sand between their fingers. Pick a blade of grass and *smell* it. Close their eyes and just *listen* to all the sounds around them. Put their noses to the ground and *look* closely at ants and beetles and flowers and stones. Watching their faces, I could see that many of them thought I'd gone mad, and merely went through the parody. But some were totally entranced. Their faces reflected a wonderment of surprise and discovery. They looked like rosebuds opening up into full bloom.

An admirer of Thoreau asked if he had travelled much. His unhesitating answer was 'I have travelled much in Concord.' Isn't that wonderful? The world is full of the most incredible discoveries, if only you would take the trouble to seek them out. I myself (though I have been fortunate enough to travel the world very extensively) believe that my most valuable journeys have been in the realms of my inner self.

T S Eliot — probably my all-time favourite poet — writes in *Four Quartets* about time as that ephemeral moment when the future passes into the past. Just think about it: even as you read this, the future is flying past you and becoming the past. Reality — the 'now' moment of truly being alive — is a fleeting moment that passes so tragically quickly. If only we could grab hold of it! If only we could hold it for a few seconds and cherish it to the marrow! Impossible? I don't think so.

I recall, when I was playing bass guitar in a Greek band, ducking and dodging the shards of broken plates as the crowd expressed their appreciation of the dancers and their uninhibited enjoyment. Fascinated, I tried to find out where the custom of breaking plates originated. A wise old man eventually explained to me in broken English that the plate represents the beauty of that moment of great pleasure and enjoyment; in time it will only become dirty and cracked, and therefore it must be broken in its moment of perfection. It is as if this is an attempt to 'freeze' moments in time for ever.

I also loved the scene from Thornton Wilder's play *Our Town*. Emily, who had died in childbirth, was allowed to return to earth in the little town of Grover's Corners to relive her twelfth birthday. For the first time, she really saw her mother and father in their simple goodness and love for her, and could realise the myriad small details which make up and enrich our daily lives. Unable to bear the pathos of ephemerality, she called out, 'It goes so fast! We don't have time to look at one another... take me back — up the hill — to my grave; But first: Wait! One more look. Goodbye, goodbye world. Goodbye Grover's Corners... mama and papa. Goodbye to clocks ticking... and mama's sunflowers... and new-ironed dresses and hot baths... to sleeping and waking up. Oh, earth, you're too wonderful for anyone to realise you. Do any human beings ever realise life while they have it? Every, every minute?' And Frank Craven, the stage manager, soberly answers, 'No.'

And what, I hear some of you asking, has this got to do with escaping my Comfort Zones? In my opinion, it has *everything* to do with escaping your Comfort Zones. With living instead of merely existing. With being fulfilled and happy. With being completely in touch with who you are. With sucking the marrow out of each moment of your life.

Think of these 'now' moments as tropical islands in the turbulent seas of your everyday life. The more you can escape to these islands and bask in their warm, rejuvenating sun, the closer you will be to escaping from the grey lifelessness of your Comfort Zones.

Arthur Koestler talks of such moments as 'self-transcending experiences' and quotes Romain Rolland's definition of it as 'the oceanic feeling of limitless extension and oneness with the universe'. (Rolland apparently wrote to Sigmund Freud to explore this; amazingly, Freud admitted 'with regret' that he 'had never experienced such a moment'.)

Koestler goes on to say that self-transcending emotions

> ... do not tend towards bodily action, but rather a passive quiescence. Respiration and pulse are slowed down; 'entrancement' is a step towards the trance-like states induced by contemplative mystics; the emotion is of a quality that cannot be consummated by any specific voluntary act. To be 'overwhelmed' by awe and wonder; 'enraptured' by a smile; 'entranced' by beauty — each of these words expresses passive surrender. The surplus of emotion cannot be worked off by any purposeful muscular activity, it can only be consummated in *internal* processes.

This, then, is perhaps a scientific or academic explanation of what I have already experienced myself. In the timelessness of these moments I have felt myself to be *outside reality* — floating in a kind of blissful limbo where all my worries and cares and doubts seemed to dissipate like early morning mist in the sunlight. Of all the things that helped me escape my own Comfort Zones, these 'islands of tranquillity' were undoubtedly the most important catalysts.

Joseph Campbell gives a rather more esoteric underpinning in comparing it to the Buddha and the lotus that was 'without/beyond words', namely

> Whenever anything is experienced that way, simply in and for and as itself, without reference to any concepts, relevancies, or practical relationships, such a moment of sheer aesthetic arrest throws the viewer back for an instant upon his own existence without meaning, for he too simply 'is'. He is, in Buddhist terms, 'thus come' ... a vehicle of consciousness, like a spark thrown out of the fire.

Campbell also tells the story of pondering a question put to him by an Eastern mystic: 'Where are you between two thoughts?', or how the Buddha, preaching, held up a single lotus — that simple gesture being his entire sermon. Only one member of the audience understood, a monk named Kashyapa (today regarded as the founder of the Zen sect). The Buddha gave him a knowing nod; then preached a verbal sermon to those who required words and meanings.

That favourite poet of mine again, T S Eliot, also explores what he calls the 'still point' in his poem *Burnt Norton*: 'I can only say, there we have been: but I cannot say where, And I cannot say how long, for that is to place it in time.'

But living in the 'now' moments isn't only for poets and philosophers and beings on lofty spiritual planes. I believe that everyone can experience them. I believe that everyone *should* experience them. But, as before, the only condition is that you need only make yourself receptive to these moments and these feelings.

THINGS THAT HELP YOU LIVE IN THE *NOW* MOMENT

Throughout history people have at times used external, or what I'll call 'unnatural', means of heightening their awareness and increasing their receptiveness to external stimuli. From alcohol to pot, from mescaline to LSD, from sexual perversions to dangerous hobbies, people have sought the magical quantum leap into the Wonderland of transcendental experience.

Creative people in particular have experimented with these methods in an attempt to improve their art or music or writing. Think of the widely publicised dabblings by members of the Beatles and particularly their song *Lucy in the Sky with Diamonds* ('See the LSD in the title?' people were quick to point out), or the Rolling Stones, or Janis Joplin with her ubiquitous bottle of amber nectar, or dozens of others, many of whose lives ended tragically.

There is little doubt that these methods can play a positive role. Though I personally have never taken any of the hard drugs, I have experienced the role of alcohol in making me more relaxed and lowering my inhibitions and resistance to overcoming external loci of control, and making me more receptive to my emotions. But too much alcohol, or too frequent usage, does exactly the opposite.

I have no doubt that these methods can be useful catalysts in helping you escape your Comfort Zones by reducing your fears and inhibitions and making you more receptive to living in the 'now' moment. They can be stepping stones across your rivers of doubt; prompts for small 'quantum leaps' that you would normally not take in a completely sober state when your emotions and reactions are ruled by over-rationality.

However, I cannot stress enough the inherent dangers and potential tragedy implicit in using – and abusing – these substances. Even a single experimental trial can lead you down the road of physical or psychological dependency and plunge you into a dungeon of despair that makes a Comfort Zone look like a toddler's playpen.

As to using sex as a catalyst, here we must differentiate between 'higher level' sex and 'lower level' sex. On the lower level, it is a purely physical act, a simple, lustful satisfying of a basic and primal instinct. And yet even at its lowest level, it is the most natural act of intimacy between a man and a woman; and even pure lust between mutually consenting adults can be a deeply satisfying experience and a wonderful release of inhibitions.

Even 'lower level' sex rightfully belongs in 'natural highs' (see next section); it is only unnatural when it infringes on the freedom and rights of others, when there is some form of coercion. This need not be the obvious – such as rape or paedophilia. There is a great deal of sexual coercion which occurs at more subtle and insidious levels. For this reason, I would never encourage sexual deviations or perversions of any kind since this is very often a manipulation in a control/ dependency sense, or an infringement of the freedom of one of the parties involved.

However, with mutually consenting adults, sexual innovations can be a way of rejuvenating a physical relationship and taking both partners on to new heights of sensation and new levels of awareness.

At its higher level, when it is the end result of a deep and committed relationship and the celebration of connectivity between two people at emotional, intellectual and spiritual level *in combination with* the physical act; when it is the purest form of communication and the ultimate expression of trust in your partner in allowing your total vulnerability, then it can be one of the most wonderful, fulfilling and transcendental experiences a man or woman is capable of attaining. And of course this is one of the best 'natural highs' you can get.

On the down side, I would be irresponsible if I didn't remind readers (some of whom may be young) that unless you have a sexual relationship with a single, dedicated partner, there's the very real danger of sexually transmitted diseases — particularly Aids — which simply isn't worth even a one per cent risk, no matter how great the ecstasy. And an unwanted pregnancy is one of cruellest emotional and psychological blows that can be dealt anyone (not to mention the child), even in this day when 'easy' abortions are an option. And if this is an option for you, remember that the 'solution' can sometimes be far worse than the problem.

So much for chemical substances and unnatural catalysts. Because there are far, far better ways of achieving the awareness levels and intensities you are looking for. I call them 'natural highs'.

Natural highs

As opposed to the 'unnatural highs' discussed above, there are infinitely more ways of achieving *natural* 'highs' that are completely safe and which enrich your life enormously. Being creative is one of them. When you are creating something — writing, sketching, building, gardening, painting, sewing, knitting — think of it as the creation of something completely unique. No matter how crude or amateurish, it will be something that never existed before you created it.

223

Natural highs can also come from culture and the arts and your appreciation of them — a book, a poem, a good film, theatre, architecture, a painting, and so on. Try to become completely immersed in them. Imagine what the original writer or artist or playwright or engineer or designer was *feeling* or what emotion he or she was trying to express at the time. Allow yourself to feel elated, to cry, to feel happy, to feel sad. Don't feel self-conscious or ashamed. The expression of emotion is what makes people *real*, and anybody who ridicules or criticises you is the loser. (It took me a long time to have the confidence to cry at the movies. After all, men don't do that, do they?) Expressing your emotions is a wonderful balm for the soul, a catharsis of your spirit, a wiping-clean of a full slate of pent-up feelings.

Try to get close to nature. Even if you live in the centre of Manhattan or Bombay or London, nature is all around you — in parks, in gardens, in a bird coming to peck at the crumbs you have put out. *Study* these things. Go up really close and really *look* at them as if you were an alien seeing them for the first time. And even if you need to create your own little garden on the window-sill, or buy a Bonsai tree, make sure that you have something living around you. It's amazing how plants reflect the ongoing cycle of growth and decay and death and rebirth, and constantly remind you how very natural (and unscary) these things are.

Whenever you possibly can, try to *escape* completely from your urban environment and get away from it all. Go to where nature is still abundant, where man has not yet imposed his crude structures of 'civilisation'. We live in such anaesthetised worlds (artificial light, processed air conditioning, concrete and glass, heating, shelter) that we have become remote from the everyday sensations of interfacing with nature.

I remember a trip to a private game reserve called Gamela in the Northern Transvaal region of South Africa. After a few days in the bush, away from the noise and the pollution and the artificiality of so-called 'civilisation', I was able to start making my senses really work again. While out driving I could actually smell the difference between the grasses and the trees we passed. I could suddenly *smell* game, and even started to be able to differentiate between antelope and rhino and giraffe and zebra and lion. My eyesight seemed to improve, so that I could spot a kudu camouflaged beneath the dappled leaves of a thorn tree, or a bush-baby leaping from branch to branch at night.

How anaesthetised we have allowed our senses to become — and, with it, a diminished enjoyment of the richness of living. I remember reading in one of Lyall Watson's books about the South Sea islanders who navigate long distances between the islands by making use of the currents. A man will stand in the front of his canoe and actually feel the current in his testicles, and adjust course accordingly.

So, whenever you can, surround yourself with nature. Immerse yourself completely in it. Become one with it. Let all your senses be alive and receptive. Isolate yourself in that specific 'now' moment and try to experience each thing first as a totality and then in its individual components according to each of your senses.

- *Smell*
  (of the sea, of rain approaching or falling on dry earth, of freshly mown grass or newly baked bread, of leaves crushed between your fingers, of decomposing vegetation in a forest, of flowers, of animals and fresh dung... and a million other things you can discover for yourself).

- *Sight*
  (A rainbow, sunrise and sunset, clouds — lie on your back and just watch them! — scenic grandeur in its countless variants, the colours and shapes and beauty of flowers, leaves, birds, bees, ants, mountains in all their changing moods, a snowflake, an icicle.)

- *Touch*
  (The wind in your hair, the sun on your skin, the rain on your face, the texture of bark, of clay between your fingers, of leaves

225

and grass, of a pig's rough bristles or a lamb's soft wool or a snake's smoothness, of a cool river or lake on your hot body.)

- *Taste*
  (Instead of wolfing it down, try to savour everything you eat and really think about it — fruits and foods, new/strange/exotic tastes, ice-cold water from a mountain stream, wine.)
- *Sound*
  (It's amazing how much more you hear when you 'tune' your ears in — to birds and insects and animals, a waterfall, a stream babbling over rocks, the whisper of wind in the grass, or just the balm of 'non-noise', the sound of silence.)

Intensification through focus and isolation

Remember, all these things can be more fully experienced and intensified when you *focus* on them to the exclusion of other stimuli. For example, you might want to close your eyes when you are lying on the beach and just concentrate on listening to the sound of the waves and the seagulls. It's amazing how much more you suddenly seem to hear.

This reminds me of some interesting customs and practices I read about in Japan. For example, guests being invited to a 'moonrise watching party' at which no conversation is expected or heard; or holding a tea ceremony in a small, austere room, completely without decoration, so that the teapot is enhanced with new, all-encompassing elegance and beauty as the only object of attention; or burning different kinds of wood on top of a small charcoal brazier at a dinner party so that guests can appreciate the different smells of peach, cherry, pine, balsam.

Probing emotional depths

I believe that some of the most transcendent of 'now' moments are to be experienced in the intensity of human emotions and feelings — love, sexual passion, joy, laughter, crying, sorrow, pain. When these happen to you, don't hold back: luxuriate in the joyful and pleasurable feelings; and use the painful ones as a catharsis, an important step in your healing process.

We've already talked about experiencing things through all your different senses. And the same goes for experiencing the full spectrum of each emotional experience — they should be felt simultaneously on different levels. For example, when you make love, try to separate the physical pleasure from the emotional pleasure from the spiritual ('floating' or 'high' feeling) from the intellectual, and then try to integrate all of these dimensions into a single multi-dimensional transcendent experience.

In what other ways can physical and emotional and spiritual sensations be enhanced so that you can get more out of them?

Deprivation-enhanced gratification

I believe that *deprivation* is one such catalyst. Firstly, because it stimulates our imagination and anticipation of gratification, and therefore the experience is heightened when it finally happens; and, secondly, the deprivation enhances the eventual experience by providing a significant *contrast*.

For example, lukewarm water feels 'hot' if you have just taken your hand out of an ice-bucket. And you know how much better food tastes when you are genuinely hungry, or how wonderful it is to have a long, cool drink when you have a great thirst. Perhaps you can try some of these 'deprivation-enhanced gratification' experiences — or, better still, try to invent others of your own.

Consciously try to create contrasts. Cartoon animators use this technique to enhance movement and actions. If they want a character to go speeding off, they will first make him take a step backwards or stand in one place and 'get up to speed'. Remember that quaint French expression quoted by Arthur Koestler? '*Reculer pour mieux sauter* — draw back to take a running jump forward — a temporary regression to more primitive and uninhibited levels of ideation, followed by the creative forward leap.' That's a perfect description of creating a negative contrast in order to amplify the positive action to come.

Change as a catalyst

I believe that any *change* is an opportunity to experience things at a new, heightened level of awareness — new surroundings (take a holiday to some exotic place!), a new job or new school, even new clothes or a new hairstyle.

And, like most of the above experience enhancements, change is very easy to instigate in your life. Try shaving or putting on lipstick with your left hand for a change (or your right if you're left-handed). Take a different route to work. Get a new hobby. Buy something outrageous to wear. There are a million ways of making small changes in your everyday life and shifting your consciousness and awareness to a new level. So take a holiday from the humdrum!

I love the poster on the wall of one of my advertising creative director/copywriter friends, directed at the people who work for him. It says, simply, *Astonish me.* So why not astonish yourself by doing something fresh, new, different, surprising, out of character even? After all, 'the only difference between a rut and a grave is the depth of the excavation'.

Be receptive on all dimensions

Moments can only become 'now' moments and transcendental experiences when you are *receptive* to them; when you maintain a balance between living in the 'now' moment and experiencing the sensuality of (for example) nature or emotion, and also contemplating them and their relationship to yourself in the context of timelessness and feeling eternity in that moment; when there is an appreciation of these moments on a physical, emotional and spiritual level simultaneously. But you also need to *isolate* these moments from thinking, analysis or rational activity — simply *experience* them as they are.

Share the experience

Having travelled much of the world on business, I was inevitably alone. During the day I usually had heavy commitments, but every chance I got I would immerse myself in the new city and culture and people. I would take local taxis and talk to the cabbies. I flitted through the sightseeing traps and spent most of my time in the poorer or less popular areas, soaking up the character of the place. I would rise at four in the morning and watch it all come to life. Once in Manhattan I even spent the entire night walking around the city, going to the latest of late-night coffee shops or delicatessens and studying the people that came and went and talking to the streetwise waitresses. I sat in doorways and watched the parade of beggars and garbage-bin pirates, hookers and cops, jittery joggers and stumbling drunks and shuffling old people taking a stroll.

It was wonderful. But it was so lonely! How many times I wished I had someone special to talk to; to share the moments and give me different insights into the experiences. Because nothing is more wonderful than when you can share 'now' moments with somebody who is completely on your wavelength.

Emeritus Professor Charles Manning Hope Clarke, whose books include the acclaimed six-volume *History of Australia*, spoke to Caroline Jones about the importance of making contact with like spirits and people you can truly connect with (soulmates!): 'You do meet from time to time the people that do understand who you are; and you recognise each other; and this is a great moment.' How very true.

THE GREATEST *NOW* MOMENTS OF ALL

As an eternal Romantic, I am always very interested (no, almost obsessed!) in finding those 'self-transcending' experiences in life — those exceptionally rare, brilliant moments when time seems to stand still; those moments talked of with awe by great poets and writers and musicians. I was happy to read that Manning, speaking with the distilled wisdom of more than ninety years of searching, talked about 'Love ... genuine, fulfilling, all-consuming love ... doesn't happen very often, but when it does happen it's supremely worthwhile, it's a great moment.'

I believe such love is only possible when both partners are in a state of fully heightened awareness and on a spiritual and emotional level where their connectivity transcends everyday life. Call it romance, call it a soulmate bond, call it whatever you will — I wish more than anything that I could isolate and reproduce at will the vital spark that kindles the eternal fire of such exquisite moments in life. The closest I have come to this answer is in finding the courage within to make yourself receptive to the moment and allow yourself to be vulnerable to whatever happens... and sharing this with someone who is equally receptive and courageous in their vulnerability, so that complete communication can happen between you.

And this is what *living* is all about; 'sucking the marrow' out of that fleeting and ephemeral moment where the future passes into the past, when future and past become irrelevant; when now is all that matters. As someone once said, 'There are no perfect endings; just perfect moments.'

Of course, such moments of transcendence of time and the world's problems are not limited to love or romantic experiences. They are the very essence of life in all its rich diversity. As one of the modern world's greatest geniuses, Albert Einstein, said: 'Whoever remains unmoved, whoever cannot contemplate, or know the deep shudder of the soul in enchantment, might just as well be dead for he has already closed his eyes on life.'

I would like to share with you some of my own experiences of such moments in the hope that they will be catalysts for you to reach into your own past for similar moments of ecstasy, or perhaps inspire you to seek them (and better ones) from now on in your own life. As you read them, try to imagine yourself in the same 'moment'; in your mind, try to see and feel and hear the same things I felt at the time. And when you have finished reading my experiences, write down some of your own in the space provided, and then in the next space write down some new ways that you are going to try to experience the 'now' moments.

SOME OF THE *NOW* MOMENTS I HAVE EXPERIENCED

I have felt it while gazing in awe for the first time at the mile-long Victoria Falls in Zimbabwe, as the mighty Zambezi River poured millions of gallons into a bottomless chasm and hung a curtain of spray hundreds of feet above untamed Africa. Years later, I watched a fairy-dance of fireflies above one of the wild, unspoilt tracks nearby. On another occasion, as I waited beside my camera and tripod at midnight to catch the full moon rising over the magnificence of the Falls, I was surprised by a bushbuck darting out of the inky-black bushes right next to me. (Remember — this was untamed Africa. There wasn't another living soul around at that time of night, Zimbabwe was still full of terrorists and at that time attacks on tourists were common-place.)

I have experienced it in the breathtaking beauty and solitude of the ghostly white Sacré-Coeur rising like some Phoenix in the Parisian night. I have felt it in the mellow quietude of a tiny and ancient church somewhere in London as the late afternoon sun streamed through stained glass windows and fell across wooden steps worn into a smooth bow shape by the passage of thousands of feet, while I listened to the choir practice and the resonance of the organ.

I have felt it as I stood opposite Rembrandt's *Night Watch* in Amsterdam's Rijksmuseum, and alongside the majesty of the *Winged Victory of Samothrace* at the Louvre, and in the midst of the antiquities of Egypt in a remarkable exhibition in New York's Metropolitan Museum, and marvelling at the exquisitely smooth Rodin hand struggling to free itself from the rough granite (or was it marble?) block.

I have felt it as I passed my hands over the walls in the Tower of London and felt myself transported across the centuries to the times of Walter Raleigh. I felt it as I silently recited Wordsworth's *Westminster Bridge* one dawn as I stood in the centre of the modern-day bridge and gazed at the same sights of sleeping London.

I have felt it when my sons were born — both by Caesarean section — and I heard that indescribable first cry of life and saw that incredible living, breathing being created partly out of my own genes.

I felt it in the early morning solitude as the sun rose over the lower reaches of the great Orange River on a canoe trip in western South Africa, a solitude filled with the cries of fish eagles and the awesome peace and tranquillity of Africa at its most primitive. Or sharing my solitude late into the night with the dancing flames of my campfire, my nose filled with the indescribable fragrance of wild African wood burning.

I felt it in the complete silence and tranquillity of floating weightlessly under water, surrounded by the fragile beauty of coral formations off the Comores Islands on the east coast of Africa and stretching out my fingers to try to touch an astonishingly beautiful fish.

I felt it as a young boy, exploring masculinity through the fork of a catapult and killing a bird on a fence, and then crying with my sister as we wrapped the fragile limpness in my new handkerchief and buried it beneath a cross of ice-cream sticks.

I have experienced it on top of Mount Evan in Colorado, with the indescribably beautiful vista of the snow-capped Rockies stretching into a 360-degree horizon; and on the Zomba Plateau in Malawi, with an endless goosedown duvet of clouds tickling my feet.

I have felt it in the exquisite timelessness of making love, and in the perfect peace that follows like the afterglow of vintage red wine.

I have felt it as I watched the power of angry storm-lashed waves crashing on the rocks as I sat alone on a cold beach in Maine. I have felt it in the crisp snow of Austria's ski slopes and the chocolate-box magic of Germany's Berchtesgarten on Christmas Eve.

I have felt it as I took off my clothes and stood, naked, with the hot African sun warming my body on a remote game farm in Botswana; and as I hiked through the oxygen-saturated, decaying-leaf atmosphere of the Sabie forests in the Eastern

Transvaal; and watching the moon rise in the desolate and ghostly beauty of the Namib Desert.

I experienced it as I dipped my hand into the waters of the St Lucia estuary late one moonless night and watched the almost magical phosphorescence of micro-organisms drip off my fingers like illuminated diamonds.

I felt it as I lay on my back, eye to my telescope, and became one with the mysterious endlessness of the billions of stars and planets in the jewelled velvet of the African skies, and felt the utter humbleness of my own puny insignificance and the incredible superiority of being able to acknowledge that fact.

I felt it as I cradled and kissed the head of our faithful dog Jackie as she lay on the lawn with her life-warmth slipping away just before dawn on my birthday, and saw it when she painfully turned her gentle brown eyes and looked at me with great love a moment before the spark of her life was extinguished.

I have experienced it many times in listening to, and playing, music; in watching great plays and musicals (Andrew Lloyd Webber's *Cats* and *Phantom of the Opera*), in reading wonderfully moving poetry and other great writing. And although I generally hate crowds, I have had the incredible experience of being one with a collective mass emotion — seeing the Beatles at Detroit's Cobo Hall and first truly understanding the meaning of the term *electric atmosphere*, so tangible I felt I could climb it like a ladder. And being caught in the middle of a riot in Johannesburg when forty thousand emotionally charged students with the smell of political freedom in their nostrils went on a destructive and anarchistic protest march.

I could go on for ever. I have in my life been blessed with innumerable moments of incredible richness. But the point is that I have experienced such moments *only because I have continually searched for them and made myself receptive to them. And when they happened, I recognised and luxuriated in them and wove them into the fabric of my life.*

I call such moments 'islands' and I believe we should all strive to find and make such islands in our lives, whether we are doctors or lawyers or accountants or writers or housewives. They are times when we can confront ourselves, when we can recharge our batteries, when we can be truly in touch with who we are, when we can connect with the Universe.

This, to me is what living is all about. And I have had some good teachers. When I had my own advertising agency, I interviewed a man (who looked like Albert Einstein!) called Richard Mooney who wanted to be a copywriter. When I read his résumé I was amazed: the man was vastly better qualified than I was. He had been creative director of several agencies in the Far East and had had a whole world of experience. When I asked him about this and why he now wanted to be 'just a copywriter', he smiled and said that was what he wanted to do; what he enjoyed doing. That was just the beginning of many wisdoms I learned from Richard who had, of course, already attained the inner peace that this book strives to teach others. The relevance of this to the 'now' moments? I asked him on a trip one day why he hadn't brought a camera. (I was and still am an avid photographer.) His answer was, as usual, elegant in its simplicity: he said that he had long since learned to use his eyes as his camera.

And now that I've let you have a glimpse into my soul, I'd like you to let me look inside yours as well.

Write down some of the 'now' moments you have experienced in your own life.

234

I hope you have filled the page. In fact, I hope you needed several pages more. If you didn't do either, just think how you have wasted your life! How much you have missed out on. The tragedy is that I would bet a lot of people wouldn't be able to fill even one page with really magical, special moments. But don't despair if your page is a little sparse: that was *then* and this is *now*. You've got your whole life ahead of you to make up for lost time.

Now write down some of the 'now' moments you've read about or heard your friends talk about, or which you can imagine yourself experiencing in the near future.

_____

_____

_____

_____

_____

_____

_____

_____

_____

_____

_____

_____

_____

_____

_____

_____

_____

_____

_____

So, what are you waiting for? Go out and *just do it*! Do something entirely new — different, startling, even out of character. Surprise yourself and your friends. *Live!*

MIND-SPIRIT-BODY: INSEPARABLE PARTNERS
FOR ACHIEVING BALANCE AND FULFILMENT IN LIFE

In doing the above exercises and reading about living in the 'now' moments, you will have noticed that the experiences are always *multi-dimensional*. In almost all cases, they involved physical, emotional and spiritual aspects. At least, that is what you should always strive for when experiencing these moments.

To repeat what I said a few pages back: the moments only become 'now' moments and transcendental experiences when you are *receptive* to them; when you maintain a balance between living in the 'now' moment and experiencing the sensuality of, for example, nature or emotion, and also contemplating them and their relationship to yourself and yourself in the context of timelessness and feeling eternity in that moment; when there is an appreciation of these moments on a physical, emotional and spiritual level simultaneously.

Balance in life is vital to your happiness. And in trying to achieve this balance in your lifestyle integration, there are normally three essential factors:

- *Intellectual*

  Activities and interests related to the mind − eg creativity, intellectual pursuits such as thinking/philosophising/discussing, reading, writing, studying, verbal communication, organisational skills, and so on.

- *Emotional*

  Activities relating to feelings/spirit − eg personal relationships, creative expression, value systems, personal esteem, sense of worth, love/hate/envy, and so on.

- *Physical*

  Activities relating to the body − eg exercise, health, physical and outward appearance, what we eat and drink, physical structures around us, such as our homes and places of work, where we live, and so on.

237

Each lifestyle factor has in itself the potential to be either *positive* or *negative* in its relationship to your life.

The ideal is to have all three in a state of perfect balance and harmony.

If they are in a state of imbalance, your entire sense of well-being and fulfilment could be affected; it could be one of the reasons why you are not achieving your goals and personal happiness. If one or more of these factors dominate and overshadow your life, or if they limit your life because one or more are too weakly developed, you cannot possibly achieve 'wholeness' in your life.

I read a charming story that illustrates very well how we in the modern world have perhaps the tendency to forge ahead in one area and neglect another, and thus become 'unbalanced'. James Truslow Adams tells it like this:

A friend of mine, a distinguished explorer who spent a couple of years among the savages of the upper Amazon, once attempted a forced march through the jungle.

The party made extraordinary speed for the first two days, but on the third morning, when it was time to start, my friend found all the natives sitting on their haunches, looking very solemn and making no preparations to leave.

'They are waiting,' the chief explained to my friend. 'They cannot move further until their souls have caught up with their bodies.'

We therefore constantly need to assess and re-evaluate the balance in our mind-spirit-body relationship in order to be happy and continue to grow healthily without impediment.

To examine how 'balanced' your life is at present, take a hard look at each factor separately.

Are you healthy, in good physical shape, happy with the way you look? (Body). This is probably one of the easiest ways of proving how our lives are affected when one of the three elements is out of kilter: when you've got flu or a hangover, it's very hard to function effectively on any other level.

Are you emotionally stable, happy, fulfilled; do you have love and laughter and joy in your life; have you got good friends; do you do things for others; how active is your social life; have you got faith and do you feel comfortable about who you are spiritually? (Spirit).

Do you exercise your mind in intellectual and creative activities, in contemplating life, in planning and thinking about the future, in self-analysis? (Mind).

How balanced is your life? It's time you found out.

I am once again indebted to Albert Koopman, and to the sources he drew on, for some of the following exercise you can try to help you examine your life balance.

My life course is balanced in the following manner

Some examples of Mind-Spirit-Body activities are listed below. Go through the columns and tick off the activities applicable to your present lifestyle.

Mind	Spirit	Body
I frequently do creative things: painting, pottery, flower arranging, writing etc.	I frequently contemplate the meaning of life	I engage in a lot of physical activities like sport, going to gym, aerobics, etc.
I am studying or attending classes or have just finished.	I often go to religious or metaphysical or philosophy meetings.	I often do physical things and work with my hands doing repairs, renovations, etc.
I read a lot of 'serious' and non-fiction books.	I often find myself discussing spiritual and philosophical subjects with my friends.	I spend a lot of time on outdoor activities like swimming, horse-riding, windsurfing, biking and hiking.

239

Mind	Spirit	Body
I spend a great deal of time thinking about and planning my career.	I spend a lot of time thinking about and planning my life.	I spend a lot of time doing things like dancing, walking, jogging.
When I think about nature, it's the species and their habits and behaviour that most interest me.	When I think about nature, it's the origin of species and their place in the scheme of things that most interest me.	What I like about nature is being in it; camping and hiking and fishing and hunting.
At parties I find myself talking to people about work and current events and practical affairs in a social context.	At parties I inevitably end up discussing serious subjects with one or two like-minded people in some quiet corner.	At a party I'm a ball of fun and spend a lot of time dancing; if I talk it's just socialising.
At work I'm the one who usually organises things to be done.	At work I'm usually involved in planning and behind-the-scenes activities.	At work I'm usually the person who actually does the work and makes things happen.

Insert the number of ticks from each column into the relevant box provided. This will give you an idea of the balance/imbalance you currently have in each life factor.

Mind ☐   Spirit ☐   Body ☐

Koopman then goes on to encourage you to adjust any imbalance by consciously pursuing activities in the 'low score' areas of your life. He also talks about the importance of integrating the 'balanced you' into all aspects and elements of your lifestyle — your family, your career, your relationships, your Faith.

Although Goal Source was primarily created for use in a business environment and thus prepared his employees for successful integration into his participative management plans, you will find that its orientation is just as relevant on a personal level as it is on a commercial level.

Dreams and Goals

Business success the world applauds; business failures the world sneers at.

Likewise, the world always looks up to winners, but scorns the losers. Why is it that some people just seem to have a 'Midas touch'? Why is it that more often the busier a person is, the more he is able to do and take on, while the person with a lot of time on his hands never seems to be getting anywhere and then still says, 'Sorry, I just don't have the time'? Organising and prioritising your daily activities is critically important if you want to achieve anything. If you simply allow your life to 'happen' by being at the beck and call of Fate or some other person, you're like a dandelion seed blowing in the wind.

Many motivational books have been written about achievement, success and discovering 'the magic'. Some are even very inspirational. Why, then, is there still such a huge demand and continuing preoccupation by people for more answers? Could it be that all of these previous approaches and suggestions fail to address the real issues?

The answer is very simple indeed, but also very complex from a personal perspective. Every person who has been searching for 'how to make it' has overlooked two critical factors. We have already talked extensively about the first of these factors — the spiritual or *Infra-ego*. But of equal importance is the second — the *emotional* aspect. The 'feeling' aspect of life which is deeply ingrained in the recesses of our minds.

These emotions can often be extremely destructive and make personal success and peace of mind and self-fulfilment unattainable without the person being able to pinpoint the reason why he is not achieving or has not achieved his goals. Likewise, a goal-orientated person achieves because he possesses less of these destructive emotional forces and limitations.

Too often we have heard that achievers have a 'positive mental attitude'. Unfortunately, this concept is very misleading, especially if one has ever tried to think positively for any substantial period of time.

The critical thing is that one has to *feel* positive.

For example, have you ever noticed how effortless it is to think positive thoughts when you physically feel good, and how difficult it is to think positive thoughts when you are feeling ill or when things aren't going right around you? Positive thinking in its real sense is not possible if you are subject to any ingrained negative personal life orientations.

In order to understand Dreams and Goals, you need to understand what they are, how they originated and what you must do to *make them happen*. And in order to overcome the obstacles that are preventing these dreams from happening, you have to discover and explore their *source*. The source of your emotional blocks, the source of your positive/negative feelings. The source of all your goals and aspirations in life. The source of your perceived purpose in life.

APPLYING THE PRINCIPLES OF BALANCE IN YOUR PRACTICAL LIFE

As you have seen from our first exercise, we consist of three states of being:

The Psychological Person	(Mind)
The Spiritual Person	(Spirit)
The Physical Person	(Body)

Stated in a philosophical sense of existence and derived from these states of being are:

Attitude	(Thoughts and Feelings)
Values	(Emotions/Principles)
Behaviour	(Action/Manifestation)

In turn, we move back and forth between these states of being through three levels of awareness (in the same order):

Pre-conscious

Unconscious

Conscious

1. The *Pre-conscious Mind* can concentrate on many thoughts at a time, especially in routine matters — such as driving a car. It won't allow new thoughts inside if they need conscious mind concentration, but it can handle all other thoughts which it has learned by dealing with frequent repetitive input.

2. The *Unconscious Mind* works both day and night. Its capacity for storing data is enormous. All your experiences, impressions, fantasies, dreams and creative thoughts are processed here. It forms the basis of your value system. All the skills and patterns of behaviour which you have learned over the years can be used unconsciously, and sometimes no need will exist for the conscious mind even to be involved in the process.

3. The *Conscious Mind* generally only processes one thought at a time during the hours you are awake. The moment you try to think of two things at once, the conscious mind becomes fatigued. Just think of the situation when you try to speak in a foreign language and must constantly 'translate' in your mind.

The key to achieving your goals lies in *connecting* the Unconscious Mind with the Conscious Mind.

Good thoughts may surface in the conscious mind and, if applied, can bring fulfilment (control over one's life), happiness and creative development. Such a person will then be seen as stable and a success in life because his or her value system is being put to use through practical behaviour.

If the value system is questionable (as housed in the unconscious mind through years of experience), bad behaviour will be the result of those unconscious thoughts in the conscious brain.

Applying different input mechanisms into one's life will determine the quality of thoughts coming to the surface of the conscious mind for conversion into behaviour. The key is therefore connecting your unconscious thoughts to practical behaviour.

And the most important thing to realise is that thoughts from your unconscious mind (via your value system) are converted into day-to-day realities in the form of behaviour.

You have to live what you are and believe in.

You have to act out your value system positively.

You have to act out your being as if you have already achieved your goals.

You should strive not to do things right, but to do the right things. Everyone on earth has exactly the same time — 24 hours in each day — to make a success or failure of their lives. How each one uses those hours is what separates the achievers from the non-achievers.

Key points to remember from Chapter 7

1. How much of your precious, precious life do you spend really *living*? Isn't it time you started living a whole lot more?

2. The more vividly you learn to see and feel, the more alive you are.

3. Time is that ephemeral moment when the future passes into the past. Grasp it. Embrace it. Make it your own. Create 'islands' in the turbulent seas of your life.

4. Seek out and be receptive to as many 'self-transcending moments' as you can. Experience them multi-dimensionally: physically, emotionally, intellectually, spiritually.

5. 'There are no perfect endings; just perfect moments.'

6. Do something completely different — fresh, new, startling. Surprise yourself!

7. Try to achieve a state of balance and harmony in Mind, Spirit and Body.

---

8. Don't just *think* positive. *Feel* positive as well. Believe absolutely in yourself — you can't do better than your own personal best; if others can't accept that, that's just too bad.

9. The key to achieving your goals is to connect your unconscious mind with your conscious mind. Act out your inner feelings. Trust your own instincts. Merge 'who you are' with 'what you do'.

10. True success and fulfilment are only possible if your life and your actions are based on a higher level value system — principles that are eternal and will continue long after even the most luxurious mansion or the most precious and expensive material possessions have turned to dust.

11. You should strive not to do things right, but to do the right things.

8

Stage 6

The Vital Importance Of A Mentor/Soulmate/Guide

People seek out retreats for themselves in the country,
at the seaside, on the mountains ... but nowhere can a person
find a retreat more full of peace than one's own soul.
Make use then of this retirement continually and regenerate thyself.

Marcus Aurelius (AD 121)

We have seen in the previous chapters how in almost every myth and legend there is the Wise Old Man who appears magically to the traveller and gives him the secret key or the magical sword to slay the dragon or some other information or device that is crucial to accomplishing the mission.

In the same way, a mentor can play a crucial role in helping you to accomplish your own mission in your own journey in life.

Hagberg and Leider confirm this in their book *The Inventurers* by saying that it is 'extremely rare for anyone to accomplish a major life or career renewal *alone*'. They go on to identify three types of people who can help you: Role Models, Mentors, and Intimates.

- By observing, studying and emulating role models (ie people we admire and would like to be), we can become more like them.

- By sharing our lives and dreams and problems with our closest, truest, most honest and trusted friends, people who will stick by us no matter what happens, we can lighten our burdens and get objective advice and perspective in our lives.
- By finding and being receptive to a mentor. Mentors have been described as 'what most people are missing to make their lives more meaningful'. They are very rare and once found should be cherished and bound to you — as Shakespeare described it — 'with hoops of steel'.

Mentors are people you consider wise and absolutely trustworthy, people who are genuinely altruistic and will not manipulate or influence your life with an egocentric motive of any kind. They can serve as counsellors, advisers, guides in helping you fulfil your potential. Mentors can be recognised by the things they do, and the way they do these things with your interests at heart.

Mentors are those people who can put your life back on track when you've gone off the rails, or help you to confront the fact that you are in a Comfort Zone by making you see through your illusions and self-deceptions. But rather than try to impose their will on you, they will offer insights and honest, objective criticism (which may be very hard for you to swallow), *but ultimately they will leave the decision to you.*

Nobody else can tell you how you should live your life. It's yours, and it's the only one you've got. And you have to follow your own instincts and do what is best for you, even if this dismays others.

But the key — and one of the main points of this book — is that in following your own interests you must be absolutely sure that they *are* your own honest instincts and convictions, stripped of obligations and guilt and emotional baggage and what others expect you to do. More than all this, they must be driven by and based on higher levels of consciousness and the desire to strive continuously for self-improvement and fulfilment in terms of these principles. To help you in your search for that special person who will help you on your journey, I have tried (again with due acknowledgement to Hagberg and Leider for part of this) to list some of the qualities and values of a mentor:

- They listen and empathetically understand.
- They ask questions, they make you confront truths and break down your illusions and rationalisations, they prod and challenge you.
- They influence, but don't dictate, your life and your dreams and aspirations.
- Rather than give you ready solutions, they help you solve problems and answer questions for yourself — ie they stimulate real and permanent inner growth. They understand that the change must come from within *you*, and that mere external 'changes' are just window-dressing.
- Similarly, they will show you that 'external' solutions are meaningless. (Like becoming financially independent, winning a jackpot, even physically moving away.) None of these will work unless there is first an *internal* transformation in you.
- They let you be who you are, but constantly motivate you to make you more of who you are.
- They recognise your potential and your limitations and make you feel uncomfortable about being content to remain in your Comfort Zones.
- They expect you to use your own judgement and help you discover your inner values.
- They are concerned with the eternal and spiritual rather than the ephemeral and material aspects of life.
- They share your ups and downs; they are critical without being judgemental.
- They support and trust you.
- They provide you with realistic personal information.
- They guide you to books, quotations, experts and experienced people and other means of gaining insight and wisdom.

- They are honest even when that honesty risks invoking your anger.

- They are characterised by humility rather than arrogance and self-importance.

- They are inevitably on a higher spiritual level than you are but constantly strive to lift you higher than themselves.

- Their concern and love and advice is altruistic and unconditional; there is never an egocentric or manipulative motive. They can give you keys without demanding that you unlock the doors.

- They are always there for you, no matter what.

- They are patient and tolerant. They are content to sow seeds without expecting to share in the harvest, knowing that those seeds will grow when your soil has become fertile only through a real inner transformation in you.

Very few people (if any!) can fulfil all the expectations listed above. But if you don't already know someone who fits the description, you should actively seek out a mentor by thinking of people you respect and enjoy talking to, by attending professional lectures in self-actualisation and spiritual growth, even by consulting a psychologist or expert in the field.

The most important key to finding a mentor is — once again — that you make yourself receptive to finding one. Be alert in every social situation. At the office. At parties (they're often the ones not dancing or getting plastered, but cornered by someone who needs a shoulder to cry on or a sympathetic ear). Ask your friends about people they know — about who *they* turn to when they want good advice. Think about teachers, lecturers, family doctors, uncles and aunts, parents or grandparents. Ask your librarian to recommend books about self-growth and adult education. Read the newspapers, listen to the radio and watch television to see if there are any courses or lectures being offered or any visiting experts in the field.

Don't despair if you don't immediately find a mentor. They have a way of just 'showing up' in your life when you are sincerely pursuing your journey of self-growth. It's as if you suddenly start sending out signals on a cosmic wavelength.

At first, I used to believe that I was very alone in the world in my thoughts and beliefs and learned to be very wary about what I said and who I talked to. But when I *did* have enough confidence to say what I believed in without worrying about other people's reactions, it was amazing how many people suddenly 'connected' with me and expressed their own relief that there was somebody else in the world who 'thought like they did'.

After reading Marilyn Ferguson's *The Aquarian Conspiracy*, it seemed that there were in fact a whole lot of people out there who thought this way. And these people are beginning to network with each other all over the world. Comfort Zone escapees of the world unite!

INTUITIVE MENTORS

Mentors aren't always consciously aware that they are mentors. Many people go through life performing this role simply by the example of their own lives and becoming role models for many others they may never meet. Great authors can be mentors long after they have died, by sharing their observations and insights with readers who take the trouble to seek out their wisdoms. (Henry David Thoreau was and still is undoubtedly one of my own most influential mentors.)

And then there are the intuitive mentors. They are people who intuitively know things that others may take years of study and bitter personal experience to learn. And yet when you talk to these people and try to get them to verbalise their wisdoms and insights, or when you try to specify or define or intellectualise them in discussion, they are often unaware or seemingly ignorant of their intuitive knowledge. The following case study illustrates this.

250

Case study: Eleanor

Eleanor was a photographic model who had momentarily reached the top in her field, at which point she was wooed by the boss of an up-and-coming model agency — which one particularly cynical social columnist saw as a blatant move to capitalise on her fame. After a whirlwind romance, they wed — yet it soon seemed the columnist was right. Eleanor was soon ridiculously overworked and over-exposed, and when she quite predictably found herself less in demand, her new husband began abusing her emotionally and sexually. Within a very short time her career was dead and the marriage was on the rocks. Yet when she tried to join another model agency, Eleanor found to her horror that she was bound by a watertight contract she had signed in the euphoria of romance, and her husband was not prepared to release her. Stung and disillusioned, she sought refuge in several affairs which were as unsatisfying as they were powerless to solve her problems.

Then at a party she met a much older man (we'll call him Gary) who was a philosophy professor at the local university. Amazingly, they found they were true soulmates; and though on the surface they were completely different, in some strange way they stimulated and complemented each other perfectly. Although not well educated, Eleanor was receptive to Gary's intellect and philosophies, while he in turn found her the perfect mentor in awakening his emotions and sexuality which he had never before been able to express. Also, for his entire life he had believed the greatest virtue lay in doing what others wanted him to do and being what they wanted him to be, but — for the first time — with Eleanor's encouragement, he discovered the joy and satisfaction of asserting his inner self.

Her influence inevitably had an impact on his private life as well. Never married, he supported his parents and younger brother who all lived with him, and believed it was his moral and religious duty to do this. But with simple logic, Eleanor demolished his excuses and rationalisations about his moral and ethical and social and religious obligations, and convinced him that he had the right to be himself and follow his inner honesty. She brushed aside his excuses about being concerned about the opinions of others, about 'not having the time' to pursue his own desires and do things for himself, about their age difference. [*Author: Completely naturally and intuitively, she was teaching him how to escape his Comfort Zones.*]

Eventually, this culminated in a physical relationship which was easily the most fulfilling, the most passionate and the most complete

Eleanor had ever had. Entranced, she saw Gary as her escape from her miserable marriage, and put increasing pressure on him to make a commitment. But Gary was trapped in his own complex web of guilt and obligations, of obedience to social and religious norms, of morality and ethics. Despite the intensity of his feelings for her, every time she got really close he would pull away and retreat deep into his castle, avoid her, and refuse even to answer the phone when she tried to contact him. Then he would confront his emotional dishonesty, reach out to Eleanor again, and the whole cycle would begin all over. Of course this couldn't carry on, and eventually Eleanor forced an ultimatum and asked Gary to marry her or leave her. Unable to face the final confrontation with its risk of change, Gary ended the relationship.

Eleanor was distraught at this betrayal of the deepest expression of her love, and while he retreated deeper than ever into his castle, she set about building unscalable walls around her own pain. She rationalised her husband's behaviour and suppressed her own real feelings, and forced herself to become heavily involved in his business, training new models and trying to make the best of things. Desperately unhappy, she sought solace in the arms of a host of faceless men, and when she fell pregnant she told her husband it was his. And her guilt only drove her deeper inside her own castle.

Now things took an ironic turn. After months of agonising over the issue, Gary finally confronted his emotional honesty and took the leap. He moved his parents into an old-age home, made his brother find a job and his own place to live, and accepted that he had a right to marry for love — even if that meant someone outside his religion. Then he made contact again with Eleanor.

But Eleanor was still angry and resentful, extremely wary and emotionally traumatised, and by now well and truly ensnared in a complex web of circumstances and psychological tangles. At their infrequent meetings, Gary tried to draw her out of herself and show her that she had become a complete mirror image of what he had once been. He had internalised and intellectualised what he had been through, and it was now his turn to be a mentor to her.

And yet she simply couldn't learn what she had intuitively taught him. Confused, she drew him closer and then pushed him away. It was a roller-coaster ride of opening the door a crack, putting a toe outside, and then retreating back into the relative security of her castle. She used denials and avoidance to escape confronting painful truths about herself and her marriage; she rationalised and made excuses for not doing the very things she had once convinced Gary he had to do; she was paranoid about her husband and friends finding out that she was seeing him again.

Deep down she simply couldn't forgive him for the pain he had caused her, despite his genuine expressions of remorse and his explanations of why he had not been able to make a commitment at the time. Secretly, she blamed him for decisions she had been forced to make, for being tied for long hours to her husband's business, for the spousal abuse she was forced to endure, and even for the child and all its restrictions on her freedom. Gary forced her to confront the hard facts: that she was trapped through circumstances engineered by her husband as well as by her own decisions and defence mechanisms, and had painted herself into a corner. But Eleanor simply didn't have the emotional energy or courage, or insight, to try to escape.

Finally, Gary had to confront the fact that although Eleanor had helped him escape from his Comfort Zone castle, there was very little chance that she would ever escape from her own. Although intuitively she had been the perfect mentor for him, she was simply not able to turn her intuition into objective wisdom and spiritual insight and apply these principles to her own situation. Although still very much in love, he walked away and plunged himself into a relationship with one of his ex-students. Within a year they were extremely happily married.

WHAT HAPPENS WHEN YOU YOURSELF BECOME A MENTOR

Once you have completed your transformation and escaped your Comfort Zones (like Gary), or even while you're still on your journey, you will inevitably find that you build enough confidence in who you are and what you believe in to start living this out in your daily life, that other people notice the 'new you' and start asking you for advice.

Of course, this is very flattering, but it's also very scary — because suddenly you find yourself in a position where you can greatly influence someone else's life for the better. The only advice I can give is that you read once again the earlier section which discusses the qualities that a mentor should have, and try to live up to each of these criteria in your own life.

And the most important thing of all is that you can only offer advice and wisdom and then leave it to the other person to make the decision. You can't decide *for* him or her. Because if you do, they will only resent you if things go wrong, even if it is entirely their own fault, or the result of circumstances that you had nothing whatsoever to do with.

You will also learn that the very last thing you can expect is *gratitude*, even if your advice and influence made a huge change in the other person's life. Unless that person is on a high enough spiritual level to truly appreciate these things, they will probably only resent you for your spiritual maturity and altruistic help — and for making them feel uncomfortable in their Comfort Zones.

Sounds crazy, doesn't it? But it's true. And I learned it the hard way. As Shakespeare put it, 'Blow, blow thou winter wind; Thou art not so unkind As man's ingratitude'.

There have been many instances in my life when I have bent over backwards to help people; to pick them up when they were really down and out; to give them 'breaks' which in many cases led to prosperity and success. There have been people I have pulled out of the gutter and helped shift into an entirely new paradigm of lifestyle and social standing which they could never even have dreamed of before. But, with a few exceptions, most of these people never acknowledged or expressed appreciation for what I did in their lives. In fact, there were some instances where these very people turned against me and betrayed me in later years. It's particularly spiritually trying when you have power over such people (as has often been the case with me); when you are in a position to retaliate and 'teach them a lesson'. In at least two cases in my life I could have utterly destroyed people, as easily as snapping a matchstick, and sent them back to the gutter where they belonged, and I would have felt perfectly justified in doing so, considering all that they had done — not only to me but to others as well. Yet, thankfully, my compassion prevailed.

What do you do in cases like this? All I have tried to do is to see them as positive learning experiences in my own spiritual growth, and the opportunity to cultivate my compassion and spiritual maturity by putting aside my own anger and simply forgiving and forgetting. I am grateful for the lessons they allowed me to learn, and for the roles they played in my development. Although I may initially have been hurt or indignant or angry, I realised the futility of retaliation of any sort. After all, these people had harmed themselves far more than they ever harmed me. Although in a temporal and immediate gratification context, it may have appeared (certainly to them) that they had 'won', they were in fact the big losers in an eternal context.

As Joseph Campbell says:

Often it seems, it is the best who lose and the worst who win. But winning, finally, is not the aim; for as we have already learnt... winning and losing in the usual sense are experiences only of the lower chakras [*Author: lower spiritual levels*]. The aim of the ascending serpent is to clarify and increase the light of consciousness within, and the first step to the gaining of this boon — as told in the Bhagavad Gita, as in many other wisdom texts — is to abandon altogether all concern for the fruits of action, whether in this world or the next.

As the Lord Krishna on the battlefield said to the warrior prince Arjuna, 'To the work alone you are entitled; never to its fruit... He who knows the way of renunciation and the way of action are one, he verily knows.'

It all comes down to spiritual levels. And all you can feel for such people is genuine compassion and hope that some day — in some future life perhaps — they will grow beyond what Hermann Hesse calls 'the slime and egg-shells of the primeval world' and become real people. But for now, you might simply have to accept that '...There are many who never become human; they remain frogs, lizards, ants. Many men are human beings above and fish below.'

In trying to be a mentor it's very hard to accept this — that some people simply don't have the insight to understand what you are trying to say, or simply aren't on a sufficiently high

255

spiritual level to appreciate what you are trying to do for them, or may be going through things that perhaps you can't understand or see, or may have very valid reasons that inhibit or prevent them from hearing what you are trying to say. In such cases, perhaps we must just accept that we're only human and not saints, that life is too short (and we are too weak) to continue carrying other people's burdens, or trying to give them insight, or make them into what we think are 'better' people.

Perhaps there are cases when you just have to walk away from it all and let it be. And yet it's one of the most painful of experiences to see someone you really care about refuse to be receptive to what you are trying to say; to watch them take the golden keys you hand them and toss them into the wastepaper baskets of their lives.

Perhaps this sounds terribly condescending and judgemental. Hesse points out that each individual has his own unique lessons to learn and that *every* man's story is 'important, unique, sacred'. And Joseph Campbell wrote:

> The joy of the quest to wholeness is not a triumph over others, it is a triumph over oneself. And the distance you have travelled in your own quest does not imply an arrogance over others who have not journeyed as far ... in our relationships with others, we should share our insights and experiences, for we will learn valuable lessons from their journeys just as much as they will learn from ours. Rather than seek qualities in ourselves that are superior to others', we should search for the qualities we share with them and use these as a common ground for under-standing and sharing.

What a wonderfully mature wisdom — and how incredibly difficult to live up to! I know from personal experience how frustrating it is when people (to quote Helen Keller) 'have eyes and fail to see' if, even when you do try to be empathetic and understanding and try to find common ground, they resist building their half of the bridge across the chasm. I'd like to share a poem I wrote to express my own frustration with trying unsuccessfully for a long time to help someone close to me. It's about a report of a proposed nuclear waste dumpsite in the desolate beauty of the Kalahari desert, home of the nomadic Bushman tribe, which I have used as an analogy for the person sinking deeper and deeper into a Comfort Zone and not having insight into the spiritual and emotional degeneration caused by the negative environment, and my seeming inability to make that person understand.

The Bushman

It was tucked into the bottom corner of page thirty:
how the birthright was sold for a handful of silver
pimped to a nuclear ejaculator by a greedy and conscienceless
caretaker.

My beloved Kalahari!
There is no deeper peace
than being One with the mystery
of You.

And so I travelled a long way
a long, long, weary way;
to sit down and talk to you of the danger:

of drumfuls of lingering death
buried and hidden in your very bosom
and I begged you to flee the seeds of your extinction.

But with maddening contempt for haste
you smiled and scratched the sand-flies from your hair
and disinterred the ostrich-egg reservoir
and offered me a drink
accompanied by endlessly friendly clicks
of sociability.

Joined by the bridge of humanity and love
and separated by the gulf of understanding
you chattered on and on
and while I implored in sign-language
you proudly showed me the tatters of your hide hut
and the crudeness of your loincloths.

257

> I walked away slowly
> with a great sadness in my heart
> And long, long afterwards I thought:
> Perhaps you are wiser than I think you are
>> but I don't think so
>> no, I don't think so.

The final words of the poem reveal my own questions at the time about the ethics of trying to help someone 'who has eyes and fails to see'. In reading it again, and with the benefit of hindsight and all the lessons I have since learned, I realise how futile and spiritually immature it is to get angry when someone refuses to use the keys you are giving them (even with the most noble and altruistic of intentions) to unlock the doors of their prisons. That decision can only come from within. As a mentor, the greatest gift you can give someone is *freedom of choice* — and that includes the choice of whether to take your advice or not. How I wish I had learned the 'Lesson of the Butterfly' a lot earlier in my life.

GETTING RID OF OLD BAGGAGE

Anger and resentment are burdens that harm you far more than they harm anyone else. Take the simple decision either to genuinely forgive and forget and walk away from it completely; or to do something about it now and get it over with. The first option is the ideal: if you can be big enough to approach the person who hurt you in a genuine spirit of reconciliation and turn that enemy into a friend (or at least stop being enemies) by burying the hatchet, this is a wonderful spiritual victory.

Unfortunately, its success depends on the other person's response. I once wrote such a letter, but the person concerned didn't even have the common decency to reply. I also believe that if you change your own perspective on events and see them in a positive way as a valuable learning experience, it can help you get over your anger and resentment. To me, the best expression of this is in a book of Sanskrit poetry:

A hundred times I learnt from my philosophy
To think no more of Love ...
this Vanity, this Dream,
this source of all Regret,
this Emptiness.
But no philosophy can make my heart forget
Her loveliness.

Dharmakirti

However, if you decide to take the second option, make sure that your actions are emotionally and spiritually mature and guided by integrity. Don't do anything you will later regret. It's the classic confrontation between the biblical 'turning the other cheek' and 'an eye for an eye and a tooth for a tooth'. But remember, that same Bible says 'Revenge is mine, sayeth the Lord'.

Before you decide to get rid of your emotional baggage by taking out your anger on someone or getting 'revenge', ask yourself how you would feel if someone did the same to you. Ask yourself whether you're prepared to take full responsibility for the consequences. Ask yourself whether your actions won't become something you will later deeply regret; something that will simply become a guilt 'albatross' around your neck.

When you allow someone to make you angry, you are simply empowering that person to carry on hurting you. The chances are, they are blissfully unaware that they are even hurting you; that they are simply not on the spiritual level where these things bother them; that conscience, morality and ethics are non-existent. By feeling anger and bitterness and resentment, you are clogging up your mind with negative thoughts that will only harm *you*.

But if expressing your anger or retaliating is the only way to release yourself from these encumbrances and allow you to progress on your journey, then do it and get it over with rather than let it keep on simmering inside you. But, as I have said before, be very sure that you are prepared to accept full responsibility for your actions and handle the consequences. Finally, before you act, ask yourself how you would feel if someone did the same thing to you. You'll probably end up not doing it!

One of the more interesting ways you can express your feelings in an acceptable way was suggested by an acquaintance who had been dumped on her wedding day and knew all about anger and emotional hurt. After months of depression, she decided to expel everything associated with her 'almost husband' by writing down all her grudges and anger and resentments of a piece of paper. She wrote straight from the heart, using the most vitriolic and insulting words she could think of. She poured it all out, didn't hold anything back. While she was writing, she imagined the man bound hand and foot and gagged in front of her while she told him exactly how she felt, exactly what she thought of him, exactly what she'd like to do to him. She kept going until she had drained herself of every remnant of anger and pain.

Then she found a place where she could be completely alone (otherwise, as she said, watchers might have thought her quite mad). She threw the sheets of paper on the ground and jumped on them. She ground them into the dirt. Then she picked them up and crushed them and tore them to pieces, put them in a pile and burned them, together with several other things associated with him — photographs, sexy lingerie, gifts he had given her, and all his letters.

She says that as she watched it all burn, all her anger and pain and negative memories, she felt the same emotions draining from inside her. She said a prayer, forgiving him for all that he had done to her, and tried to concentrate on what lessons she had learned from the experience, even if it was just that she was determined that she would never allow herself to be hurt in the same way again.

Then, when nothing was left but ashes, she spoke out loud, calling him by name and saying something that went like this: 'I am not going to allow you to hurt me any more. I have burned all the pain you have caused me. All the influence you had on my life is now nothing but ashes, as are the chains that bound me to you. I have burned our past. I could have hurt you as you hurt me and even worse, but I choose not to. Instead, I forgive you completely. If and when you can also do that, you will not only have my forgiveness, but also my respect. I don't care if you have the insight to appreciate that or not, but from this moment on you have lost someone very special in your life. And if you don't know just how much you have lost, then I have truly lost nothing.'

Then she turned her back and walked away. Physically, emotionally, spiritually. And got on with her own life. She says that every time painful memories or anger creep into her head, she just thinks about watching everything burn and disintegrate, and repeats her prayer that one day the man will gain insight and understanding.

You may not want to do anything as radical or dramatic, but you *must* find whichever way you can to get rid of painful and traumatic emotions that are blocking your happiness and not allowing you to lead a normal life.

One of the best ways of doing this is to involve yourself in activities that keep you busy and occupy your thoughts, so that you literally don't have the time to think negatively or feel depressed by painful memories. This works best when that activity is fresh or different and stimulates you, or when you are doing something for other people who are a lot worse off than you in many other ways.

I know that's just a 'physical escape' in many ways, but trauma needs a natural period of 'mourning' before the intense pain can dim and become just a sad memory. Think about it: in some ways you are simply 'acting yourself into a better way of thinking' by engaging in these activities.

Of course, this relates specifically to a recent traumatic experience — but many people carry such burdens around with them for years. The experiences may have been long forgotten, or suppressed in some deep cavern of the brain to avoid pain, but they will continue to exert the same negative influence on your life until you confront them and come to terms with them intellectually, emotionally and spiritually. And put them for ever in the past where they belong, retained only as catalysts for a positive growth experience for your future.

To end this section on emotional baggage on a lighthearted note, I'd like to share the wisdom of a Chinese proverb with you.

> *That the birds of Worry and Care fly above your head,*
> *this you cannot change.*
> *But that they build nests in your hair,*
> *this you can prevent.*

THAT'S GREAT — BUT WHAT HAS ALL THIS GOT TO DO WITH ESCAPING MY OWN COMFORT ZONES?

Firstly, I hope it will teach you the lesson it taught me: that failures and mistakes and frustrations are often the best lessons in life. It was only through making my own mistakes, feeling my own anger and frustration, experiencing the bitterness of ingratitude and betrayal, that I learned to grow into genuine acceptance and be able to get rid of my emotional baggage and sincerely forgive and forget those who had caused me pain.

But the most important lesson of all was that these incidents made me realise that — no matter how altruistic or noble I thought I was being — my *real* motivation was probably a kind of intellectual arrogance and a stroking of my ego, or some egocentric motive that I was not prepared to admit to at the time. It took me a long time to learn the lesson of true humility; of realising my utter insignificance in the greater scheme of things, of striving to be *genuinely* altruistic.

Overcoming your ego is an incredibly difficult process. The ego with its collection of qualities and convictions dreads its own demise. And true transformation in life is suicide for the ego.

Although I myself am a Christian, there are many elements of the Eastern religions that have given me great insight. For example, in terms of the importance of overcoming the ego, Joseph Campbell talks about the literal meaning of the Sanskrit word 'nirvana' (which I always interpreted as 'heaven' or perfection) as being 'blown out', and Campbell uses its reference in the Buddha's sense as 'an extinction of egoism'. As he says, 'The *released one* is beyond ego and is moved from within, not by any external authority, wiping out desire for earthly goods, fear of death and deprivation, all sense of social obligation, and above all, every thought of *I* or *mine*.'

It's a difficult goal to achieve. But it's one you must strive for — and a hurdle you are sure to encounter — in your journey of escaping your Comfort Zones. As psychologist Erich Fromm said, 'Happiness... can be achieved only when man has achieved inner freedom.' Remember, that's freedom *from* constraints, and freedom *towards* future growth.

To end off this section, I'd like to share a case study with you to illustrate how short-sighted I was in trying to help a friend. (Like all the case studies used in this book, I have changed names and places and taken creative licence in embellishing them to protect the identities of the people and respect their privacy.)

Perhaps you can learn from my mistakes as I did myself.

Case study: Donny

Donny and I had been friends since we were teenagers. After school we went our separate ways, but periodically visited each other. Having left school early, he never progressed very far in the forestry company where he worked all his life, and got trapped in the total security of a small salary but all the needs of his life being taken care of by the company. This total dependency extended into his private life as well, where his wife — a very strong and domineering woman — took care of everything.

Then one day she decided she'd had enough, and divorced him. I got a call from him one afternoon, and over the phone I could hear that apart from being utterly distraught, he was slurring his words and being frequently incoherent. Alarmed, I found out where he was and arranged to fetch him. I cancelled all my appointments and rushed off. (He was living in a forestry settlement some 100 km away.)

When I got there, he was in very bad shape. He had been drinking non-stop, and told me he had swallowed a whole lot of aspirin the previous night. When I put him in my car, he had his entire worldly possessions in a plastic shopping bag.

To cut a long story short, my wife and I took him in and started the long process of re-humanising him (it's the only way I can express it). We let him live in a cottage on our property, gave him clothes, helped him find a job, taught him how to use a bank account, put down the deposit for a small car, and bombarded him non-stop with life skills and positive thoughts. We gave him dreams and all the elements of a new life.

Donny responded magnificently. Soon he was walking with a spring in his step, head held high. He won a prize for the best manager at his job — the first award he'd got in his entire life. He bought new clothes, a TV, a radio. He started paying us back the deposit for his car. He was ready to go out into the world on his own.

We found another cottage on a large property nearby and helped him move in. We kept up the visits and the advice and the positive thoughts. Then one night he gave me a personal and rather secretive invitation to supper (my wife was away at the time). He prepared a barbecue, we laughed and drank wine, and halfway through the evening he sat me down and said he had something for me. Standing like a nervous schoolboy in front of me, feet together and hands behind his back, he recited a poem from a book I'd given him. It was a wonderful timeless moment that brought genuine tears to my eyes. I was incredibly proud of what he had achieved, and it made me feel really good inside knowing that we had been catalysts for this remarkable recovery. For the first time I believed that a 'quantum leap' was possible.

Then suddenly it all fell apart.

He had been secretly meeting a woman he'd found at the local singles bar, and we found out through a third party that they were engaged to be married. A whirlwind later, he gave up his job and moved to a nearby city where her brother owned a block of apartments. We didn't hear a word from him — not even a phone call.

Then, a few months later, he was back. He hadn't been able to get a job; his wife was out of work, and her brother had kicked them out because they couldn't pay the rent. When my wife and I visited them, we were shocked. It was as if he had taken a quantum leap backwards, and it seemed that everything we had taught him had been totally forgotten and discarded. Soon afterwards he disappeared again, and we have not heard from him since.

At first I felt very angry and, somehow, betrayed. How could he do this to us? I thought. And then one day — it was about the time I found the 'Lesson of the Butterfly' and took my own quantum leap in spiritual maturity — I realised how incredibly small-minded I was being. What did it matter what he did to us? We had helped out of pure compassion, and genuinely expected nothing back. But, on that day of revelation, I realised that we *had* expected something back; we wanted him to continue to be the person *we thought he should be*; the 'new' person we had made him into. How small, how petty, how ignorant, how insensitive we had been.

And so, Donny, wherever you are, please forgive me. I acknowledge and respect your right to be who you want to be. I know now that the 'external changes' that I encouraged (no matter how impressive they were), stopped far short of what I should have given you: the keys to an inner transformation, and the freedom to choose if and when you would use those keys to open the doors to a new life.

At the end of it all, you taught me far more than you ever learned from me.

Key points to remember from Chapter 8

1. A mentor can play a crucial role in helping you escape your Comfort Zones. But don't expect or allow them to make decisions for you. It's up to you and you alone to make those decisions based on your own honest instincts and convictions.

2. For you to make a real escape and undergo a real inner transformation, these instincts and convictions must be driven by, and based on, higher levels of consciousness.

3. 'External' solutions are meaningless; at best, they are short-term catalysts for real change and inner growth.

4. True mentors will sow seeds without demanding that they grow or expecting to share in the harvest. But it's up to you to make sure that those seeds fall on fertile soil by being receptive to growth.

5. The more tuned in you are to their wavelengths, the easier it will be to find a mentor.

6. When others start using you as their mentor, make sure you measure up to the criteria.

7. Anger and resentments are burdens that harm you far more than they harm anyone else. Take the simple decision either to genuinely forgive and forget and walk away from it completely; or to do something about it now and get it over with.

8. If you decide to take the latter course of action, make sure that your actions are emotionally and spiritually mature and guided by integrity — don't do anything you will later regret.

9. Burn the emotional baggage and pain of your past and genuinely forgive and forget those who caused it. Walk away from them for ever.

10. Failures and mistakes are often the best lessons in life.

11. True transformation in life is suicide for the ego. But overcoming your egoism and attaining humility are essential steps in escaping your Comfort Zones and moving on to higher spiritual and consciousness levels.

12. Remember the 'Lesson of the Butterfly'. No matter how compassionate you are, no matter how good your intentions, helping someone else to be who you think they should be could be the most harmful act imaginable. Give keys without demanding that they be used to unlock the door; sow seeds without expecting to see (or share in) the harvest.

9

Stage 7

The Final Nudge — Action And Integration

Full circle from the tomb of the womb to the womb
of the tomb, we come: an ambiguous, enigmatical
incursion into a world of solid matter that is soon
to melt from us like the substance of a dream.

Joseph Campbell, The Hero with a Thousand Faces

We've come a long way together in our journey through this book. If the journey you originally saw in your mind was a thousand steps, then we've already walked nine hundred and ninety of them. Just over the hill is where you wanted to be... but perhaps you feel you're not actually there yet, and that those few final steps are the most difficult of all to take.

That's not unusual at all. Because although you have learned many things and gained great insights into yourself and your Comfort Zones, the most crucial steps of all are actually *putting those things into practice.* Going through the gate. Crossing the drawbridge.

All along the journey I've tried to help by telling you how important this is; how you have to act yourself into a better way of thinking, how you must just *do* something (no matter how small) to start the process. And I know as well as anyone just how difficult this sometimes is. In fact, I am still very cautious and reluctant to hurt anyone or cause pain in anyone else around me — which, unfortunately, is often absolutely necessary as part of the process.

Yet I have found that the story about how to eat an elephant ('One bite at a time') is probably the advice that works best for me. Even the biggest decision or action can be broken down into small pieces, minimal actions that can be taken without causing too much stress or pain. But the critical thing is that *you must start doing them and continue doing them.* Once you have set a goal, be absolutely determined to keep it in front of you and work your way towards it. Each step of a thousand-mile journey takes you closer. Each bite of elephant takes you closer to finishing off the entire animal. But you will *never get there* if you stop or start skipping steps or bites.

Remember that we are talking about a *process*. I know it's the umpteenth time I've said this. So, forgive me, because it's so very important to internalise this and make it an automatic way of dealing with any task — including escaping your Comfort Zones.

But no matter how much or how little you may think you have progressed since page one, there is one inescapable fact: you are now a different person from the one who first picked up this book. You have made progress, whether you are aware of it or not. The seeds have been sown, and I can promise you that they will grow.

If you want proof of these things, one of the best ways of gauging progress is to look back on your journey. So, I've prepared a short synopsis to help refresh your memory, as well as to imprint the stages of the process on your memory so that you can continue your journey for the rest of your life.

LOOKING THROUGH THE PHOTO ALBUM

When people want to relive their vacation experiences, they get out their videos or slides or photographs. So, to help you relive your experiences and the things you learned on your journey of escaping your Comfort Zones, let's page through the photo album, so to speak.

The first step to escaping your Comfort Zones was *recognising that you were trapped in one, or more than one*. And while you were trapped, you couldn't possibly grow or progress in your life or become fulfilled as a human being. You learned that Comfort Zones can be material, or emotional, or spiritual in a religious context, or psychological, but usually they are a complex interwoven web combining all these things. You learned that your castle walls — your obstacles to escape — almost always exist only in your own mind, but that often they have been so warped and magnified by years of rationalisation that they are hard to recognise.

To identify the nature of the Comfort Zones you were trapped in, to scout out your castle walls as it were, you learned to be truly honest in scrutinising every aspect of your life; your job and career; your relationships; to ask yourself what you really want; what you would do or where you would be if you had no physical or financial restrictions, no responsibilities, no obligations, no guilt feelings. You learned to separate needs and dependencies from wants and desires, and temporarily mentally discard the needs and obligations, and concentrate on your inner feelings, on what you idealistically want or what you would do if you could wave a magic wand over your life. And you learned that you hold that magic wand in your own hands — that you are the only one who can bring about these changes.

You learned that even a thousand-mile journey begins with the first step. It was up to you to make the decision to take that first step; that the *intention* and *desire* to grow and better your life was the most crucial step of all. *Most importantly, you actually took it.*

You learned physically to isolate yourself in order to discover who you really were, to get in touch with yourself, to learn to live in the 'now' moments. You went away by yourself for a day or a weekend, you spent some time alone where you could be free from outside influences and your life's complications, or perhaps you confided in a friend you could trust completely. In short, you 'took time out'.

Concentrating as much on what you *felt* as what you *thought*, you wrote your dreams and wants and desires down in a sentence or paragraph starting: 'What I really want in my life is . . .' (If you didn't write it down, do it now!) You learned that, no matter how valid or important they may have been to you then, material goals and self-empowerment are superficial and ephemeral and only rungs on the ladder of true growth — the lower levels of Maslow's hierarchy and of human development generally — and that they must therefore always be seen only as a means to an end. When they are an end in themselves, you know that they will become even greater obstacles to your growth.

You learned that, in fact, material possessions and their inevitable human companions of pride, status and power, are some of the prime building blocks of Comfort Zone prisons, and that the higher the walls get, the more difficult they are to escape from. And of course you know by now that the deeper someone is inside his or her castle, the harder it is even to acknowledge that there is a better world beyond the walls.

Once you knew what you *wanted* — even if that was difficult to identify (it might have been simply that you knew that you were not happy or fulfilled and wanted to change) — you identified what was stopping you from attaining your desires — ie what the *obstacles* were that were preventing you from achieving your goals.

You discovered (to your annoyance, probably!) that escaping your Comfort Zones was not a magical, instant 'quantum leap' but rather a long, slow, and always painful process, that it was a gradual orientation rather than a sudden metamorphosis which almost no one could cope with psychologically or emotionally. And in confronting the risk and pain, you learned that some discomfort is a necessary and inescapable component of any change — like paying a highway toll before you can continue on your journey.

Once you identified the obstacles that stood in your way, you examined them very carefully and identified which of the obstacles were genuinely unrealistic or physically impossible to change. You recognised that, with minor adjustments to your desires and objectives, even these 'impossible' obstacles could be overcome. For example, Douglas Bader lost both legs, but he carried on flying a fighter plane. Helen Keller, though blind, 'saw' more clearly than most people by developing her spiritual insight.

You have learned some techniques of self-affirmation, but you also learned that you must never manipulate other people in order to help you achieve your objectives or overcome your obstacles. You learned that this is true even in an altruistic context — ie where you want to help someone for their own good. At best, you can make them aware — you can 'give them the keys' — but you cannot demand, or even expect, that they will open the door. The bottom line is to give them complete *freedom of choice* to do only what they genuinely want to do.

You confronted the fact that there can be no 'rebirth' (ie of the new you) until there is 'death' (ie of the old you), that one cycle has to end before another can begin. You accepted that *any* transition is turbulent, that the quantum leap in your life would be painful, and the leap into the unknown scary. But once you recognised that it is an essential and inevitable step, you learned to accept pain and risk completely, and even to welcome it because it is the mechanism *necessary* for change.

You confronted the truth. You separated realities from illusions and self-deceptions. You learned that, by a process called 'cognitive dissonance', we tend to believe only what we want to believe, rejecting even hard facts because they don't fit into the picture we have painted for ourselves, rejecting anything that threatens to burst the bubble of security around us. (One of the best — if extreme — examples of this is that of a battered woman telling you what a wonderful and loving and caring man her husband is while she tries to pull her hair over a black eye or a broken jaw.)

You learned to confront negative emotions and painful memories, to recognise that you cannot change historical facts but that you can stop them from burdening and negatively influencing your life by seeing them as learning experiences that have enriched you and made you wiser in some way.

You learned that resentment and anger and hate are some of the most powerful obstacles to growth and inner fulfilment, and you made a commitment to genuinely forgive and forget, and not allow them to continue harming and hurting you. Perhaps you even followed my suggestion and 'burned your past', getting rid of the poisons in order to begin the process of positive growth.

You set yourself goals and deadlines — and you set your sights high. (Remember the old Arapahoe Indian saying that if you aim at the moon, you might hit an eagle ... but if you aim at an eagle, you will probably only hit a treetop.)

You found yourself a mentor or guide, a soulmate or kindred spirit. Someone on the same (or higher) spiritual level as yourself with whom you can truly share your experiences and learn from in a mutually beneficial synergy of growth; someone you can trust totally and who will truly understand you and empathise with you. You have committed yourself to having regular contact with this positive and guiding influence and influencer, because you realise now that the more time you can spend with him or her, the faster you will grow. You have also learned to be open and honest and genuinely receptive to confronting painful truths and learning new wisdoms that may at first seem uncomfortable to you.

You started taking action. Doing things. You stopped sitting on the platform of indecision and got on to a train. You know now that no matter how small or insignificant, each positive step you take is a step in the right direction. You set yourself small, easily attainable goals. And you just *did* it.

You learned the importance of constantly moving ahead and no longer standing still or going around in circles. You are now determined that you will continue growing all the time; that you are going to continue improving your life and are not going to stop until you have achieved that objective. You learned that perseverance and patience are very important; that, above all, you will never give up. You know that failure is the last rung on the ladder to success.

(There's a lovely story told by Charles Westrill of how, as a young aspiring writer, he had the audacity to make an appointment with a certain T J Watson (whose name and number he had got from a friend) to meet him at the Zoo cafeteria to 'pick his brains' about a project. Watson suggested the alternative of lunch at his own office. When Westrill arrived he realised to his horror that T J Watson was president of IBM, and one of the most powerful men in the country. Showing the kind of humility which often characterises great men, Watson nevertheless had lunch with him and said he liked his spunk and, in the course of conversation, imparted his formula for writing success [and any other kind of success as well, I say] as follows: '*Double your rate of failure.* Failure is a teacher — a harsh one, perhaps, but the best. You can be discouraged by failure — or you can learn from it.')

You learned the importance of integrating your spiritual growth with the realities of the world around you, with other aspects of your life, with other people in your life, and how to integrate your 'Who I am' with 'What I do'.

Most of all, by the simple act of reading and stimulating your thoughts about yourself and your life, you gained important new perspectives which will for ever be a part of who you are and how you see the world around you.

So, now that your destination is right before you, or already behind you, or has been discarded for a better destination; now that you have become 'unbundled'; now that the walls of your castle have been broken down and are forgotten ruins in your past; now that you are more confident and assertive and emotionally honest and real; now that you have become yourself (perhaps for the first time in your life), you know where you are going, and your journey has begun in earnest. Now you are an experienced traveller and you will be able to share your knowledge with others along the way and see things with new perspectives and insights.

Like Thoreau returning to Concord after his time beside Walden Pond, you can now return carrying a message to your own 'fellow countrymen' — your friends and colleagues and family — and 'be a Columbus to whole new continents and worlds within you... explore the private sea, the Atlantic and Pacific Ocean of one's being alone.'

CONTINUING THE PROCESS

How long is a 'process'? When does your journey end?

It ends when you have reached a state of perfection. And I think that's beyond even what is variously called Heaven or Nirvana or whatever name your particular religious belief uses. Unless we are already Gods (which we very obviously aren't), I don't think the process of improvement and striving for perfection ever ends.

And so, for us mere mortals here on earth with our multitude of imperfections, the process or journey you have just been through is only the beginning. And yet, as I have said several times, the journey and the destination are really the same thing. The one is inextricably part of the other. The destination cannot be reached *without* the journey. And the important thing is that you are already *on* your journey.

I know you had a lot of questions when you started reading this book. And if you were hoping to have all the answers by the time you reached this chapter, I apologise. Because you have only some answers... and possibly a whole lot more questions. There will *always* be new questions. But by now you will know yourself how to find the answers (that is, if you have conscientiously followed your map and absorbed and internalised all the experiences along the way).

But any way you look at it, by undertaking this journey you will have progressed quite a long way towards self-fulfilment and inner peace, and you will have achieved some quite wonderful things and made some very important changes in your life. You have gained a completely new perspective. And so the new lessons you will learn, and the lessons you can teach others, are completely different too.

One of the most important things is that you are now *aware* that there are such things as Comfort Zones, and from now on you will know how to recognise them for what they really are — inhibitors and suppressors and castle walls and dungeons preventing people from being truly themselves. And once you start 'thinking Comfort Zones', it's amazing how you begin to recognise them all around you.

One of my copywriter colleagues said that after discussing Comfort Zones with me he suddenly realised that although he loved his job and was very fulfilled, he had fallen into a Comfort Zone as far as his daily work was concerned. He was conscientious, always met deadlines, always delivered the goods — but he was just churning out what was needed. With his new insights and inner changes, he started 'going the extra mile' by trying to make each headline, each ad, special and fresh. The results were amazing.

The twenty-six-year-old son of one of my friends told me that after hearing me talk about Comfort Zones at a dinner party at their home one night, he had finally confronted the fact that he had been postponing leaving home because he was inwardly afraid of being alone in the wide world. He confronted the fact that he had become a perpetual college student not so much because he wanted to continue studying, but rather because this gave him an excuse to continue living at home and being supported by his parents. This confrontation and self-honesty had brought about an internal change which motivated him to take a full-time lecturer's post and complete his doctorate part-time. He has since moved into residence at the college. (I congratulated him but warned him about *this* also becoming a new Comfort Zone!)

Having written this book, and having the most noble and optimistic aspirations about its worth, I was nevertheless amazed and humbled when people started telling me that it actually *works*. It's the most sobering experience imaginable, knowing that something you've written has the potential to make dramatic changes in other people's lives.

I got a call one day from a friend who told me he wanted to meet me alone. Since we served on the same committee and had a few weeks previously returned from a conference, I assumed it was work-related. But when I sat down, he told me he had a terrible confession to make.

I was completely taken aback. Terrible confession? Had he embezzled funds? Killed his wife? Was he having an affair with mine? But he was such a nice guy...

Then he told me that he had intercepted a copy of my Comfort Zones manuscript that I had sent with him to a friend in Australia whose judgement and criticism I valued a great deal. He apologised profusely, but explained that he was so intrigued that he had started reading it and simply couldn't put it down. Then he went on to explain how it had changed his whole life; how he kept nodding as he read, saying 'Yes! Yes! Yes!' as he found me expressing things he had always felt deep inside but had never been able to verbalise. Needless to say, I forgave him – as I did his wife, who phoned me a couple of months later to report that she had grabbed the manuscript and was reading it, and how dramatic an effect it was having on her life as well.

Then there were the guinea-pig volunteers for our first Comfort Zones course. Out of the ten people who attended, three wrote that it was the most valuable thing they had done in their lives (one said for the past fifteen years). Two asked if they could buy the franchise for South Africa. One man in his early fifties took the plunge two weeks after the course and opened his own business after spending his whole life working for a boss. A woman confronted the fact that she was very unhappy in her relationship and left her boyfriend within a month, moving to her own apartment. Another woman, who had been entirely dominated by her mother, resigned from her job and went to live on a kibbutz in Israel.

As I said, it's a very sobering and humbling experience. But I cannot really take the credit for any of it: together with Albert, I was merely the mentor and the catalyst. What these people did was simply to have the courage to confront honestly who they really were and what they really wanted in life, recognise their freedom of choice, and assert that right. I applaud their courage, and I am deeply grateful that I could have played a role in their spiritual growth.

Comfort Zones in the workplace

Apart from the most obvious cases — mentioned earlier in this book — of people being stuck in dead-end jobs or unfulfilling careers, you can see Comfort Zones in business relationships of all kinds.

Picture a corporate boardroom, the huge polished table surrounded by nodding heads as the chairman (the ultimate figure of authority in the company context, the controller in the dependency relationships of each employee) makes a statement, or laughter when he tells a joke. The nodding heads feel obliged to nod and laugh because if they didn't they would risk the disfavour of the boss. So even if the joke's not funny, or if they disagree with his statements, they would rather stay in the comfort of their corporate Comfort Zones than speak their minds or be emotionally honest when they don't find his humour funny.

Picture a brand manager listening to a bold new approach for a dying product. Perhaps he's just seen a new campaign from his ad agency. He has to weigh up the recommendations of this long-haired arty type with an ear-ring (heaven forbid!) against the proven formula of his predecessors. Inevitably there's a weighty document gathering dust somewhere with Strategic Guidelines that are the Bible for the product. No matter that they were written twenty years ago, no matter that the world and the market-place have undergone dramatic changes since then, he feels terrified of the risk of discarding these 'comfortable' rules in favour of taking his own gut-feel decision. Will he cross the drawbridge, or will he retreat inside his castle?

Picture a company with a thirty-year record of successful growth. Let's say it's in South Africa, where socio-political changes have been dramatic, to say the least. Worldwide, corporate structures have changed shape; traditional autocratic hierarchies have had to make room for participative management and involvement by the lower rungs of employees. The unions are making strong noises. And instead of being receptive to change (change which will ensure the ongoing success of the company), the greyhairs feel threatened and indignant. Why should they give up their perks and power, the privileges they've worked so hard and so long to enjoy?

And so the nodding heads go on nodding in the control-dependency relationship. The brand manager rejects a risky new approach and carries on running his 'safe', boring advertising, shackled by the rules of some long-forgotten Ghosts of the Past. And the grey-haired hierarchy retreat behind the walls of their entertainment accounts and company limousines and directors-only canteens, where they will stay even as those walls crumble around them and the company commits suicide.

MY FINAL WORD: AN APOLOGY!

When Albert Koopman and I originally put our heads together, our intention was to write a book specifically for corporate and business use. Our working title was *The Inner Shift*. We simply wanted to formalise Albert's original Goal Source into a fully structured and integrated programme to facilitate change in the workplace. To help break down old-paradigm corporate hierarchies. Make people (employers as well as employees) more receptive to inevitable changes.

Our premise was that organisations have traditionally only recognised the 'material' side of employees. And the failure to recognise and attach value to those employees' individual needs and desires and ambitions, their basic human values, and finally their relationships to others not only within the workplace but also at home, in a social environment, and especially in a

278

spiritual context, inevitably lead to the vital elements of productivity and quality being sacrificed on the altar of corporate materialism.

We believe that individuals are starting to reject authoritarian rule and the old-wave hierarchical management pyramid and are seeking greater participation and self-actualisation in their jobs and careers — which, after all, consume a major chunk of their lives. We believe that unless managements recognise and address these dramatically changing needs within this shifting paradigm, they will find themselves and their companies left far behind the standards which are making the Pacific Rim countries world leaders. By doggedly pursuing methods which are doomed to be increasingly ineffective and even damaging, they risk losing the very things that they are trying to achieve.

The Inner Shift was planned as a guide which will help any company not only achieve its commercial objectives through greater synergy between management and workers at all levels, but will also enrich the lives of employees by incorporating their personal and social values and aligning their aspirations with the corporate needs in the working environment.

So much for following the brief! Unfortunately, as I started writing, this book leaned more and more towards growth on a personal level. The more I wrote, and the more research I did, the more I realised how widespread a problem we were attempting to resolve. It seemed everyone I spoke to was trapped in their own private Comfort Zones.

The result was that I eventually presented my friend with *How To Escape Your Comfort Zones* by Lee Johnson *with* Albert Koopman. And I look forward to the day when he retaliates by following our original brief and presenting me with *The Inner Shift* by Albert Koopman *with* Lee Johnson.

The Castle lagers are busy frosting!

279

CONCLUSION

Now that you've reached the last chapter, you may find to your dismay that you still haven't escaped some — or all — of your Comfort Zones. Does this mean you're a failure? Or a coward? Or that you lack the courage or ability to grow and progress in life, and attain inner peace and self-fulfilment?

Not at all.

It simply means that you've chosen to exercise your freedom of choice and remain temporarily in some of your Comfort Zones. This may be because you don't want to hurt someone in a relationship, or you are too responsible to change jobs right now and abandon that mean old fool you call a boss, or there may be a million different reasons for your decision. For example, you may simply be emotionally too fragile right now, and you need to rest in a safe harbour a little longer to build up your strength and courage before you set out on your new voyage. Or you may have decided that, right now, the Gain simply isn't worth the Pain.

That's OK. As I said, at least you have chosen to exercise your freedom of choice. And that's a victory in itself.

But at least in reading this book you've gained *many new insights*. At least you are now aware of Comfort Zones, and you know how to recognise them. At least you are aware of how they are inhibiting your life and your growth. At least you now know a whole lot more about *yourself* — your true, inner self. At least you have now learned the importance of self-honesty, and of expressing that honesty to those around you. At least you are now aware of the inevitability of change, and that there can be no rebirth without the death of the old. At least you now know how to confront realities; overcome your fear; accept risk and doubt as inseparable from growth. At least you *know* that your decision is only a temporary postponement of the inevitable and the inescapable.

But, most of all, at the very least you now carry with you the keys to unlocking the doors to your castle. You know the mechanisms for escaping your Comfort Zones, the magic combinations to the locks — and you can use them, and will use them, one day when you are ready.

The seeds have been sown. One day they will push through the hard crust of soil and grow into mighty trees.

So, take courage and have faith. I'll be praying for your rain.

Write to Lee Johnson and Albert Koopman at:

InfraManagement
Suite 516
1489 Marine Drive
West Vancouver
British Columbia V7T 1B8
CANADA

References

Bach, Richard (1973). *Jonathan Livingston Seagull*. London: Pan Books.

Bhaktivedanta Swami Prabhupada, A C, His Divine Grace (1984). *Bhagavad-Gita. As It Is*. Los Angeles: The Bhaktivedanta Book Trust.

Burns, David D (1981). *Feeling Good: The New Mood Therapy*. Signet Books.

Campbell, Joseph (1994). *Myths to Live By*. Souvenir Press.

Campbell, Joseph (1973). *The Hero with a Thousand Faces*. Princeton, New Jersey: Princeton University Press. Bollingen Series XVII.

Davies, Gail. *The Blind Spot*. Papers and correspondence with the Author.

Eliot, T S (1970). *Selected Poems*. London: Faber and Faber.

Ferguson, Marilyn (1982). *The Aquarian Conspiracy: Personal and Social Transformation in the '80s*. Paladin Grafton Books.

Fishbein, M & Ajzen, I (1975). *Belief, Attitude, Intentions and Behaviour: An Introduction to Theory and Research*. Boston: Addison-Wesley.

Fishburn, P C (1972). Personalistic Decision Theory: Expositions and Critique. In H S Brinkers (ed.) *Decision-Making*. Columbus: Ohio State University Press.

Fromm, Erich (1951). *Psychoanalysis and Religion*. London: Victor Gollancz.

Gerdes, Lily C *et al.* (1988). *The Developing Adult*. Durban: Butterworth, second edition.

Gibran, Kahlil (1946). *The Madman*. London: William Heinemann.

282

Hagberg, Janet & Leider, Richard (1978). *The Inventurers.* Reading, Massachusetts: Addison-Wesley.

Hesse, Hermann (1969). *Demian.* London: Panther Books.

Howarth, William (1981). Henry David Thoreau: Following the tracks of a different man: Thoreau. *National Geographic* Vol. 159, No. 3.

Hurlock, Elizabeth B (1959). *Developmental Psychology.* McGraw-Hill, third edition.

Jones, E *Sigmund Freud*, Vols I and III, London, 1953-57. (Quoted by Arthur Koestler in *Janus*).

Jordaan, Wilhelm & Jordaan, Jackie (1984). *Man in Context.* South Africa: McGraw-Hill Book Company.

Kleinmuntz, Benjamin (1980). *Essentials of Abnormal Psychology.* San Francisco: Harper & Row, second edition.

Koestler, Arthur (1978). *Janus. A Summing Up.* London: Hutchinsons.

Koopman, Albert (1991). *The Corporate Crusaders.* Johannesburg: Lexicon.

Koopman, Albert. *Goal Source.* Unpublished material used for staff motivational courses.

Kühn, Thomas (1962). *The Structure of Scientific Revolutions.*

Laing, R D (1967). *The Politics of Experience.* New York: Pantheon Books.

La Mar, Donna F (1992). *Transcending Turmoil.* New York and London: Insight Books, Plenum Press.

Mandino, Og (1985). *The World's Greatest Salesman.* New York: Bantam Books.

Marrs, Texe (1988). *Dark Secrets of the New Age.* Westchester, Illinois: Crossway Books.

Melody (1992). *Love is in the Earth: A Kaleidoscope of Crystals.* Arvada, Colorado: Earth-Love Publishing.

Miller, Arthur (1961). *Death of a Salesman.* Harmondsworth: Penguin.

Reader's Digest Association (1965). *How to Live With Life.*

Rieff, Philip (1965). *Freud: The Mind of the Moralist.* London: Methuen.

Sheehy, Gail (1981). *Passages.* Bantam.

Spielberger, Charles D (ed.)(1971) *Anxiety and Behaviour.* New York: Academic Press.

Spielberger, C D *et al* (1986). *Stress and Anxiety (Vol. 10): A Sourcebook of Theory and Research.* Washington: Hemisphere Publishing Corporation.

The Search for Meaning. Conversations with Caroline Jones (1992). ABC Enterprises for the Australian Broadcasting Corporation (in association with Collins Dove).

Thoreau, Henry David (1986). *Walden (And Civil Disobedience).* Harmondsworth: Penguin. (First published in the USA by Ticknor and Fields, 1854.)

Wann, T W (ed.)(1970). *Behaviourism and Phenomenology.* Chicago: University of Chicago Press.

Watson, Lillian Eichler (ed.) *Light From Many Lamps.* New York: Simon & Schuster.

West, Morris (1977). *The Shoes of the Fisherman.* London: William Heinemann Limited (in association with Octopus Books).

Wilder, Thornton (1972). *Our Town.* Harmondsworth: Penguin.

Williams, Margery (1958). *The Velveteen Rabbit.* Doubleday.